Defending Andy

One Mother's Fight
to Save Her Son from
Cancer and the
Insurance Industry

Marilyn Azevedo, R.N.

Health Communications, Inc.
Deerfield Beach, Florida

www.hci-online.com

Library of Congress Cataloging-in-Publication Data

Azevedo, Marilyn
    Defending Andy : one mother's fight to save her son from cancer and the insurance industry / Marilyn Azevedo.
        p.   cm.
    ISBN 1-55874-906-3
    1. Azevedo, Andy—Health. 2 Sarcoma—Patients—California—Biography. I. Title.

RC265.6.A94 2001
362.1'96994'0092—dc21
[B]
                                                                    00-053991

Publisher: Health Communications, Inc.
          3201 S.W. 15th Street
          Deerfield Beach, FL 33442-8190

Cover design by Andrea Perrine Brower.
Cover photo of wheelchair by Pulitzer Prize–winning photographer Annie Wells.
Cover photos on football field and under hood by Ron Bath.
Inside book design by Dawn Grove.
Inside photos by Pulitzer Prize–winning photographer Annie Wells and Ron Bath.

This book is dedicated to

Andy,

Who showed us the meaning of love,

laughter and courage

Whose spirit remains on the top of mountains,

Within the sea

With butterflies in my summer garden

In rainbows

and

Singing through the sky as meteor showers

Contents

Acknowledgments

*T*he love and support of so many helped this process through to completion. Without them, I know this book wouldn't have been published. Their collective "How's the book doing?" kept me going.

Special thanks to Annie Wells, who was brought into our lives on a job assignment and stayed as a dear, dear friend. She was my gift from Andy. She willingly shared my pain. Her photos are extraordinary; her heart is even more so. Her gentle spirit let me know I could do it!

To Kathy, who helped me through the terror and shared my heart and tears.

My gratitude goes to Anne Sheldon and Michael Vidor, my literary agents. Anne first saw the possibilities of this work and guided me to Larry. She moved me along with strength and care. They had faith in me and in Andy's story. I couldn't have done it without them.

I will always be indebted to Larry Kearney, first my mentor and now my friend, who brought such literary talent and truth to this book.

I will never forget Alex, whose supposed carefree teenage years were interrupted with such violent realities. She gave her love to Andy and all of us throughout the hardship and pain. I will always adore her. And to her parents, Carlos and Rebecca, Andy's other mom and dad. He loved you so. My thanks always for such care and tenderness.

I will love always Andy's support group: Jacob, Frankie, Fred,

Howard, Lisa and Matt. You managed to help Andy laugh and shared his fun when others were too frightened to stand by his side. You continued to be there for Andy and listened to his fears. You held him together while his heart broke. And looking back, it's wonderful to know you didn't leave us when Andy did.

Bob Lewon read the manuscript years ago and critiqued the book with insight and wisdom.

Jeff Rubnitz, who is now Bob's son-in-law after marrying Karin, but as one of Andy's pediatric oncologists was the gentle man who came into our lives in the midst of terror, saw Andy for who he truly was and now calls me Ti Tia.

Tansy and Bob Goodman shared Make-A-Wish and Piper's Dinners with me, and through their own pain, helped me take steps to live again.

Carey Sakai, who cried when she met me, remembering Andy's story, and shares her aloha with me in so many ways.

Jules Jaffe, who gave such tender care, spoke the truth no matter how hard and treated Andy with such love. He is the epitome of what every doctor should be.

I could never forget Andy's Memorial Hospital 3-West Nurses, who could joke and play, be tender and compassionate and do their difficult job while giving Andy his dignity.

Peter Vegso and Christine Belleris at HCI, who worked hard for the publication of this book. To Allison Janse, senior editor at HCI, who took over as editor and dedicated herself to make the book perfect. She always listened to my feelings and point of view, then adapted them into this work. She is a rare gem.

As always, my most profound thanks and love go out to my family. I wouldn't have been able to even begin without their love and support.

My husband Simon, for the tenderness he allowed himself to show and the growth that was so difficult for him. And for always being there for me, letting me fight in the only way I knew how. He may never be able to read Andy's story because it is too painful, but he cooked when I was too engrossed to even think of food and understood that I needed to write this even if it was difficult for him.

My children and grandchildren, the joy of my life, who helped so much during Andy's battle and in giving me hope after Andy died. They supported and loved me, sometimes with rolling eyes, sometimes with sighs and jokes, but they made me live! They stood by my side when I couldn't stand to have others near. They were always doing what needed to be done, even when I couldn't ask. I feel so blessed to have them in my life.

Andrew and Ali, grandchildren who came to us after Andy died and made it possible for me to open up my heart again. They both gave me someone to hug and hold when the rest of the world thought I should be ready to move on and snap out of my grief. They asked nothing in return except to be loved, and they are. And our brand-new grandchild, Andy Michael Azevedo, a new life that will bring further joy to our family and to my heart.

Thanks will always go out to my sisters, Maureen and Mello, who are constantly there for me no matter how angry or sad I become. They always give me a boost when I need it or let me cry for hours until I am finished. They have been my best friends: my truest confidants, and gave me their strength when I had none. Their hours spent with the book and my discussion of it must have seemed interminable. They shared beauty with me when I thought there was none left in the world, and waited until I was able to see it for myself. I never felt abandoned when they were with me.

And last, I must acknowledge those unlucky enough to follow Andy, who will need courage, love, strength and humor to get them through. I wish it weren't so.

My thanks and love go out to all of you.

Foreword

$\mathcal{A}$s a pediatric oncologist, I have the opportunity to work with the most courageous and resilient children in the world. I now realize how special these children and their families really are. They are thrust into intolerable situations without permission or choice. The cancer dictates their path. As their physician, I mediate, aware that the knowledge and energy I give is necessary to save each child. Through all of this, the child shows great courage and general acceptance of what must be done. Younger children with cancer adapt amazingly well to their disease and its treatment, taking it all in stride. Adolescents and teenagers, however, often have more difficulty accepting their situations.

What it takes on a personal level is astounding for both the patient and their family. The parent, with strength and determination, offers support throughout the treatment of their child. Without the patient, family, and physician's active participation—watching, guiding and fighting for what the patient needs—the medical system can become much more convoluted. I witness and understand the difficulty cancer patients and their families' face.

During the many months or years that a child is under my care, I practically become a part of his or her family. I see them in the most difficult of situations. I share their pain and their joy. I understand their determination and the need to fight. My contribution is sometimes more emotional than medical, and I believe that I often fill a need as much for the parents of my patients as for my patients themselves.

When I lose a patient, I lose a small part of myself. But, I never lose the bond that I established with his family. When I first met Andy, he was sixteen years old and had just learned that he had clear cell sarcoma. Andy was incredibly strong, both physically and emotionally. At the same time, he was caring and sensitive, often supporting other patients around him. One of my fondest memories of Andy is the time I saw him at the birthday party of a young girl with leukemia. Although Andy was quite ill himself, he took the time and energy to travel to her house and join in her celebration. I'll never forget the joy in her eyes when Andy walked in. That is part of the joy, one of the hidden benefits of cancer. The support of patients and families for each other is an important and valuable gift—one that strengthens the patient in innumerable ways. Even when the family loses their child, the support they received remains. As I watch this process with my patients and the families, I also gain strength.

There are also times after a hard day at work—when a patient dies or when I have to give parents some bad news—that I come home at night and lie in bed next to my own children and cry. My love and appreciation of my own children has been strengthened by my career. At the same time, having children of my own has helped me to focus my feelings at work and to understand what my patients' families are going through. I pray that I will never be the parent of a patient, but if that should happen, I hope that I can have the courage and grace that Marilyn, Andy, and all of my families have shown.

Jeffrey Rubnitz, M.D., Ph.D.
Director of Fellowship Training Program
Department of Hematology/Oncology
St. Jude Children's Research Hospital

Introduction

*D*riving home from Stanford Medical Center in the fall of 1990, after we knew the tide had turned and we wouldn't get out of Andy's cancer unscathed, Andy and I talked about the lack of information available to help us through the fight.

"Once we get this done, Mom, we better write a book. I'll write one chapter, you can do the rest." We decided that day to name the book, *When You Can't Pull the Covers Over Your Head.*

The title has changed, the determination hasn't. And I need you all to know, I didn't write this book, Andy did—through my fingers. Good job, Honey.

Author's Note

*T*he people and events portrayed in this book are true. Some of the names have been changed and a few of the situations portrayed have been broadened, since without Andy's input, I can only guess at the exact context.

Photo by Annie Wells. ©*The Press Democrat,* Santa Rosa, CA.

Easter gathering on the ranch in 1990. From left to right: Andy's dog Opu, Cheryl with puppy, Simon, Andy, Marilyn, Nick, Kerri, Linda with Stefanie, John, Brenda and Paul.

1

WHISPER GRASS

Andy was my youngest child, my darling. He died after a three-year battle with cancer.

I had two convictions firmly in place in my head when I suddenly had to deal with Andy's cancer, and both had come from my life with my parents. The first was that I was weak and couldn't be trusted not to panic. The second was that I was very strong because I had always endured without running to anyone.

They were both true.

Today, I'm at the lake we used to come to when Andy was just

1

a little boy. I know the things I have to do when the memories emerge. I know I have to accept and honor them and stay busy. If I don't do the things I have to do, I'll find myself going around in circles, trapped in the images of loss.

I've come to the conclusion that maybe I can do some good, and shore up my life a bit, by making an offering of my youngest son's battle with clear cell sarcoma. I don't want to leave anything out because I need the story and the feelings to be complete if they are to help anyone else, or me.

I developed my panic from my relationship with my father, an imposing, intellectually dominant man who had always been able to do whatever he wanted to, and expected you to be able to do the same. He scared the hell out of me. There were three of us: myself; Maureen, my twin; and Melouise, the youngest.

Dad had a violent temper that he indulged physically. We went to Balboa to swim when I was five, and he wanted us to go out past the surf and dive for rocks. The first time I tried, I was caught in the waves and bashed and ground on the bottom. When I came out, I refused to go again, so he beat me and made me sit in a sandstone cave at the top of the beach for the rest of the day.

All of us had to be ready to handle the sudden explosions, but I never quite got the knack. My bowels would collapse as my temperature surged. The related problem was that I loved him to distraction.

My father gave us the sense that we could do anything if we wanted to enough, and we all wanted desperately to meet his expectations. He was a military man, a seaman and an adventurer. He sailed his sixty-three-foot sailboat around Antarctica in 1973, and wrote about it in a book called *Blue Water*.

Our mother was beautiful and aloof, with her own range of

intimidating mannerisms. If I were going to panic, there would be little use in running to Mom.

I remember swimming and going underwater once and when I tried to come up a big hand was on top of my head, holding me down. I turned and twisted, but I couldn't get away. Through the deadening water, I could hear the other kids laughing. It went on forever. That's the panic of Andy's sickness: the helplessness, the rage, the endlessness.

We've always lived in Sonoma County in California, dairy country. From our windows, we can look across the valley and watch the hills change with the light and the seasons. In winter, the hills are dark green and, during the early summer, the unharvested fields are marked out in green rectangles.

We're dairy farmers, and our farming moves with the seasons. Once the hay and silage are out of the fields, Simon, my husband, plows for the next crop. I used to drive the silage truck, but I loved baling hay. I'd be alone with the hay, and the sky, and be able to turn back anytime to see the hard results of my work laid out in rows.

Simon is the epitome of a dairyman. He has huge hands and strong arms from years of manual labor, but his physical power doesn't mask the softness at his core. In high school he was a shy, dark boy, and I was completely thrilled when he asked me to go to the movies with him in Petaluma. Simon has always worked hard, and sometimes maybe he didn't have enough time for the kids. But he loved them, very deeply, and they knew it.

When Andy got sick, Simon barely knew what to do. He grew very quiet. In my head forever is the picture of him bending down to pick up nineteen-year-old Andy in his big arms.

"Honey," he said, "I don't want to hurt you, but I have to pick you up."

There were tears in his eyes and just the one, unlikely word, "Honey," said all he ever needed to say.

Andy was our fifth child, the last, and special to all of us. John was just seven, Paul and Linda were almost teenagers, and Cheryl was thirteen when Andy was born.

I had already had my success with my children and I was feeling confident, but I was shocked and not at all happy to be pregnant again. Abortion was an option, I guess, but I thought it over and decided against it. I knew we had room for one more in our house. Our children had all been loved, always.

We made it through the pregnancy all right, long months of my confinement to bed with Cheryl and Linda taking care of the house and cooking as best they could. John was still small enough that he needed some watching, and Paul was mostly outside with Dad. Those nine months must have seemed like an eternity to them.

When the time finally came, my girlfriend drove me fifty miles to the hospital on a Wednesday night because Simon couldn't leave the cows. Andy wasn't born till Saturday morning.

I was so exhausted that when Simon was suggesting names, I couldn't have cared less. We finally agreed on George Anthony, after two of Simon's adored uncles. We found out later the baby had actually been born on the anniversary of his great-uncle George's death.

There's an Indian belief that if you are born on your namesake's death day, you inherit his spirit. I'd met Uncle George when I was ten. He was the first person in Simon's family I had met. He was a dairyman on Point Reyes (way out at the lighthouse), part of the area my father had covered as a veterinarian.

Uncle George had died of a brain tumor, but that fact hadn't crossed anyone's mind. It crosses mine now. We had wanted to put all the best of Uncle George into this child, but not the cancer, certainly not that.

Andy was always an athlete; it was what he wanted to do with his life. It wasn't fun for me to watch him getting thrown around in the football games. I cringed and winced and held my breath. His worst injury came in high school, when he caught his finger under another kid's helmet. He shrugged it off. It wasn't a big deal.

Andy stayed busy in high school. He had to keep his grades up if he wanted to keep playing football, and though his girlfriend, Alex, was away that season, his buddies weren't. There was a lot of talk about his college potential, and the pros. Things were coming together, and his future looked like it was going to skyrocket.

I congratulated myself. I'd done the right things again.

By the beginning of October, his finger hadn't healed and was causing him a great deal of pain. I made an appointment with my friend Michael, a plastic surgeon I'd worked with in the operating room.

Two days before the appointment, Andy came into the kitchen, holding his hand half up and out as if it were some separate, living thing. It was a bright morning, and the kitchen curtains were breaking up the early sun.

Simon was out already in the fields and I was washing dishes. I turned when Andy came in because he'd come in fast and stopped abruptly. I looked at the way he was holding his hand and straightened up.

"My God, Mom," Andy said, "look at my finger!"

I looked. The nail had split, and tissue was coming through the hole that had initially been used to drain the supposed blood blister. The bright morning turned sickly, and the sun suddenly picked up every flaw in the kitchen. There wasn't any safety, not in my kitchen and not in my chest.

I was ten years old again, lost in a cornfield, the high corn all around, and the slightly swaying tops all alike against the bright sky. I'd push through a row to the next and find I hadn't moved at all. Everything was just the same: the sky above, and the cornstalks standing like guards.

Of course, all I had to do was follow a row to its end—it had to end—but my panic took over and I thrashed in circles without purpose. When my father found me, he told me that all I'd needed to do was follow a row.

When Andy came in that morning, my safe kitchen was suddenly endless, with no row to follow. So it all began. The mind shuts off and runs the odds for a while. "Odds are it's nothing." You walk through the developing information as if you were following a fugitive trail through quicksand. You talk with friends and you watch for the healing, and you pray just to be normal. Nothing abnormal can happen to *you*.

When it's over, all you do is remember. I remember his enthusiasms spilling in all directions. I remember his voice, the precise intonations. I remember how he'd say "remembery"—*remember* and *memory* rolled together for a five-year-old's convenience. I remember how his smile was the first thing you'd notice about him.

The lake is very blue, just as it was before, and I'm lying out of the wind to get dry. I'm here at the lake with Annie and Kathy, friends who helped through the long fight for Andy's life.

I imagine him, I can *see* him, a little boy coming out of the water and running toward me: dripping, golden brown and full of energy.

I remember the day he came out of the water and stopped to bend and look at something on the granite. He was just five. When he reached down I shouted, "Don't touch it! What are you looking at?" I thought it might be a snake.

"Whisper grass!" he yelled, and I stood up and walked over, wondering what he meant. He was standing on the granite with his leg swinging over the tops, smiling, and looking down at dried stalks of mountain wheat bending in the breeze.

"Look Mom, whisper grass."

When I reached down, I could barely feel a whisper of stalks brushing at my hand. If I hadn't been paying attention, I'd have missed it entirely. It had the delicacy of memory, of remembery.

The world is implacable, and sometimes hope just breaks against it like a confused bird against a window. When that happens, there are two ways to go. One way is to withdraw into rage and resentment. The other way is to draw together in love for each other and everyone who suffers. If you continue to read, you'll probably decide for yourself which is best.

But for me, right now, the lake is very blue and the clouds are white and I'm standing by myself, looking down at the whisper grass and crying.

2

REMEMBERY

We're a dairy-ranch family. It's not an easy life, but there's a lot about it you wouldn't trade. The kids woke up in a beautiful world every morning. Just pull back the curtain: rain, shine, fog; it was all beautiful.

I liked to imagine myself as my grandmother in those years: utterly competent and adored by her children, family and friends. *I wasn't the child I had been*, I thought—never wanted, never good enough, never liked. I was going to make sure that my kids felt the emotions I hadn't. I wanted them to feel consistent, reliable, durable love.

It wasn't a bad motive, but the fact is, I wasn't my grandmother and I was still seeing myself through other people's eyes, imagining what other people saw.

My children were happy and secure, though. They built tree forts in the eucalyptus grove, they skidded on ice-covered ponds in the early morning and rode their battered yellow and orange Tonka trucks down the knobby hill in front of the house, howling with laughter. They had the freedom to play and the freedom to invent. The dairy ranch was a great place for youngsters.

But, all things considered, we couldn't handle any more children. On the day after Andy was born, I decided to have a tubal ligation. It's minor surgery.

They gave me a spinal anesthetic and soon I found myself drifting, warm and protected. A voice was calling me, but I had no need to answer. I didn't want to answer. I was floating comfortably down a dark tunnel toward a bright light, totally supported and enveloped.

I knew I was dying, and it felt good.

I knew that once I reached the light I wouldn't be able to return, but I couldn't have cared less. My husband and my kids and the new baby and my life and the world weren't important. All I needed was to go where I was going. Then I started floating back.

For the first time in my life, I didn't panic when I wasn't in control. The voice grew a bit louder.

"Marilyn, Marilyn!" Then, "Oh shit, we lost her."

I could see myself on the operating table. The doctors were pumping my chest and raising the head of the table. I could see and hear, but I couldn't say anything. The doctors clearly were scared, partly for me, but also, I feel, for their own reputations. After what seemed like a long time, I could feel the panic in the room ebb away and the operation continued.

I've been a ranch woman and an operating-room nurse, and my preference has always been for hard, reliable information. So with that thought, I offer you my outlook on death as part of Andy's book and his lovely spirit.

What I felt of death was exactly as I've described it. Everything is taken out of your hands and placed into the care of a perfectly comforting force.

Death isn't frightening at all.

Simon didn't believe my story, so he's never quite understood the impact it had on my life. Over the years, the near-death experience has become a well-described phenomenon, so I don't worry anymore about being crazy. I never really thought I was anyway.

Subsequently, the rhythm of life returned to normal, and we all went through that tentative trying out of the new baby's name. "George" we called him, and "Georgie," "Georgie Porgie," "Curious George"—but "George" just didn't fit. The name we finally came to was Andy. When a baby's name comes that way it's almost magic. It's like *you* haven't said who he is; *he's* told you.

His smile lit up the room. He smiled with every fiber in his being, and the smile said there was nothing sly or cunning in him. There wasn't, either. He was a trusting little boy, with all the goodwill in the world. He was my prize and perfect. I adored my other kids, but something was different about Andy from the beginning.

He was born having to tag along. The other kids knew their

routines—school, chores, 4-H, swimming—and Andy went along, imitating, learning, pulling on his rubber boots with the others when work needed to be done outside.

The other kids were great with him and let him help. In helping, his character began to form. He tried everything. He wanted to be a big kid and called himself, mysteriously, "Big Andy Zedo."

He went to school with me when I volunteered to help with first-grade reading. He thought he already knew how to read. He'd grab a book and sit back in the big blue chair in our living room. He was two. It didn't matter to him that the book was upside down; he knew how to read. He read me his own wonderful stories from the upside-down book. One story had me chopping rocks with a pitchfork.

1974. Andy's first mud puddle, discovered at age two.

"Honey," I said, "that story's not really in the book."

"Me know," he'd say, a little bored with me.

He took swimming lessons and learned almost immediately, moving through the water and across the pool like a dolphin. You could tell he'd be an athlete. Eventually, he'd play basketball and baseball and football, and the one thing he'd require of me was, "No matter what, no matter what happens, don't ever come onto the field, ever." I'd smile and say, "Okay," but I was lying.

When Andy was two, I went back to school to complete my nursing degree. Simon wasn't very happy about it, but everything seemed to push me in that direction. I'd been in nursing school when I got pregnant at seventeen. My father cried.

You couldn't be in nursing school in those days if you were married or had a child, and when I left, I thought the door had closed behind me for good. My father was crying because my life was over. In his eyes, I was a failure, a stupid girl who'd compromised her life.

Simon didn't want me to go back to school. He stopped just short of forbidding it. But after my near-death experience, I felt that I'd been suddenly presented with my life on a platter, as a gift, and now I was expected to do something with it.

And there was money to think of. Extra money wouldn't hurt; we could hire a man to take some of the burden off Simon. So my return to school was a good idea all around. I started with a course on death and dying, not only because I was interested, but also because I wanted to offer my experience and perhaps make contact with someone who had shared it.

I managed to overcome the odds—I had five kids, a business to take care of and minimal support—and graduate with a B-plus average. After graduation, I found a job as an operating-room nurse. We had the extra money now for family things and the hired man. The day-to-day grind eased a little, and the kids were more able to participate in school activities: sports, jobs, clubs and fairs. I could even afford trips to Hawaii to visit my family.

1977. Andy's first backpacking trip into the Sierra Nevada Mountains at age five, with his cousin Meredith.

1981. 4-H electricity project: Jesse, Andy and Matt in cap.

June 1981. Andy taking his 4-H calf, Misty, to show in his first fair.

Andy was ten when he went to Hawaii to visit his grandparents. His brothers and sisters had been telling him about it for most of his life. Hawaii was already heaven to him, the water and the culture. We had a family legend about a mysterious Hawaiian in my grandmother's heritage, and Andy believed it wholeheartedly. No one else really did but Andy said, "It's true," and took it into his being, whole. He'd read the myths, and listen to stories, and gather up bits of information he felt were important.

On that first visit, he bought a great white shark's tooth to wear around his neck. It looked out of place on his immature body, but it meant a great deal to him, and gradually it became an important part of who he was. It was always around his neck, an image of his faith and his physical grace. The tooth was supposed to offer the protection of Moho, the Shark God. Andy believed, and during times of stress, he'd finger it absentmindedly.

His early school years were okay. He liked his teachers and he worked hard at whatever interested him, though he did find schoolwork hard. I remember in the fourth or fifth grade he had to write a paper and didn't want to. He dug in his heels with a ten-year-old's bravado.

First, there was, "Don't worry, Mom. I'll get it done."

Then I pushed. I took him to the library.

"Geology?"

"No."

"Animals?"

"No."

"Airplanes?"

"No."

"We have to find *something*."

"I wish I was in Hawaii and then I wouldn't have to do this."

"Okay, how about a paper on Hawaii?"

He looked at me, trapped. Finding the topic didn't end the resistance and the temper tantrums. Simon stayed out of the whole thing. As far as he was concerned, Andy could write the paper or not. When Andy finished, it was like I'd put down a sack of bricks. It was wonderful.

He got an A and learned a great deal about hard work, the need to finish what he'd begun and pride in results. He learned I could match him even-up for passion and stubbornness and—most importantly—that even if he couldn't spell, he could write.

It was a wonderful experience for him. As he grew older, he wrote a lot: stories, speeches and accounts of his dreams. When an English teacher took an interest in him, his talent for communicating his feelings grew.

I was working as a nurse–case manager with a small, nonprofit hospice in Petaluma. Going to work felt like entering a safe place every morning, and my mind would shift effortlessly from the problems of home to the problems of my patients. No matter what was going on, I knew that at work I was at a place where I was respected and my opinions mattered.

Working with the dying is a delicate and sometimes exhausting task. You offer what you can, but you're always just outside—you have to be—and sometimes the vortex of family emotions can pull at you with considerable force. It's difficult, painful, intimate and intense. Generally speaking, I felt privileged to be at hospice, a wonderful experience in a special place. But in that type of environment, you wear down in secret places without even knowing it, and a time comes when you have to heal.

Just before I had to leave, I had a terrible, difficult case. A young boy was dying and the way things were—the way things had been for him, I guess—he was reluctant to try to do anything to ease either his physical or psychological pain. A person can come to the point where pain seems like a currency that needs to be passed along. It's like a token of rage.

All the time he was in hospice care, he and his family sank deeper and deeper in a dysfunctional spiral. Seemingly, I could do nothing at all. I couldn't reach anyone. I wasn't adequate.

When he died, nothing had been resolved and the whole family blamed me. It was a horrible, grinding experience. What do you do with the blame? The way my childhood had been— the way I'd lived expecting the sudden explosion or revelation of some weakness on my part—I hadn't become one of those adults who only needs to know themselves that they'd done nothing wrong. I was conditioned to generally feel like I had erred, and I couldn't shake off the blame.

I was walking into the grocery store in Petaluma a few months later and saw the boy's mother in the parking lot, drawn and tired with slumped shoulders and flat, angry eyes. I walked over to her and asked her how she was doing. She looked at me for a long time, not saying anything, then spat on the sidewalk as crudely and violently as she could. She walked away. The sun was shining and people were passing, some noticing, some not. I looked at her back stupidly, unable to move, until she was gone from sight. Then I went back to my car, the shopping forgotten.

It was time to back away. After eight years, I was clearly burning out. I didn't want to leave; I had to. I was carrying the loss of my patients and the pain of their survivors, and the load was becoming very heavy. I was talking about my patients all the time at home.

I told the director at hospice that I wanted to spend more time with Andy while I could. He would be graduating from high school in a few years and would then be gone. I didn't hear anything ominous in what I'd said. Why should I? Surely, the work I'd been doing had lent me some kind of protection, a few brownie points on someone's scoreboard? I knew things about life and about death. I had a deep involvement with the real world and had shared myself as best I could with people who needed comfort and assurance. I believed what I'd told them, and I'd helped. That had to be worth something. I had that notion tucked away somewhere in the back of my head, as a charm of sorts, something like Andy's shark's tooth.

I was wrong, though. No action can keep bad luck away. You can only deal with bad luck when it comes. I can see now that almost dying, then living with death at hospice, had given me all the world can offer in terms of dealing with a parent's grief, which lifts and twists the heart as if it were a rag doll.

3

*D*ISCOVERY

*A*ndy treasured his friends. Frankie was a kind, trusting kid, muscular, with blond hair. Matt was impish, Irish and freckled. When Matt's eyes were open, you could see right into his heart and its flicker of altar-boy devilishness.

When he was just fourteen, Matt went on a hunting trip with his father and died in the woods of an asthma attack. When Matt's mom called, I rushed out without saying anything to Andy. I couldn't bear to do it. The kids were so close they'd called themselves triplets. Matt's death was devastating.

There was a hole in their world where Matt had been. Andy and Frankie vowed to be best friends forever. "Forever" was suddenly a new word.

In the wake of Matt's death, Andy began playing soccer. His first coach was big, burly Larry Dido—kind, loving and positive—who made clear to the kids everything he believed in: how to win, how to lose and how to be a member of the team. So Andy learned skills, conditioned his body and met town kids whose lifestyles were completely different from his. It was a great time.

In high school, though, there was no soccer team. Football was the game. Andy couldn't wait. At fourteen, he was a coach's dream: big, fast and a team player (thanks again, Larry). The world was opening for him. He couldn't *just* play; he was very good.

The kids teased me continually for not understanding football. I remember once excitedly calling a dribbling penalty and how they shook their heads slowly. No matter how hard I tried, I couldn't get it down. My only understanding was that if one of my kids was hurt, I was going to be in the ambulance.

"Why are you going to the game, Mrs. Azevedo?"

1986. Andy's eighth-grade graduation, at age fourteen. He wore the tuxedo in memory of his best friend, Matt, who had worn one for his eighth-grade graduation the previous year.

"Oh, I just want to be there to ride in the ambulance"—the frolicsome world of the sports mother.

On cold Friday nights, when the winds surged and the rain poured (we're close to the ocean and the storms come howling in), we'd head to the gym for the basketball games.

In the spring, with the new green all over everything, we'd drive out to the baseball field. I wish I could accurately describe the green that comes over the Sonoma/Marin hills. It's so sudden and bright, it's like someone draped the hills with a sheet of green light.

We'd park close to the fence so we could see the games without having to be out in the sharp wind that felt colder than any winter storm. When I had to work, Simon would go alone or with other parents. So he was there for the last game of the season when Andy slid poorly into third and hurt his ankle. Andy rode home on the bus with the team, but four hours later he said he thought he should have it checked. It turned out to be broken. Broken or not, I was still relieved. The season was over.

Mom had made it through another year of high school sports, and Andy's only injuries had been a broken ankle and a jammed finger. I felt like I must be doing the right things. That's how you stay in control, you know, you do the right things. I think I really felt that in some way I was in control.

Learning can be very painful. It can hurt so much you think you're going to die.

Colleges started noticing Andy and sending him recruitment letters. His grades were good, and there didn't seem to be any problem. So he was making plans. Should he stay with us on the ranch after college, or fly search-and-rescue with the Air Force or the Department of Forestry? He loved his options.

Things were going well, generally. Paying bills was still a

struggle, but the dairy was getting bigger, the older kids were moving on with their lives and we had a new daughter-in-law and son-in-law. Paul had married Brenda and given us our grandchildren, Nick and Kerri. Linda married Les and, after a few years, had Stefanie. We were a big, boisterous, happy family and our house was always full.

Kids were always stopping by to see Andy or John, and we never knew who would be there for dinner or staying the night. During harvest, buddies from the football team would come out to work, stacking 120-pound bales of hay in the barn. They toned their muscles for next season, and we received some very valuable help.

Our son John was getting married to Toni, a shy, adorable local girl who meshed into our family easily. There were parties and preparations and a whole range of family run-arounds. It was also the summer when Andy's girlfriend, Alex, was leaving to study for a year in Puerto Rico.

Alex was sixteen then, a sparkling, dark beauty with Mexican/Puerto Rican roots. She knew who she was and what she wanted from life, and she worked hard to get it.

To round the summer out, Andy was showing beef at the Sonoma County Fair. His ankle was still in a cast, but he seemed to be moving around well enough.

Before Alex left, we—Andy, Alex and I—organized a Sierra camping trip. The ankle was too sore for backpacking, so we went by boat. We swam and laughed and cooked at night over a fire. As always, when you're away from the camouflaging light of cities and towns, the stars were incredible. My father taught me about that, the rocking motion of the sea with the stars the brightest light.

We lay back and watched them at night, waiting for the

Perseid meteor showers to begin, and in the mornings, Andy taught Alex how to fish in the still, blue waters. In the afternoons, they went off by themselves. It was a bittersweet time. I suppose, looking back, life has been bittersweet. That might be the only word that covers everything. No tragedy, no comedy, just the day-to-day events and the sudden wrenching or ecstatic flashes of emotion.

The families were probably more worried than Andy and Alex about how they would handle the separation. They were sad, but they were also looking ahead to a year full of adventure and changes. If they weren't in love at the end of it, well, they had shared a wonderful experience. These were kids you couldn't help but respect. They both seemed in control of their lives: powerful, adult, ready for whatever came.

Football would help fill the void.

His ankle was still sore, so we went to the doctor and discussed how best to repair a break that wasn't healing. He didn't want to miss too much football. The doctor decided he wanted to pin the ankle, and Andy decided to wait to have it done till the day after John and Toni's wedding.

The day of the surgery, we were bleary-eyed heading for the hospital. It was short and uneventful, and Andy was home that afternoon. When school started, Andy was still waiting for his ankle to heal.

I went on a trip to the East Coast with some girlfriends, and near the end of the trip, I called home and talked to Andy. He said the ankle was fine—the cast was coming off—but that the bruise on his finger was starting to hurt. I told him to have Simon take him to the doctor to have it looked at.

"Nah, it's nothing, Mom," he said. "I'll have the orthopedist look at it when he takes the cast off next week."

When I got home, his ankle was much better, but the finger was really sore and the nail bed was swollen and blue-black. The orthopedist had said it looked like a blood blister, so he tried to drain it and relieve the pressure. Nothing much happened.

In hindsight, this diagnosis was the first of the mistakes, the first of the "what-ifs." He thought we needed to give it a bit more time to heal, so we went home. The best part of the appointment was the doctor's okay for junior-year football.

It was hot when Andy started his conditioning. The running exhausted him, but he was enthused and tried to catch up quickly. School started, and with it, the pressure to keep up his grades so he could play football. He was missing Alex a lot, but all his buddies were around him and more people than ever were noticing his football skills and talking about his college potential. By the beginning of October, his finger was causing him a great deal of pain.

And then there's the moment.

"My God, Mom," my beautiful son says, "look at my finger!"

So it begins. The big hand grabs your head and pushes you under and you can't breathe, and the real world is up behind a silvery barrier and laughing at you, carelessly.

I replay it all the time. "My God, Mom, look at my finger!" he says, and I turn from the sink again in slow motion. This is a precise point in my life: the first step on one of those long journeys you hear so much about.

Like most truisms, "the longest journey begins with one step" doesn't address the nature of the trip—where you're going, whether or not you want to go, what sort of country you'll pass through, whether it's worth making. The trip through the valley of the shadow of death begins with one step.

The finger hurt so much Andy couldn't think of anything else on the way into town to see Michael, the plastic surgeon. He looked at the finger and scheduled Andy for surgery the next day. When it was over, Michael came out and told Simon, Cheryl, Linda and me that the mass of tissue was a tumor like none he had ever seen. He thought he had removed it all, but it had wrapped itself around the bone and it was hard to say.

We were all quiet. I had to say something. I had the medical experience. What could I say? Simon was quiet—that wasn't a surprise. But Cheryl was quiet, too. Linda's mouth was just slightly open. I had to think of something to say in order to regain control. If you don't say something, you give up control. Michael was looking at me. I couldn't say anything. My heart seemed to pull loose and sink.

"Could it be a melanoma?" I said, softly, finally.

"Well, we'll really have to wait for the pathology report."

There was a brief silence and Cheryl said, "Leave it to us to have something no one knows about."

She said it brightly and I was very grateful. She tried to work our humor. "Maybe they can call it Android's disease after Andy."

I couldn't think. Why should I think? The tumor was gone and his finger would heal. Our luck would hold. Regardless, thinking or not, my fear was palpable—a real, live thing beating inside of me.

I knew Andy was special. I always had. Was this what "special" was going to mean? Was "special" just a concentrated quality in a life destined to be short?

After he healed for a week, we went back to have the stitches removed and find out about the tumor. But the pathology report wasn't in yet, and no one locally had been able to identify the cells.

"Is that bad news?"

"There's no use panicking when we don't know anything," Michael said.

I wished he hadn't said "panic." Andy seemed sure it wasn't going to be anything bad. He wasn't panicky. I tried to stay calm, but my ghosts were stirring and grinning.

The slides from the tumor were sent to the Stanford University Medical Center for identification. I told a friend how scared I was, but all I received were platitudes that were helping her more than me. I knew that the tumor was bad news, but no one around me was interested in validating my fears. Why should they be?

I knew too much and I was afraid. Bits and pieces of operating-room knowledge kept popping into my head.

And I felt guilty.

Was this my punishment for not doing a better job with the young boy in hospice? Was this a payback? The fear dogged my thoughts for months, and I carried it alone. I couldn't tell anyone about it.

Andy's surgery had been in October 1988. By early November, we still hadn't heard a thing. Finally, Michael's secretary called and asked us to come in. Simon and Andy and Fear and I waited in the office.

When the normally cheerful Michael saw us, he was quiet. He looked at Andy's finger and said it was doing fine. Then he turned with what Andy later called "a shallow kind of sorrow in his eyes," and looked at each of us in turn. I took a deep breath.

"It's a rare tumor. It's called clear cell sarcoma. We don't know much about it, but it is related to melanoma. It's highly malignant." He stopped.

I didn't have to look around. I could feel everyone in the room. I knew I wasn't understanding everything he was saying.

We sat. None of us had said a word. Andy was looking at the floor.

Michael cleared his throat and started to turn, then turned back with his arms apart and his palms out.

"His arm will probably have to come off at the shoulder," he said. Silence. "I've already started calling the teaching hospitals to find out what's new in the field." Silence.

Michael was distraught. He was a friend, with children of his own.

"Whatever I can find out, whenever I find it, I'll call you right away. I'm so sorry."

Andy might die. Andy would have his left arm amputated at the shoulder.

The thoughts I had in my head were rolling and thudding from side to side like heavy ball bearings. We left and crossed the parking lot like zombies. At the car, we cried and tried to draw strength from each other. Driving home was driving to safety. That's what it felt like, at least. Outside was the nightmare and home was the safe place. Things could be as they were at home. We didn't talk. I don't remember seeing anything.

At home, we called the rest of the family and they all came to the house. Nobody knew what to say. We just needed to be together in a familiar place. The house drew in around us and we were cut off.

The atmosphere grew thicker and thicker and finally Andy had to get away, so he drove over to Frankie's while the rest of us just sat there, hashing and rehashing what we knew and what we didn't know. It was a long, long night, and even after it was dark, it seemed to keep getting darker. When I finally turned off the lights, it was like they were the last ones anywhere.

4

Shattered Dreams

I think back now to who I was then, and there's a strange dislocation. I know I've changed, but it's hard to pin it down. It's almost like you disappear into a crisis and come out the other end and something is different, but you've been inside so long you hardly know. You have things to relearn.

I'd already been through times I thought were difficult. When Simon and I married I was just eighteen, and Simon's family were traditional, old-fashioned Portuguese who didn't think of me as the ideal bride. But I couldn't go home (my father was at sea and my mother was unavailable), so before the baby was born I left nursing school and moved into Simon's parents' home. It wasn't a wrong-side-of-the-tracks problem between us my family was well-to-do—it was personal. Simon was away doing his required military time. He came home on leave so we could get married. Then he went back and left me with his parents, afraid and alone. He was able to come back again when Cheryl was born, but he had to leave as soon as I came home from the hospital.

Among the notes of congratulations on Cheryl's birth was a letter with the date of our wedding on it, the date of Cheryl's birth and a handwritten note that said, "Who do you think you are fooling?" I can still see it.

When Simon came home for good, things were easier. His parents had bought the neighboring property so we were able to have a place of our own. Life was still difficult, though, and I acted in ways that would have been normal in my own family, but which brought the "We don't do things like that" rebuke from my in-laws. I'd never felt so isolated and visible.

I had no one to turn to. I'd sit out in the field thinking about my options. There weren't many, and one time I sat in the bright green field with a shotgun. The moment passed, though, and I endured, and finally, after years in a mobile home with five children, we moved into the main house.

I was the woman up in the main house now: a good mother and wife and, I like to think, a tough woman who knew how to dig in and fight. My grandmother's blood was in me, and my father's too.

If Andy had cancer, well, we'd fight it all the way.

Andy didn't talk about it much in the first days.

"Mom, it's fucked; it's just fucked."

I remember that, the pure rage. My answers were simple.

"We'll beat it. We'll find out everything we can about it and we'll beat it."

We'd always talked in the afternoons after school, and especially in the mornings, when we'd sit in the kitchen. But this wasn't chitchat and this wasn't the kind of topic for which we even had a vocabulary. We weren't able to tell him, "We'll do this, then that, and this will be the result." He was coming to terms with the fact that sooner or later all the decisions were going to have to be his.

I remember him calling Cheryl one night, and she came out half an hour later in her Nissan and picked him up. Linda loved Andy very much, and she had been old enough when he was born to feel that special sense of responsibility for him, but she was a new mother and Andy didn't want to burden her with his thoughts just then.

And God knows if you needed to talk to someone, Cheryl was the one. There wasn't anything unspoken with Cheryl. I spoke to her about it the next day.

"Andy wanted to scream at God," she said. "We went out to the coast to the PG&E site and parked at the cliff because that's where he wanted to go. He said he wanted to scream at God but he didn't, not at all. We just talked for a long time."

We began a hunt for anyone who knew anything about clear cell sarcoma. We didn't know how or where to start, but others were doing it for us, calls going out in every direction. We entered the world of cancer, a societal substratum with its own words and rules and images. The children dominate the images: the crying and the silent; the children with no hair and pale faces and vocabularies not just beyond their years but beyond, you like to think, their understanding.

We needed to know where to go. That afternoon my sister Melouise (Mello) reached someone at St. Jude Children's Hospital by telling them she had donated to them and needed help now. Someone on staff talked to her and gave her a name at Stanford Medical Center.

My sister Maureen called them and started the process through the radiology department. I was surprised how easy it was to set up an appointment. We didn't even need an original physician's referral. I called Michael and he said yes, this was the way to go. All we had to do was make it through the weekend and Monday. Then we'd see someone who could help.

Around the house, Simon was quiet and I cried.

I had all the pathology, surgery and X-ray reports ready to take with us. I started a journal for important information and bought a tape recorder to record whatever was said. Maureen, a nurse in Sacramento, and my friend Sharon, who had graduated with me, were coming along. Andy, Simon, Cheryl, me and two more nurses. We formed a solid wall of support.

I figured we'd be able to make it through the day.

As I stepped forward to the radiology window, Andy watched, hanging behind like a frightened rabbit. Both he and Simon were ready to run at the first chance.

This was the first step in what was to become our pattern. I would swallow my fear and step up to see what we needed to do. I couldn't hang back; we each had our role to play. Cancer opens a world where you come to have a role. It may be similar to the one you always took, or it may be completely different. The family has to shift and adapt.

After what seemed like hours in the waiting room, we were

ushered into Dr. Chandler's office. She told us flat out that we were dealing with a rare and deadly cancer.

"There's probably going to be surgery, I want you all to know. There are other treatments, but surgery is the first consideration. There's radiation and chemotherapy, and in combination they have been effective. I won't lie to you. Chemotherapy is still controversial for this type of cancer. But there is hope."

We heard "hope" clearly. Probably each of us didn't hear other things, chose not to on some level, but "hope" we heard clearly.

"The tumor's in the end of his finger and that's good. Andy says he's feeling good and can do the things he's always done, and that may mean it just started."

"Can we start right away? I need to start doing something," Andy said.

He asked good questions about surgery, radiation and chemo. He was so afraid he'd lose his arm at the shoulder, so afraid that it would be just the beginning.

"You know, I'm scared and I want you to tell us where to start because I just need to know what to do and I'll do it."

"There are some things I just can't tell you," Dr. Chandler said. "I can't lie to you. I know what you're going through, but I can't give you any clear answers. Most cancer treatment isn't cut-and-dried, and the rareness of yours makes it all the more difficult."

I was glad he'd brought it up, but I knew Andy hadn't exposed all his fear. He couldn't.

As far as the doctor could see, nothing had spread. We were going to be immersed in tests. Other doctors would test and evaluate, and out of the assembled data they'd hope to be able to adopt an effective treatment plan. Andy said, "How long will all this take?"

Dr. Chandler looked at him with considerable attention.

"It's going to take a week, longer for the results. But you're one of my kids now and no matter what, you're always going to be one. If you need to talk, call me. Anytime. Do you understand me?"

"Yeah."

"Anytime, believe me about this, anytime."

She was very kind, but it wasn't enough. I didn't want to leave without her. She was our anchor on a stormy sea.

We followed the signs to Pedi-Onc, as the pediatric oncology clinic was called, and traveled the hallways that would soon become familiar, though never comfortable.

In the clinic area, we sat where we could, scattering around the room. We would have preferred to be together but couldn't, so we sat there quietly and watched the sick children. There were lots of them. None looked like Andy. They looked sick and he looked well—handsome, big, strong.

This can't happen to my son. He doesn't belong here. How could he possibly belong here? We'll just go home. If we go home everything will be all right.

The image of Cheryl and Andy in the tiny car in front of the ocean at night came to me. The car was lit inside and seemed warm and safe. *This can't happen to us. Why are we here? Run.*

Runrunrunrun.

The other parents offered tentative smiles. They recognized our newness, fear and pain. The kids played and didn't notice us at all. The kids in their parents' arms looked at us, but showed no interest. They seemed submerged. In what kind of misery? In what kind of pain?

A nurse came for us and, with a look of reassurance and a touch on the arm, showed Andy the way. We went along, all six of us. As she was weighing him, the nurse directed control to him.

"This is your battle, Andy. This is your cause. Your family can help, but it's your fight."

The next room had an examination table, a stool and cupboards. There were bright children's posters on the wall, but they only heightened the sterility of the room. They also heightened the fear, because they let us know how far we had moved from the pleasures of the child's world.

The new doctor was colder. Dr. Schlemmer, a pediatric oncologist, gave us less hope. He wasn't at all what I had expected in terms of demeanor or empathy. He seemed battleworn, and he didn't connect with us or even seem to want to. I didn't like him and I was suspicious. I felt like I needed to protect Andy from him. I wondered if he was typical of the doctors who treat childhood cancers. I would find out later he wasn't.

I recorded our whole conversation.

"Let me go over some things you may have discussed already."

He opened a folder and pursed his lips, dropping the corners of his mouth. "I talked to the radiologist, and I have to tell you, I take exception to some of the tests she's suggested."

He sat back authoritatively.

"For one thing, these tumors begin to spread immediately. They might not be large, but they're probably there already. So we're going to have to look for spread aggressively."

No one said a word. This had the momentum of a performance, and it didn't seem possible to interrupt.

"We're dealing with a cancer for which the literature is inadequate. It's old before it even gets published, so throw away any notion of a simple, prescribed treatment. And whatever we find when we look, you have to avoid being automatically against chemotherapy. Kids react better to it, forget what you've heard."

Dr. Schlemmer was looking at Andy's cancer differently from the radiologist. His experience was different, and his opinions were harsher. What he told us was much less hopeful. Worse than that, it sounded like the truth. I was beginning to hate him. Hatred is not an everyday emotion in my life. Hatred is beyond anger, and I hadn't even really explored my anger yet.

He thought chemotherapy was what we should look to first. Andy would lose his hair, become permanently sterile and have periods of not feeling well. But he would probably do fine in the long run, and he wanted us to start just as soon as we could. He hadn't yet been able to read all of Andy's reports.

"The tumor's been in Andy's body for at least a year, and there are probably small cells in Andy's lungs and lymphatic system. There's no way the previous surgery got all the tumor."

Silence.

A year. All the time we'd been waiting for it to go away, we'd been giving it time to grow. My head began to scream.

"Oh," Andy said.

"What does that mean?" I said.

"Just what I said. The previous surgery didn't get all of it."

The journal we had was a battered yellow tablet with an orange and blue quicksilver sticker of a pair of surfing shorts on its front. I looked at it in Sharon's hands. She was scribbling in it.

We left the office and made our way delicately past the sick children and their parents. Our faces were white, and on the faces of the staff we could see that they knew what we'd been told.

Outside the building, in the sunlight, I started to cry helplessly. The tears just streamed down my cheeks. It was all hopeless. The world had broken in, and it was destroying us.

Everyone talked except Andy. Can you imagine what a terrible thing that is to have to say? "Everybody talked but Andy." His silence comes back now like a voice.

I cried, and Andy just stood there as if he were waiting for someone to take control and stop the nightmare. He resisted hugs and small talk, and I could see him sinking deeper into himself. He was surrounded by us and silent. Somehow none of us were normal people anymore. We weren't healthy; we never would be healthy. We must have done something wrong. I must have done something wrong.

Other people let you know that, tacitly. Not all, but some. They treat you as if you're a token sacrifice—as if your life is not only over, but it's a possible source of contagion. You can prove that cancer isn't physically contagious, but the fear remains, a deep, almost primitive fear that contact with the unlucky produces unluckiness. They're scared and they don't know what to do or say. Some of our friends and neighbors would gather around, some would pull back. That's just the way it is.

The formal patterns don't mean much. The casual acquaintance may turn out to be a pillar of strength, while the longtime friend fades out of the picture. You learn that you're in a slightly different world, just off to the side, and that some will acknowledge it, some will just look and some will run away.

In the places where your weaknesses are, cracks will form and radiate. Are you a touch paranoid? Are you chronically frightened? Are you angry and impatient? Be prepared for the empowerment of your defects and the guilt that comes with knowing you've given them power.

You can learn to live with all of it. You have to. You learn, too, that at night, when you're scared, pulling the covers over your head doesn't help at all.

5

_A_ GLIMMER

You know how it is when something has happened and you push it out of your mind but it stays, it's right there, and every once in a while you'll be doing something—good, bad or indifferent—and suddenly there's a push in your head that makes an opening and there it is, and you're stunned and fearful.

It happens in dreams a lot. The whole dream is framed by something awful and you keep trying to forget it, but then you seem to wake up, though you're still inside the dream, and you remember to be afraid.

Well, that's how everything was, every day, after we knew Andy was sick. In the dark, I'd suddenly be awake with nothing else in the world but Andy's disease and my helplessness. It's like your eyes open up in order to make you remember.

Tomorrow is another day of effort and it won't be enough and my baby might die and it's dark, it's always going to be dark, and the moonlight is cold as ice.

You absolutely fear tomorrow and the next day and the days after that, but all you want in the world, anyway, is for the night to be over and for there to be some piece of hope. I lie there looking at the dark. I plan and I try to gather myself.

We all have different ways of handling the fear. In the evenings, we cry differently. Some choke it back and some are loud and some are silent. Simon's tears are big, and they roll quietly down his cheeks.

But the main thing for me is that I have to be ready. Every time the sun comes up, I have to be ready. This is how the days go: We get up before the sun. Maybe the sound of the tractor is the first thing I hear, the sound of the milk pump in the barn, Simon calling the cows. Simon is up and out already, and the dairy work has to go on as ever. When we have to go to the hospital, Andy doesn't get out of bed till the very last minute. He doesn't eat, either. When it's a day of tests he's edgy and abstracted. I try to be businesslike. I try to be together and matter-of-fact. It's chilly in the house, and the air is full of the small, distant sounds of the countryside. The only heat is from the kitchen woodstove. Sometimes we see Simon and sometimes we don't.

The ride to Stanford takes at least two hours. When we have to be there at eight, we hit the rush hour and it's going to take a lot longer. When Andy's ready, I drink my coffee and gather up my papers and notebook and tape recorder. My attitude, too: I put that together as if I were picking out clothes for an occasion. I use everything I have.

The hills around the farm are very low and gentle. They roll over and up and down again and in the first pale light it's like being in a fairy-tale country, the twisted silhouettes of the live oak just like the trees in some children's book.

There isn't a lot to say, and we take the earliness of the hour and the breaking of the light as quiet time. We drive toward the sun and its glare.

At Highway 101, things change. Commuter traffic has started to move, and there's the inevitable jam where the road narrows through Petaluma. The sun is out, and we're caught up in the highway mechanism. At the other end is Stanford. (Go slower? Go faster? What happens today? Rush for good news? Don't go at all? There's the turnoff to San Rafael. Do something else? Wouldn't that be nice, just the two of us in the morning.)

I drive very fast when the traffic lets me. Andy calls me Marilyn Andretti. But then there's the time, and if I realize I'm going to get us there early, I slow down. We may be going for a lumbar puncture and I know exactly how it's going to hurt, but I can't tell Andy that. I always tell him exactly what will be done and I'll say, "Yes, it'll hurt," but I never say how much. I never make comparisons. Andy gets lost in his own thoughts. Sometimes we talk about when it's all going to be over, about college and what he'll do when he graduates. The more we can project it, the more real it becomes. It's like building a house out of imaginary materials. We try to make the future solid, with no room for accident.

I drive fast and erratically and, more often than not, I'll cut at least one person off while changing lanes. I know I change speeds too much, and I look at my watch compulsively. We don't want to get there early, and we don't want to get there late. The truth is, we don't want to get there at all.

We cross the Golden Gate Bridge. That's always a kind of marker, a shift from one world to the other. We drive through Golden Gate Park and out the other side and south. The traffic thins out past San Francisco State. The highway is 280 now, a wide, fast expanse.

Not too late, not too early. If we spend ten hours at the Medical Center, and that's an average time, seven of those hours will be spent waiting. Just waiting. Sitting in a variety of chairs in a variety of waiting rooms. Some are comfortable and some are savagely uncomfortable. All of us waiting watch each other. Not blatantly, but we pay attention. Once in a while, you catch someone's eye and there's a flicker of recognition, but generally we respect each other's pain and what is there to say, anyway? I have seen good news on faces coming out. Those who have had good news can't hide it. Their joy is an alien presence and they leave the building as quickly as they can. They'll be flying by the time they're outside.

The very first day we start at the main building. It's stark. The stucco walls shoot straight up into the sky, with nothing for the eye but the rows of windows. The entrance seems huge, like the mouth of a monster. I want to run away. There's a doorman, a nice man, who'll remember our faces in the future.

The children's hospital, where we'll spend the most time, is not far from Stanford Stadium. The fields around it and the parking lot have been plowed to minimize the fire risk. Every car we drive by has people in it who aren't going to the oncology unit. They don't even know they're lucky. They don't know much of anything. Not if they aren't going to the pedi-onc clinic. How could they know anything? It isn't their fault. Why would they want to?

We have some time one day and drive to the stadium. We step out and look around. Football. Sunlight and a game and what? A hundred thousand in Stanford Stadium. They had a Super Bowl here. Andy looks around longingly.

On the weekends, he goes out with his friends—waterskiing, working on the truck, hunting, four-wheeling. During the week, he's a sick child surrounded by sick children in a place of stunned, disbelieving pain.

There's a businesslike receptionist who'll gradually warm to Andy and our situation. People can't not warm to Andy. I'm sure she's done it many times before—it's her job—but it still feels good to get a smile and an occasional pat on the arm.

When we finish the paperwork and go to sit in the lobby, she comes by to touch my shoulder and say, "I know he'll make it. He looks so strong and has such a positive attitude."

Thank you, thank you, thank you, I think. There are long halls to walk, small talk filling the silence, none of us caring what we say. We don't want to think. We need to keep from thinking. We work at it.

The building has levels. You move through levels toward the antiseptic heart where there's nothing but you and your child, and the flat facts of the disease. The softness of the reception area gives way to shining halls and floors and gleaming stainless steel.

In the clinic area children are clustered around a bright green play table in the center of the room. An aquarium sits on a shelf, and tiny chairs in primary colors are arranged along the wall and bunched at the table. Orange adult-size chairs are clustered off to one side.

We sit quietly. There are lots of kids: little kids, big kids, sick kids, thin kids, babies in their mother's arms. Most have no hair, some are listless, many pale and wan. *He's too big for the little chairs,* I think ridiculously. *Do they expect him to sit in one of those little chairs?*

In the main building, where the radiation department is, we saw mostly adults. Now we've reached the place where the ravaged children are. It's impossible to face. It isn't acceptable to the human mind. The mind needs shields and buffers and there aren't any, really, not if you're going to be sitting in plastic chairs for ten hours surrounded by sick children and their terrified parents.

The occasional, flickering recognitions are almost major communications, one parent to another. From the waiting rooms, the crying and screams cut right through the walls. The little kids sit there. Andy sits there. The kids communicate across a room more readily than the parents do. Perhaps there's a hideous, inexplicable trace of guilt in the parents—that it's their fault, that they did something wrong. Our eyes don't meet as easily.

Andy sits bravely, smiling in return to the smiles given to him by the little kids, watching and absorbing everything that's going on around him. He acts as if he doesn't hear the screams. They all do. But he hears, they hear, we hear. It's something you feel should be stopped, that you should be stopping it.

Right through Andy's smile, I can see what we're waiting for: all the answers to all the questions. Would he lose his arm? Is his chance at high school and college sports over? How will he work if he has no arm? Will he die?

We had to drive a few miles for the MRI. I had directions, but I began to panic as I tried to find my way through traffic in a town I'd never been in before. I thought I'd been in control when I left that morning. The cornfield stretches out for miles, and hostile things are moving in it, crisscrossing, threatening. I thought I'd be able to handle the day alone, but I wasn't. I was lost in heavy traffic. I panicked.

I'm the Mom, I thought. *I'm supposed to be able to handle this.* But I didn't know where I was, and I didn't know where to go, and I was driving south when I needed to go east. I started to cry behind the wheel so I pulled off the freeway and looked at the map through a wet blur, but the map that had looked so clear to me before was a cipher, a drawing of hell.

Andy dozed beside me, exhausted, getting some rest before the next test. I didn't want to wake him. I didn't want him to feel responsible for my tears, and I didn't want him to see how frustrated and broken I'd become. He needed to know someone was able to care for him, someone to be in charge when he couldn't, or didn't want to. I wanted that someone to be me. Good start.

I breathed deeply, picked up the map and laboriously figured out where we were. Finally, we pulled up to the gray stone building. I breathed deeply again and said, "We're here, Honey," and Andy stirred and sat up. He didn't know. Only I knew.

The MRI would tell us if any tumors were in his brain. It was terrifying. We registered and waited. His name was called, and he bravely walked away with yet another stranger. I could hear his voice and another's, and then it was quiet for a while. When I heard Andy sobbing a moment later, my heart broke with that sudden falling of parts in your chest that you never become used to.

Alone in some small room, waiting for his life, his composure was broken and my sweet child was crying. I heard voices again. It was hard not to run to him, but the voice sounded reassuring and I didn't want to barge in. I didn't want to embarrass him.

It was all insane. My reactions were from a partly remembered stable world. At the bottom of everything was the desolation you feel when you know you can't protect your own child. I listened for any sound that might mean something.

Another woman was in the waiting room with me, but I didn't care. When I finally looked at her, I sobbed that my son was in there and they were looking for brain tumors. I needed to explain. She nodded sadly. I didn't know why she was waiting. Her reasons might have been worse than mine. I don't remember her leaving, but finally, I was alone in the room as the dark filled in the windows and the minute hands crept. All I wanted was to take my son home.

It was after 8 P.M. when Andy finally came out and said we could go. He was drained. The time spent waiting weighs with a heaviness you think will never lift. In the car, Andy slumped back in his seat.

No news would come for a few days, but at least we would be home and Andy could go back to school, see his friends and have someone besides me to talk to.

This was a template for what will come. We'll move in the right direction and we'll get the information we need to fight. We'll walk the hallways and sit in the waiting rooms and talk to doctors, and Andy will face the tests and the pain.

If you've ever had something alter the patterns of your life, you know how the new realities don't ever quite become the ordinary, how behind what you're doing there's always the specter of how things were in the place you're going to go back to as soon as you can. But for a while there's this other world, and it has to be handled coherently. That's my job.

On the weekends, I catch up on running the farm. I do all the paperwork, pay all the bills and meet the payroll. Things keep running. The bills that used to worry me don't matter.

After an average day at the clinic, Andy and I drive back with more hope, or less hope, or just the hopeless exhaustion in the dark that comes with not knowing enough and having to make decisions based on what you don't know.

Simon tries to have dinner ready for us. Coming up the driveway, the lights in the windows are heaven. There may be family inside, and we'll all sit and talk and bounce bits of strength and encouragement back and forth. On the darkest nights, when the news is bad, we'll each cry again in our different ways; Simon, as always, silent, with big tears filling his eyes.

The days are lined up in front of us, as far as we can see. When we don't have to go to Palo Alto, I clean. Clean and clean and clean. I vacuum and dust and mop the floors. I wash the walls. I shampoo the carpets.

If you walked into my house tomorrow, you could tell how my mind is by the relative neatness and cleanliness. If it's messy, I'm okay. If it's spotless and orderly, I'm floundering and faking control.

Day after day is the highway/hospital, or vacuum cleaner/mop.

In between is trying to sleep.

6

Pandora's Box

I already knew a lot about cancer. As a nurse I'd seen and handled cancers. I'd seen patients wheeled into the operating room for exploratory surgery, and wheeled out again without a hope of survival. I'd worked with dying cancer patients in hospice and watched, over and over again, the strange and always-different dynamics of families in crisis. I probably knew more about cancer than was good for me. But I needed to know more. I needed to know everything.

I knew there was hope. Treatment had advanced. Cancer

wasn't a death sentence anymore, not if it was caught in time. The patients who had left surgery under sentence of death were the ones who had come too late. We hadn't, and hope always existed. I believed that to my very soul, and I knew enough about the attitudes and problems of the families I'd dealt with to think that ours would be okay. As it turned out, I shouldn't even have bothered to worry about that. Everyone pulled together.

Brain tumors leave a road map on the head: scars running left and right on little, bald heads. Sometimes you can see the marks of the drill.

The children in chemotherapy have a different sort of baldness. The hair has fallen out by itself, and sometimes wisps are left behind that the children don't want to part with. It's their identity.

Cancer and its treatment are a world to themselves. The world of cancer isolates, and grows more isolated, as the disease progresses. The progress is logical. Not necessary, perhaps, but logical. Patients together in the hospital are a natural group, even if they don't talk much. But what begins is a gradual, insistent withdrawal. Patients withdraw from the world, families withdraw from patients, friends and acquaintances withdraw from families. Cancer doesn't eat away at just the flesh. It consumes social fabric and hollows out families.

In hospice, you see it all and you do what you can. That isn't a lot, really. You offer what you can in terms of facts and support and emotional honesty, but in the final analysis, everyone handles it on an individual level. Whatever resources they have, or don't have, are going to be attacked by the sheer force of the disease.

You see miracles of courage and love, and you see dull, fragmented misery as families pull away from the patient and each other. At some point, the general range of friends and well-wishers always starts to fall away.

You move into an artificial world where every move is dictated by the necessities of treatment, which quickly becomes a treadmill. During those times when you can get off, you tend to the requirements of your previous life in a quarter of the time they usually consumed. You can't think about the future every minute, because the fear and the helplessness will kill you. You can't sit around thinking about the past because that will kill you too, with its own soft misery. You have to stay *right there*, prepared and tough and in motion. You go up with good reports and down with bad reports. You have a family raised to an impossible power of alert tension, and you have an outside world that seems to be moving imperceptibly away, every day a little farther.

You know you're pulling back; you can feel it. The frames of reference shift, and a close friend may no longer see or want to see the world the way you do. People have their reasons, their own adaptations and their own accommodations. You know that. You don't want to push it. So you withdraw just a little and friends withdraw just a little, and pretty soon you're in parallel universes. I can't remember ever becoming angry about it.

It was easier to vent at random strangers, people in the street, shoppers at the supermarket. You think you see a lack of appreciation for the ordinary everywhere, and you seethe. You want to reach through the telephone line and choke the man who calls to remind you your payment is late. He's so vapid, so self-satisfied. He has no right.

You know this is wrong, too, but it can't be helped. On top of everything else, you're exhausted. Everyone you're close to is exhausted. And your son is going to sleep every night in absolute, hideous uncertainty.

There's another fight that goes on at the same time as the fight against cancer, and it takes a huge amount of your already committed energy. You have to fight the insurance company for coverage of the treatments the doctors have recommended.

Our insurer wanted us to do as much as possible locally. They question every test. If approved, they push to have it done locally. The person making the decisions is neither a doctor nor an oncology nurse, and the system can drive you mad.

That's the way they want it to be.

By hampering spontaneous moves and slowing the process, the direction of treatment can be controlled in a way that is cost-effective, but doesn't necessarily do anything for the patient.

They understand that your child may die, but they expect you to understand that they have accountants to answer to. The cancer itself may not always be a killer, but the insurance carrier can be. They trade on the ill-informed trust of a terrified family who has to believe that everyone cares.

And the insurers tell you their good reasons.

"What can we say to the shareholders? That we've taken their money in good faith and thrown it away on expensive treatments for a boy who's going to die anyway?"

And their expenses are just overwhelming. Consider their executive pay scale. Consider their one-year advertising budget. Consider what it costs to handle Washington in the style to which it has become accustomed.

This is the greatest health-care system in the world, we're told, and it should make you proud to be an American. But when the money isn't there, well, another way has to be found. The insurance companies are just like us and have to live within budgets. They have to make the difficult choices.

Which of the giant corporations lives within a budget? How

many families, for that matter, live within budgets? The hypo-
critical rhetoric could make you vomit. The bought-and-paid-
for congressional shills know. They just don't care. "We all have
to live within our means," they intone. "We have difficult
choices to make." Not really. There's one significant choice, perhaps. They could return the rate of corporate taxation to where
it was in the 1950s, when things were pretty good, and stop
telling us entitlements are the problem.

America's health-care system isn't the greatest in the world. As
a matter of fact, we rank near the bottom of the industrialized
world in basic services. Also as a matter of fact, executives are
being paid hundreds of times what the actual, involved, skilled
staff member earns, and "necessary" cuts are being made at the
bottom, at treatment level.

Doctors are told not to recommend alternative, more expensive remedies. Health insurance companies don't take the
Hippocratic Oath. Lives, to them, have a basic monetary value,
and treatment needs to be evaluated in terms of cost over the
expected lifetime of the patient.

The idea that human life can be measured economically has
been creeping into our political system for a long time. Nowhere
is it stronger than in the health insurance industry.

Consider it this way. Your child contracts a disease requiring
expensive treatments. It isn't fatal with the proper treatments, but
they're expensive. The insurance company won't cover the treatments. The reason they give you is that your child is going to
require an expenditure for treatment that will exceed, over the
likely span of his life, what he can reasonably be expected to earn
(his worth) as computed on the basis of his class, intelligence and
compromised physical condition. What would you do? Probably,
you don't know. Few of us have had to deal with anger on that level.

I like to think I understood what was going on pretty quickly. So the fighting on our flanks and the endless skirmishes began. We needed approval from them to continue at the medical center, but they had their own contracts with hospitals and labs in our county. At the medical center—an institution with no contracted discount—the insurance carrier pays the full rate.

In short, they wanted Andy treated where the services were the cheapest. The quality of the service doesn't enter into the equation.

I understood their problem, loathsome as it was, but my problem was saving my son's life and that was going to take the best care possible. Here's what you need to know first. *In California, it is against the law to deny any child life-saving medical services the child needs!* Remember it.

I telephoned anyone and everyone I thought might give me information on how to handle the insurance company. While working for hospice, I *had* learned how to beat the bushes to get things done, and the skills were coming in handy. I called friends from the operating room—doctors and nurses alike. I called medical secretaries, the American Cancer Society, a lawyer and my family. I called them all before I called the insurance company. I knew I needed to convince whoever I talked to of the overwhelming reasons that Andy needed to be treated where he had begun.

You need to have your facts together before dealing with insurers. Remember this fact also.

With my plan set, and anchored by the fact that there were no pediatric oncologists practicing in Sonoma County, I called our insurance company. I asked for a person whose name had been given to me as someone who might listen. I hoped she'd want to work with us after hearing Andy's story. We talked, I pleaded our case, and finally, I received verbal approval to continue Andy's care at the medical center. I felt that the woman on the other end of the telephone was feeling some empathy for me as a mother and was swayed by my begging for Andy's treatment chance.

So, while the insurance company had wanted us to do all that was possible in local facilities, we were clear for now to have all the surgeries, scans, MRIs and bone marrow tests done at the medical center. It would all change later, though.

People with catastrophic illnesses absolutely must hook up with someone in the medical authorization department who is willing to work for them. You have to make a personal contact, someone who will remember your name and your story when you call again. You might find someone who cares. You might need to go through a whole list of possible contacts until you get someone who feels right.

Health insurance problems plagued us throughout Andy's battle and, as awful as it seems, *when you are fighting cancer for a life, you also need to fight a life-and-death battle with your insurance carrier.*

If you don't stay ready to fight, constantly watching and pushing and guiding your insurance company, they will direct the care for their own benefit, not yours.

You must be clear and stand firm!

Forget the feel-good commercials. The insurance company is looking at the bottom line, and your child's life isn't on it.

To the health plan professionals, an expensive patient is an expendable patient. Your treatment is an expense they are trying to control, and a catastrophic illness with continuous, expensive treatment and tests screws up their equations. Complacency won't get you by.

If you are complacent, if you accept what you're told, you lose.

There's a kind of exhaustion that settles over you without making you actually tired, or less able to continue. "One foot in front of the other" becomes a way of life. The situation takes over, and you have to fight it with an ordinary, common-sense voice in your head. "This is not forever. The hallways at the medical center are not forever. We'll go to sleep and wake up in the morning and do what has to be done, no more, no less. We love each other and we're strong. Andy is strong. The end is uncertain and you have to keep moving."

After a long day with nothing to look forward to but scans, we drove home and pulled up the dirt driveway. The lights were on as always, and the house looked warm. Andy was crying and he didn't want to talk. He didn't want to do anything except maybe run away, step out of the car and be away from us.

He just wanted to be normal. That's the feeling you get when you see ordinary people going about their ordinary business as if it were nothing, to be in the world and untargeted. God, you want to be like them.

Normal? What's that? You wonder about it in a shifting, unreal place. Normal? What was that like? Who remembers?

7

OPTIMISTIC TOKEN

*F*ear was all over Andy's face. Would he lose his arm? Was his chance at sports over?

Dr. Tobias, the surgeon, smiled broadly, said "Hi," and gave Andy's shoulder a squeeze as he passed by his chair. He examined Andy from head to foot, paying particular attention to his finger.

Breathe and breathe and breathe. I could hear each breath in the quiet room. Finished, Dr. Tobias turned to us. "There are still cancer cells in Andy's finger, even though the tumor is out. An amputation is necessary."

Breathe, pause.

"But I don't see any necessity to amputate the whole arm, Andy. I think taking the finger will definitely be enough."

Andy smiled. I breathed again.

Dr. Tobias gave us a great deal of frightening information, and we listened and scribbled and recorded. But we did it all with less dread, and his attitude helped a lot. He wasn't tired, or dry, and it seemed that Andy's survival mattered to him. He was on our side.

We made the plans for the amputation of Andy's finger. It's to be taken off back to the second joint. The doctor has described an alternative, ray amputation, which wouldn't leave a stump but that would compress the hand. Andy would rather not go that way. But first things first. The operation will be after the big football game.

It's *the* game, the last game of the season and Andy's last chance to make his varsity letter. I can't tell you how important it is to him. He hasn't been able to play, hasn't even been able to practice, not really, and if he doesn't get some playing time against Potter Valley, he won't make the letter. So he's going to play. This doesn't sit very well with the mother of the boy who's been replacing him, but I can hardly worry about that. My worry card is full.

I wish I could tell you about the game so it would make sense in a football way, but I really can't.

I can tell you that this was the last game of the season, that we were playing Potter Valley High School, and that Andy was going to be a running back on offense and an end on defense. If Tomales could win, it would give us a chance to go to the play-offs. In high school ball, this was a very big deal. And Les, our son-in-law, was the assistant coach.

So the air was full of nervous expectation. Andy seemed fine about it. The doctor had cleared him to play as long as he wore a metal finger guard wrapped in bandages. So many things were rolled into a three-hour high school football game. Football was a link between where Andy was now and everything he wanted. If he could do it, if he could play well and rise above the fear, what could stop him? Football was a train he could ride right through this misery. Everyone knew it, everyone felt it.

You get superstitious, even if you haven't been before. You look for signs and omens. The weather on a crucial day may be important. You hold on to every little thing you can that lets you say, "We're going to make it. It's going to be all right."

So the possibilities and the attached emotions were immense. The trip to the game was like a pilgrimage to an oracle. We felt like we were going to receive some privileged information about the future.

Potter Valley is in Mendocino County, north of Sonoma. It's typical Redwood country: forest and lakes and small towns in the hills. Andy went on the bus, and the rest of us piled in the van.

I've been scared in the past at ordinary games, games before I knew my son had cancer. Now I'm in some place just on the other side of abject fear. I've always hated that sudden realization that someone is down on the field and not getting up, and the way the players go to see what's wrong—but not too fast because they're afraid to know, too.

Hot dogs and popcorn and soda and the junior varsity game going by, the formal green rectangle with the moving colors on it. The low autumn sun has a directed heat, as if it's shining just on your face, and an edge of cold is in the air even as you get hot. As it goes down farther the effect is more pronounced, and the color gets heavier, mixed with red.

The grass is from another world entirely. It looks like it floats a little, an inch or so off the ground, and it freezes a special day in the mind with unreal clarity.

The JV game is almost over and the varsity team is out on the sidelines, stretching and limbering up. I can see Andy in his white number-32 jersey. Around the far side of the field are eucalyptus trees, just behind the low chain-link fence. I know all the kids. I can see Frankie's number 33, and Fred. Fred is number 74, a right tackle, and he'll be Andy's main blocker.

The stands are almost full now, and more people have come over to say hello and ask how Andy is doing. People are a bit easier in the larger crowd. My heart is beginning to race with anticipation. I don't know how I'll stand it, minute to minute, the sudden jumps into movement and the bodies colliding, and Andy in the middle of it. I have to keep him from getting killed.

His finger is like a sore spot in my head that I have to try not to touch. Simon can't sit still, and he goes down and stands with some other fathers along the sidelines. When the JV game is over, I take my two grandkids over to the refreshment stand. Nick is mischievous, running away and out on the field. I keep him busy as best as I can—talking, walking and eating. The game is starting as I get back to the stands, drop the kids off and start my prowl of the sidelines.

From ground level, the game is impenetrable. Andy appears and disappears, bodies flying all around him. I'm walking around the sidelines like a cat, and everything is pushing me into a strange isolation: the pounding of the game; the peculiar, directed heat of the sun; and the small groupings of old friends who don't seem to know who I am anymore.

This game is rough, and these kids aren't small. They're rural kids, ranch kids, and they're big and strong and they make loud noises when they hit. It looks very much like what the guys watch on television, the college and pro games, although maybe not the passing. Even I can see that when the ball is thrown, the receivers tend to be standing still when they catch it, not like on TV where the ball is caught in full stride.

But in the middle of the field, where Andy is, kids are getting hit real hard, just like on TV. There's no score in the first quarter, but the Potter Valley quarterback runs it for a touchdown early in the second quarter.

I finally stop moving and get lost in watching Andy play. Only my vigilance is going to keep him from getting hurt. I know that. I believe it. I don't know how he does it. I know he's strong, but I don't know how he takes the pounding. He's thrown and bounced and piled on. He's a right-through-the-middle runner and seldom, if ever, goes around the end. He does have quick feet though, and an instinctive ability to angle himself through a crowd. He seldom takes a hit dead-on.

The fact is, he's having a great time (he gets up from a pile of bodies and smiles in my direction) and he's playing well. I can tell by watching Les, who is ecstatic.

It's not that we're winning. The first half is close and Andy runs well, but everything is hard-fought. At the end of the half a fumble ends a promising drive. We're still down 7–0.

It's halftime and Andy is playing wonderfully—bandaged, rigid finger and all—and suddenly it's all come down to the second half. Everything has become symbolic.

I wander back to our section in the stands, a row full of moist eyes. My sisters and I would like to talk, but down front is a madhouse—people getting up to stretch; heading for the refreshment stand; kids, ours included, running up and down and jumping from level to level—so we all head up to the top rows where the action is thinner. We sit about two rows down and talk about the week: the doctors, the hospital, the future.

When the game is ready to start again, I'm aware of trying to be reasonable. *This is a football game. This is not a picture of the future, this is a high school football game and it means nothing except for today.* It doesn't work. The game is the precise image of Andy's fight against cancer. Everything is riding on it.

The game goes on much as before: punishing. The sun gets low down in the sky, and the light is thicker and more golden. Tomales runs back the kickoff, but the kicker misses the point after and the score is 7–6, Potter Valley ahead. That's the way it stays till there are three minutes left.

Potter Valley has the ball at the Tomales forty-yard line. They fumble it and we get it back, and the tension moves onto a higher plane. A field goal could win it. Cheryl tells me that, but the kicker missed the point-after on their first touchdown and Les can't be feeling too good about trying it. Potter Valley holds them pretty well on two running plays, and it's third-and-eight when they pull off a pass play down to the fourteen-yard line.

Andy's been running right into the line all day, so they must be ready for him. Certainly the last running plays didn't achieve much. But they give it to Andy again, and this time he's through the hole and downfield, tumbling into the end zone and righting himself to throw his arms in the air. There's some time left to play, but you can't tell that from the team or the crowd. It's pandemonium, and I can't think of anything but his pure joy and determination. I hardly notice the rest of the game, and when it's over, Andy trots toward us caked in grime and sweat and pride, so proud it's shining all around him.

"Pretty good game, huh?" he says to me, and I hold him for as long as I can in the swirl of players and fans.

That night he goes out with his friends to the rock quarry. They go there to drink beer, but Andy doesn't drink anymore. He just needs to be with them and celebrate. When he comes home, like always, he yells, "Hey Mom, I'm home," from the bottom of the stairs, then goes straight to sleep.

In the morning, he wants bacon and eggs. I'm so excited I won't stop talking about the game and he says, "Sure, yeah, but did you see the block Fred threw for me? I mean it wasn't just me, Mom. It was everybody. Frankie had a great game, too."

I know that's all true, and I love them for it, but I don't care. I think I'm allowed not to care. It's the morning, and the sun is shining, and the game was protective magic, an omen. It only reads one way. In an utterly uncertain world, it only reads the one way.

My son is the toughest kid in the world and nothing, nothing is going to beat him, ever.

November 1988. Andy with his brother-in-law Les, exiting the football field after Andy's game-winning touchdown.

8

*D*ECISIONS

*T*hey'll take off the top of his finger and that will be the end of that. The cancer is right there, and when it's cut off it can't go anywhere else. It's like we're getting rid of something unsightly, restoring a damaged work of art.

The exhilaration of the football game helped a lot, and a few days later Dr. Schlemmer called to say that all Andy's test results were normal and there was no evidence of tumor spread. His brain looked fine, though there were a few hot spots on his left ring finger and left leg. The hot spots on the finger were to be expected from the surgery, and the leg spots were probably old sports injuries. "Don't write home yet, but things look pretty good," he said. I could hear excitement in his voice.

All the doctors agreed that the best way to treat Andy would be the above-the-knuckle amputation. They wanted to biopsy some lymph nodes, and the surgeon could do it while Andy was under anesthesia. Dr. Schlemmer said that if there were no further suspicion of disease, they thought Andy would be a great candidate for a protocol study being done by the National Cancer Institute. In the protocol, after the tumor-removing surgery, patients would be chosen at random to receive chemotherapy and provide some hard data on its effectiveness. It was something he wanted us to think about.

A bone marrow aspiration was scheduled for the next day to check his blood for cancer cells, and an X ray of his leg was to follow. We were told the surgeon would see Andy right after the tests. The doctors wanted both the surgery and biopsy done at their hospital so they could have all the tissue information at hand.

We arrived at the hospital anticipating the painful bone marrow aspiration that would indicate whether or not Andy's cancer was in his bone marrow. Andy was nervous. He knew it was going to hurt. The nurse in me reassured him, but the mother in me didn't believe her.

I watched as the nurse prepared Andy, explaining the procedure as she worked. The test was difficult to watch. When someone hurts your child, on a simple level it isn't acceptable and you want to say, "Stop doing that." The doctor probed and pushed, pushed harder, then finally pulled with considerable strength to get a sample from Andy's hip bone. They put bandages over the puncture sites and allowed him to sit right up.

I was light-headed from watching. How could a child not panic faced with going through it again? There may be no medical reason for a general anesthetic, but as a mother, I wished they'd use one. There's no medical reason for kids to have to hurt.

Dr. Tobias finally came in to join us. He'd received the approval from our health insurance and set the date. Moving quickly was good because the waiting never becomes easier.

It gave me less time to have the "drunken monkeys," as I called the thoughts that ran around my brain at night. The night becomes a huge, open room where all the possible horrors cluster and hover. Everything at night would be wrong: what I thought, what I did. During those times, I wasn't competent at all. I was a frightened little girl.

Dr. Schlemmer wanted to set up a treatment plan. He told us we were dealing with the limits of detection, that even though all the tests came back negative, we still couldn't be 100 percent sure there wasn't metastasis. Metastasis is the spread of cancer from the original site to other parts of the body. There is no way to test for microseeding. The previous surgery might have started the process. Draining the supposed blood blister might have, too.

We asked if any chemotherapy results made a strong case for treatment. He said that question hadn't been answered yet, and that was why he wanted Andy to join the protocol study. The Institute was interested in whether or not chemotherapy could help cure a sarcoma like Andy's. The studies so far didn't indicate whether or not it would work.

We got a quick course on chemo. The advantage of chemotherapy is that it works better early on in the disease. If the cancer recurs, the chance of a cure is significantly less. With any cancer treatment, chemotherapy is best used in the very beginning.

He told us there was a 49 percent chance of cure for Andy with surgery alone, and a 51 percent chance of cure with chemotherapy. With the chemotherapy, though, there also came a 2 percent chance of death from the treatments! We all looked at him, and I asked if he meant that the choices were statistically equal? He said, "Yes, that's what I'm saying."

Cheryl blurted, "Then it's all just a crapshoot?" The doctor held her gaze and said, "Yes, that's exactly what it is." Here we were seeking help at one of the most prestigious medical centers in the United States, and they were telling us that the best they could offer was a protocol chemotherapy study to find out if chemo would work.

Andy could help himself if he happened to choose the right course, but no one knew which course that was. He could help the kids who were unlucky enough to follow him because as his treatment either cured or failed, answers would become available.

Andy needed time to think. He had made enough choices for one day. First, he would have the amputation.

Later that week, Dr. Tobias called and told us the bone marrow aspiration had been normal: no cancer cells. Things were looking better and better. It seemed to be a localized tumor.

We arrived for Andy's surgery early in the morning and waited in the outpatient surgery area for our turn. The surgeon came by, checked Andy, joked a bit, and said things would get going soon.

We had a Gary Larson cartoon that Andy wanted to give Dr. Tobias, but he'd forgotten. It showed doctors operating and during the surgery, trying to decide how many chambers the heart has. Cheryl wrote the surgeon's name in the caption, and we taped it to Andy's chest before he left the waiting area. Cheryl also drew an arrow on his left hand pointing to the correct finger saying "THIS ONE!"

Simon and I walked alongside Andy to the operating room. The OR nurse introduced herself and had us kiss Andy good-bye before she rolled him off through the OR doors.

The time ticked by. Finally, the surgeon came out and told us things had gone just fine. Andy had done well and the tumor was out. We went into the recovery room when things had settled down. Andy was groggy, but looked good. He didn't seem to be having any pain or excessive bleeding, so we were able to take him home early that evening.

While dressing him to go home, we saw the cartoon still taped to his chest. It had been altered by the surgeon and his staff to read: "Was it his finger or his arm?" "His right arm, right?" "I'm not sure. I thought you said to take out his kidney!"

Thanksgiving was the following week, so Andy had a break from school and time to recuperate. It was such an appropriate holiday. We sat around the kitchen table discussing what the day meant for us.

Our next appointment was with Dr. Schlemmer. Nothing was back yet on the biopsy, but everything looked fine. The oncologist examined Andy and explained the protocol study for soft tissue sarcoma. No studies had been established yet specifically for clear cell sarcoma, so Andy would fall into a broader classification. The study was being done throughout the United States.

The choices we had to make were listed for us again:

1. To be randomized for the study by the computer;
2. To be nonrandomized, in or out of the study;

3. To let the computer decide which chemotherapy treatment to be used, not on judgment of the doctor, but by random selection;

4. To not be in the study.

I had thought the oncologist might help us a bit, might give some hint about how he felt. To tell you the truth, I thought it was his responsibility to guide us, but he didn't. Since the study was designed to see if chemotherapy worked, there wasn't any body of knowledge to help us. All we had to help us were our gut feelings.

The threat hanging over us seemed to lessen as we drove home. We didn't talk about the chemo decision on the way home. There wasn't any point. The next morning, Andy and I sat at the breakfast table and talked about the hard stuff. The sun was already up.

"Have you been thinking?" I asked.

He didn't say, "Of course," though he could have. He said, "Yeah. I can't decide. I don't want the chemo if it isn't going to help. I don't know enough."

"We could listen to the tape."

"Yeah, I need to do that."

"I'll give you all I can, Honey. I know some things, not much, I'll find out more. I know you know, but I just have to keep telling you it's your decision. You can't do it on emotion. You have to live with what comes out of it."

"Or not live."

We listened to the tape, listened to it as if there might be things hiding in it, privileged bits of information we'd missed. But there weren't any. He'd said what we'd thought he said, and it still wasn't enough.

"No help," I said.

"How am I supposed to do this? God, Mom," he said with a rising voice, *"I don't know anything!* They don't even know if it's a sarcoma or a melanoma. What do they know? This is the best hospital? Maybe there's someplace else."

"It is the best," I replied, looking at the window. "It is the best. Here we are and we have to come up with something."

"Sure we do. So I'll give up sports, and lose my hair, and be sick all the time, and never have kids, and maybe, I never needed to. Maybe it's all for nothing. Two percent. A 2 percent difference between a cure and no cure is 100 percent shit."

"It's your *life,* Andy. The odds don't count."

"It's gone now. Nothing's showed up anywhere else. It's gone. *I* think it's gone."

"If it isn't?"

"I'm scared of the chemo, all right? I'm really scared of the chemo. If it comes back, we can do it then. I don't want to give it all up." He started to cry. "I want sports, and I want children, and I want to watch my children play sports, and I want to be a great dad. I don't want chemo. They haven't told me shit, and if I'm going to die anyway, I want to live the best I can."

I noticed I was crying, too.

"I don't want to cry about it anymore. I just want to know what I'm doing. There's no reason to start. I can start later, if I have to."

"Okay, you can do that. Okay. But if we hit it hard now that might be what does it. You know, Hon, that might be just what we need to do."

Andy had his forearms on the table and his head down.

"I don't know what to say. Listen to me, Andy, if you died I don't know what I'd do. I don't know what I'd do. The thought of losing you kills me now."

"Look at it this way, Mom," his voice was rational and under control again, "if you could force me to do it, would you? Would you be able to do that?"

"No. I wouldn't force you to do anything."

"Yeah, I knew that."

"I love you, Honey."

"I know. I know that, too. I mean, I love you, too."

Sitting here now in Andy's old room, the sadness creeps over the late afternoon. But there's no second-guessing, because the fact is we were right.

We *were* really strong, and if it could have been beaten, we would have done it.

9

FAULT LINES

Andy made his decision not to start the chemo and told Dr. Schlemmer that if anything changed, if any metastasis showed up, he expected a rapid change in treatment. The doctor assured him.

He played catcher for the baseball team that spring. He liked the strategy involved in catching, and he loved being part of the team again. His finger, now healed, wasn't any problem until he put on his batting glove. The unfilled finger of the glove flapped around and got in the way. Out came the scissors and the sewing machine, and the glove was adapted to three and a half fingers.

Maybe there were no playoffs, but for Andy it was a winning season. It felt to me that Andy was positive and things were positive and the family was positive, but that I was odd man out. My sister Maureen had compiled all the medical studies she could find, but wouldn't show them to me.

You're in crisis, and until you get your bearings, you're not going to be the best mother in the world. You want to be, but you can't. You make mistakes. You make people cry. You raise the tension level.

None of it is out of the ordinary, and you shouldn't waste time beating yourself up.

The kids knew what was going on, and they'd talk to me about it.

"It'll be all right, Mom. C'mon, give yourself a break."

But I couldn't give myself a break. I was terrified. And, I felt sorry for myself.

I hate to say that, but it was true. I can hear Simon now saying to me that it was time "to quit feeling sorry for myself." I couldn't quit because it wasn't something I had chosen. I was consumed with fear for Andy, and when fear and responsibility become your life, you feel sorry for yourself.

Andy was a perfect child, and our family had always been lucky. But the whole thing felt like a test, and I'm never able to handle tests. Even a driver's license test scares me. I'm never ready, I never feel like I'm ready. When I was building my credits for the nursing program I had to take an algebra test, and driving on the way to it, I remember thinking that if I had an accident I wouldn't have to take it.

And Andy's illness was a test, without a doubt—to see

whether I was worthy of our good luck, to see whether or not I was good enough to save Andy's life.

I couldn't shut up either. Simon didn't want to talk about Andy's prognosis. He needed to know that the right people were doing the right things, but he didn't want to go over and over the details. We moved gradually to opposite poles.

By the time Andy had become sick, Simon and I had already been married for thirty years. So though the sexual passion in our lives was hardly the "can't get enough" of our early years, it was still alive and a regular, pleasurable part of existence. Then Andy became sick, and the door slammed on sexual relations in my marriage.

There's an implicit, physical vulnerability involved in a woman's sexual response, and that wasn't possible for me. It wasn't possible for me to be vulnerable. It wasn't possible for me to open on any level, or the fear would break through and drown us all. It wasn't possible for me to risk losing control, just for pleasure. Anyway, pleasure would tempt the fates.

I kept my face as firm and still as I could. I had a dam on my face, a smooth, curved Hoover Dam with millions of cubic feet of fear on the other side. Once a trickle broke through, it would never be contained again. I knew that. I felt it deep inside.

We'd go to bed, and while Simon would be romantic, I would be locked in my head, wanting to be left alone. For Simon, sex was communication. He wasn't a verbal man. His caring and tenderness were best expressed sexually. There's plenty about the male/female split in the cancer literature, and we fit the profiles perfectly.

I wanted to be held and comforted, which was hard for Simon. The strain was growing between us. I would not be vulnerable, and the discussions between us sometimes ended in acquiescence and sometimes in rejection. Either way, the strain kept growing. I guess I was in the stronger position because while Simon had to deal with anger and a tacit rejection, all I had to deal with, on this level anyway, was the conviction that I had no choice and that the world, as it was, required that I not indulge in vulnerability.

I had enough to deal with, and taking care of Simon wasn't on my agenda. It was, I guess, a kind of traumatic shell shock. I was tunnel-visioned and staying that way out of emotional, physical and deeply superstitious necessity.

John and Paul were quiet and pretty much stayed away from me. I guess I was overwhelming. Given a hug, I would cry. It was easier for them to be with Andy and to indulge in the kidding and joking as they always had. They were willing to do anything for him. When his truck motor needed rebuilding, they did it quietly then parked it one day in front of the house, running, so we saw it when we came back from the hospital.

Cheryl and Linda were more emotional and willing to talk to Andy about anything, anytime. It was more difficult talking to me. Linda would listen to me, but I could see her eyes filling up with the pain. Cheryl didn't show as much, but I'm sure it was just as hard for her. It was my panic they couldn't handle, which is perfectly understandable. Panic is not an emotion anyone wants to handle.

I'm afraid of everything—the cancer, the IRS, the DMV—all external power. I'm afraid of my father and the faceless, nameless figure at the edge of my life who chants, "Stupid, stupid little girl," in a simpleminded monotone.

It isn't unusual now that I can't relax. I never could. I had too much to live up to. I am aware, and I know just how much I have to do to keep that drone out of my head. I have to do everything, because nobody else has this particular awareness of how suddenly things can fall apart—how fast power can turn you upside down so the sand is suddenly running in the opposite direction, and everything you thought you knew or had is falling and spilling.

When I was a little girl, maintaining control meant I was just barely good enough. Losing it meant I was worthless and a disappointment to my father. My incompetence was an insult to him, like I was hitting him in the face. When I lost it as a child, I lost it alone, where no one could see or hear. When I was weak, only I knew.

Now I was strong. I had to be. Only in secret, at night, did the weakness come out: the whole, haunting and humiliating range of feelings around incompetence, stupidity, inadequacy and femaleness. In the dark, I'd always known the truth that my father would have thought better of me as a boy.

The dark I was carrying around in the daytime was locked in a trunk with chains around it. And that's where it was going to stay. My fear of helplessness and humiliation was my strength. And it worked. It's only later you have to pay for extended emotional paradoxes.

Through my marriage, I'd come to understand that it wasn't necessary anymore to please everyone. I didn't fear exposure to the degree I had. I found that staying in control and doing things successfully could be a lot more interesting than instinctively attempting to please.

And it was, until the dreaded, moving spotlight picked out one of my children and said, "Here. Control this."

The fact is, I guess, the kids thought I was overprotective of Andy; that I was making his life miserable trying to protect him.

I questioned him every time he went out. I took a step backward in the way I tried to control him. The kids finally told me
what I was doing and I handled that right, at least, and watched
myself like a hawk, catching the words before they came out of
my mouth.

The things I had to do for the business were getting out of
hand, too. I was making bookkeeping mistakes, bad mistakes.
Simon would go through the roof.

"For Christ's sake, can't you do the bills right?"

"I have a lot on my mind, Simon. I leave early and get home
late. I can't think. What do you expect me to do?"

"I expect you to get this stuff right."

"I can't concentrate. Nothing seems important. Nothing else
matters. What will they do, put me in jail? Give my son cancer?
Nothing else matters but Andy."

"It matters to me if you screw up."

"I don't give a shit."

"*I* can't do the books, Marilyn. You know that. I don't know
how."

"Maybe you should learn."

Back and forth, in and out. The learning is slow and painful.
But I learned. We learned. And the strength we started with grew
deeper.

You have to see things as they are, and during an extended
period of death hanging over your child, that's very hard to do.
You won't be the best mother in the world. Try to put it aside.
You will get better. You certainly won't be the best wife in the
world, and your husband will probably have to deal with mar-
ginalized anger and feelings of rejection. But if you're lucky, and
you have a husband like mine, love will persist.

10

IMPACT

*E*arly that spring, a volunteer called from the Make-A-Wish Foundation. Andy had been referred to them. Make-A-Wish is an organization that grants wishes to children who have catastrophic or life-threatening illnesses. Would Andy like to have them come out and interview him, she asked? Andy said sure and began thinking about what he'd most like to do. He finally came up with a fishing trip to Alaska.

He felt uncomfortable accepting, since he was sure his cancer was cured. He worried out loud that if he took a wish he didn't deserve, his cancer might come back. Everyday events, lapses and sins of omission all seem tied up with the cancer.

But we talked to the volunteers, who assured him that his condition need not be terminal for him to be granted a wish. The fact that he had cancer at all qualified him. He wasn't taking anything away from someone who might be more deserving. After a few weeks, the news came that his wish had been granted and that a two-week Alaskan fishing and sightseeing trip had been arranged for the following summer.

His buddy Frankie, Simon and I would be going, too. A limousine would pick us up on the appointed day.

Photo by Annie Wells. ©*The Press Democrat,* Santa Rosa, CA.

Andy feeding a Jersey calf in 1989, after undergoing surgery on his finger.

A friend of mine called in April to talk to Andy. Laurel was a cancer parent, too. Even though her son was considered cured of leukemia after a five-year battle, they were still unable to buy health insurance except at an inflated rate. He was nine years old and considered a risk.

She had started a group called Parents of Kids With Cancer and was in the forefront of the battle to end health insurance discrimination for all kids with cancer. Paying for chemotherapy, she and her husband had lost their home, their cars and all their possessions. Their insurance company had fallen so far behind in hospital payments that their son's treatments had been in jeopardy. And even though their son was three years out of treatment, the insurance company had increased the premiums for his coverage. It was impossible for them to get coverage elsewhere, because he had a pre-existing condition.

The California Finance and Insurance Committee and the Subcommittee for Health were going to be holding a hearing in Sacramento on health insurance problems. Andy was asked to come the following day and talk to the Committee about the health insurance problems he was going to have as he grew older.

Andy said he'd like to. It occurs to me now just how remarkable that was. There probably isn't anything else quite as moving to a parent as a child who suddenly goes past the person you knew and shows something of his own, some strength that's been growing in private.

Andy had no background in public speaking and he had always resisted the academic, but there he was. Something important presented itself, and Andy was ready.

The next day, we ate breakfast around a cafeteria table in Sacramento. Andy asked questions, and health industry problems were discussed as he scribbled notes. It was his own story she wanted him to tell and asked him what he already knew. It was clear from his answers that he was able to speak from his own experience and be compelling.

We arrived to an already crowded chamber. Speakers followed one another to the platform. Heart-wrenching stories were minimized and discounted by lobbyists for the big-money insurance interests. The tactics were so simpleminded that after an hour or so of listening to them, you became aware that their effectiveness had to rest with their willingness to spend money. They evade, they create straw men, they drag in patriotic fervor as if there were no higher good than making America safe for its executive class. Money changes hands, and that's that. There is no other explanation.

The lobbyists were resisting any change and downplaying the pain of the speakers, right to the edge of contempt. Sitting there watching, you can almost be seized with pity for these guys. They don't have a clue, and when they finally come to the end of their machinations and lives, what will they have? A new set of golf clubs? A Lexus and a membership in one of the better clubs? Probably.

Love? Respect? Closure and acceptance? Not likely at all.

The committee itself seemed bored. Members paid brief attention and talked among themselves. Some stood and left the room. Laurel was first to speak for the kids and talked about discrimination against sick children, and how it will follow them for the rest of their lives. She cited statistics, gave examples and caught the room's attention. She added her heart to the facts and had no need, as the lobbyists did, to cloud the issues or cover up the facts. This woman knew what she was talking about.

She talked about dead children, children who had died because a multimillion-dollar industry didn't think they were worth spending money on. When finished, Andy was called.

He walked down an aisle packed on either side with lawyers, lobbyists and representatives from every side of the health insurance debate. The Assembly Committee wasn't paying much attention as Andy prepared to speak. He took a deep breath and introduced himself.

My son had become someone different and hadn't bothered to let me know till right now. He easily told a bit about himself, where he lived and why he was there. He was low-key and relaxed enough that when he said that he had cancer, you could have heard a pin drop. I was astounded and brimming with love for who he was, for what he had made of himself.

He told them clearly and effectively about the prognosis, about how rare his cancer was and how difficult treating a rare cancer is. He explained his reasons for not choosing chemotherapy, and why it would be necessary for him to have insurance coverage for the rest of his life. He told them about his plans to go on to college, to fly search-and-rescue for the Air Force, and he ended by explaining how not being able to buy health insurance would limit him.

After five minutes, he had the complete attention of the committee and the audience. He looked straight in the eyes of the politicians who were supposed to find an insurance solution for California. His voice was strong, his presence was powerful and he projected an easy, athletic grace. And it was clear that he was telling the truth.

He made a difference.

When Andy left the microphone to walk back to his seat, someone started to clap. As he made his way up the aisle, hands came out to shake his and to pat him on his back. Smiles all around wished him luck. When he reached his seat, he smiled at me; Andy and the new guy, too, and sighed a deep sigh of relief.

At that moment, I don't think he was aware yet how he had affected the crowd. We were, though. He had stirred the room. People were still talking and clapping as the next name was called. A ranch kid, telling his own story honestly, had reintroduced clarity to the hearings and cut through the professional smoke.

As we drove home that afternoon, we told Andy how proud we were of him. He grinned and said, "It wasn't bad at all. Maybe it was the new clothes."

A few weeks later, he received a letter from an assemblyman thanking him for his testimony and saying that by speaking out, Andy had helped the legislation pass the committee on a 6–2 vote.

The day after the speech came our April visit at the hospital. Everything was reported as normal. We were both breathing easier. We shouldn't have been.

The doctors had now decided Andy's cancer was a clear cell sarcoma. Dr. Schlemmer didn't change anything he'd told us before, though he did point out that Andy would need to be followed for at least twenty years. Clear cell sarcomas have a significant history of return, even after many years. It would take that long to be sure Andy was cured.

He would always be followed in the pediatric department because no matter how old Andy might be, his cancer would always be considered a childhood disease. His case would be used to help any other children with the same disease. Andy said he didn't mind coming back to the medical center, but had some questions on what he would do when he went away to school or the Air Force.

He asked about flying search-and-rescue with the Air Force after college. The doctor told him that the armed services wouldn't accept him, even if he was considered cured. Andy was crestfallen.

Just the day before, Andy had told the Assembly Committee that he planned to go into the Air Force. Now he was facing a specific example of the kind of discrimination the committee had met to discuss. This was the exact point Andy had been trying to explain: the huge impact even a recovery from cancer can have on a child's life.

The doctor told him, however, not to put limits on any other college option, and that no matter where he went to school, the medical center would be able to find someone to follow him.

Andy's girlfriend Alex returned in May to hugs, tears and our hearts. She and Andy spent long hours together talking and getting reacquainted, wanting to see how everything felt. Alex came with us to that month's appointment at the hospital. We could see her gradually coming to terms with the reality as we went through our now-routine doctor's visit. I watched her carefully. Alex was a wild card, and she could hit Andy very hard, blindside him, if she pulled away or recoiled. It was one more thing I figured I'd have to get a handle on. She was white-faced as she sat and watched the doctor examine Andy. In fact, I didn't have to worry about Alex. I'd find that out.

The doctor startled us by saying he was leaving to go into research and didn't know yet who would be taking his place. We wouldn't have a problem with whoever took over Andy's case; the new doctor wasn't something we should worry about, he said. We would find out before our next visit who he would be. But we were disappointed. It had taken a long time to come to trust this doctor, and now he would be leaving. We felt uneasy. Before we left, we needed to make sure our plans weren't going to interfere with Andy's treatment.

We were going to Washington, D.C., in June to lobby for health insurance reform in the Congress and Senate, and after we returned, we were planning a vacation in Hawaii with a group of Andy's friends. The doctor said that would be fine, and we could see our new physician when we came home.

During the spring, the bills had started to pile up. I couldn't figure out what was happening. Bills would come with attachments saying our insurance company had denied payment. There were bills for pathology reports, the Melanoma Board visit, doctor visits and all the tests we'd had done. Everything. Nothing done since Andy had started being seen at the medical center had been paid for.

Many telephone calls to the insurance company later, the woman who was handling Andy's care told me I hadn't followed the process to the letter and they weren't responsible.

The bills were due. I had failed in some way, and I started to cry. Six months after the fact, I had to figure out what to do. I discovered that everything that I thought I'd been doing correctly, I'd done wrong.

I called our family doctor and asked his billing secretary if she could figure out what happened. She asked me to compile all the dates of visits and procedures, and give them to her to resubmit for authorization.

The woman at the company was reassuring and said things would be worked out, and not to worry. But the bills kept coming, threatening action. The bills were for thousands of dollars. I was assured with each telephone call that things would all work out, but I stayed nervous.

In the middle of a crisis, the bills mean nothing. After things settle down, they're devastating. My confusion was complete. I was involved with three hospitals, two outpatient radiation facilities and two state agencies. I was at the hub, directing mail and calls back and forth between billing agencies. One of the agencies involved was Medi-Cal, which we had never had nor qualified for. The agency had been billed anyway. It was a huge, tangled mess, and I knew I was going to have to become a lot more vigilant.

Finally, after months of phone calls, letters and hard work, the bills were paid. In the end, we only were responsible for a small share. We worked out a clearer method of billing. I had learned something else:

Double-check each request for services and every authorization from the insurance company to make sure all the papers are in hand before the services are given.

With our trip to Washington nearing, letters were sent out to members of Congress and senators we planned to meet: Barbara Boxer, George Miller, Dana Rohrabacher, Henry Waxman, Alan Cranston, Robert Matsui and others. We explained what we wanted to tell them.

These were our arguing points:

1. The unspeakable disregard of the insurance industry for children going through painful, frightening treatments and years of therapy;
2. The emotional upheaval of family life; the threats parents received when insurance companies failed to pay prompt attention to the billing for which they were responsible; and the unearned, adverse credit ratings families had to deal with in the wake of nonpayment;
3. The interruption of life-saving services for sick children when bills were not paid on time;
4. The escalation of premiums during the years of a child's treatments and for the years that follow;

5. The insurance company's certitude that no matter what they billed a family, the family would have to pay it because, with a pre-existing condition, no other insurance company would touch them.

A pretty good agenda, don't you think? It sounded a little like a criminal indictment. I had the energy that comes with specific goals, and I wasn't sorry for myself anymore. Maybe I wasn't the best mother in the world, but I had one of the best sons.

11

*P*ASSAGE

*A*ndy needed clothes for Washington, so we spent three hundred dollars we could ill afford on a very nice sport coat and slacks. I suppose it would have been more honest for him to go dressed as usual, but we didn't think it would have been comfortable for him, not in the hallways of the Capitol. Inevitably, I was worried about the differences between Sacramento and Washington, D.C.

He looked perfectly wonderful. No one would have picked him out as a cancer patient. No one could have picked him out as anything but a remarkably healthy, handsome, vigorous teenager. It would remain to be seen whether or not that would help or hinder our presentation.

When we reached Washington, D.C., the plane banked and we were looking down at the green lawns, white buildings and blue water of the Potomac town. It was moving in a way I hadn't really felt since being a schoolchild. I felt a very simple, bright and overwhelming kind of patriotism.

Our hotel was at the southwest end of the Mall, not far from the old Smithsonian. All around us was the formal history of Washington: the Lincoln and Jefferson Memorials, the Kennedy Center, the Potomac River, Arlington Cemetery and at the eastern end of the Mall, the Capitol. It wasn't a sightseeing trip, but it was impossible not to be affected by the seriousness of the surroundings.

We had to sign lobbying papers, and once that was done the real work of making and keeping congressional appointments began. Some we'd made already and some we hadn't. We hailed taxis, took the subway, ran and walked the endless old tunnels under the Capitol as we rushed to meet every appointment. We'd ask directions and someone would say "through that door," and the door would open into another whitewashed, chipped and cracked tunnel that would run a solid quarter mile without an exit.

We weren't completely naive. We knew the Bush administration had a less-than-compelling interest in health-care reform. Actually, if they had any interest at all, it was pretty well hidden. Our strategy was to focus on the California delegation and to try to build serious support there. Complete naivete wouldn't have lasted long in that environment. There we were, radiating pure motives and armed with nothing but heart while in every corner of the Capitol, dark-suited, briefcased lobbyists were sidling and whispering, nodding and smiling.

My first reaction was surprise that they were so obvious. Something was so patently dishonest in their voices and body language that I felt as if their actions were openly illegal. Gradually, we were coming to understand that Washington is not a very nice place, and that the salaries we pay our representatives don't buy nearly as much allegiance as corporate money does.

Later, when the Clinton administration tried to get its health-care reform agenda through, we were as high as kites. Barbara Boxer and Jay Rockefeller were also enthused, and they were sure reform was coming. Now the convenient, official version of what happened is that the Republicans mounted the brilliant "Harry and Louise" ad campaign and turned people against reform.

Andy lobbying in Washington, D.C., in his "good suit."

Sometimes we were cordially met, sometimes not. The status of the citizen in a building full of politicians is not always what it should be. Sometimes the best we could do was a meeting with an aide. Alan Cranston sent his staff to meet with us, but they couldn't have cared less and made that quite clear. Robert Matsui never showed, and his staff was entirely unhelpful.

But generally, in dealing with the California delegation at least, we got a plausible reception. They clearly knew we were coming and what it was all about. We saw all our representatives from California, and we met with twenty-one congressmen and women, three senators and four legislative aides.

We spent as much time as we could with people with power, never something to do if you want to preserve your illusions. It was sometimes depressing for Andy. He went to Washington thinking that if your cause was right, and you stated it clearly and honestly, people would have to respond. That turned out to be true in a limited number of cases. In terms of the overall picture, our approach meant little.

Andy would wait his turn quietly, smile, shake the hand of whoever we saw, then calmly tell his story and his reasons for being there. He spoke from his heart, and he wasn't there for himself or for money. He was there because he wanted kids to be cared for.

He talked about their paradoxical strength and helplessness, and how they were being betrayed by a corporate structure that didn't care what happened to them. He didn't need to project what someone else had told him, because he knew for himself.

About half the people we met were interested in what we had to say. It was a beginning. Andy had impact, and his maturity, eloquence and straightforwardness gave our group weight. We were there for six days, and our message was heard by some people who would be guiding the future of insurance reform. (See Barbara Boxer's comments about Andy in The Congressional Record in Appendix B.)

Barbara Boxer was wonderful, and she remained so through our whole battle. Henry Waxman was also wonderful. George Miller, Dana Rohrabacher, Nancy Pelosi and Vic Fazio, whose daughter had had a bone marrow transplant—all of them were fine. Their staffs were particularly responsive to Andy's lack of guile, and sometimes they'd talk with us for an hour after our meeting with the boss.

Barbara Boxer met us in a whirlwind of enthusiasm and whisked us out the door to meet other representatives. She was interested and caring, and from that day on she kept in touch with Andy. She called the hospital to find out how he was doing when things were critical, and she made herself available for a fundraiser, speaking at length to those who came to support him.

She made a real difference in Andy's life, and he in hers. I remember Barbara holding a meeting in Petaluma one day. We waited through the long morning for it to break up. When it did, Andy caught up with Barbara at the door. Her bodyguard blocked his way, so he said, "Barbara, it's Andy," and she turned quickly, grabbed his arm and told her guard, "This young man is walking me to the car."

For a few rushed minutes they talked about how he was doing, how his insurance company was responding and what she could do to help. We had found an ally who really cared how he was being treated, and about him as a person. She had to stretch on tiptoes to give him a hug good-bye, and he had to lean down to do the same. They liked each other.

Six days in Washington, D.C., I guess we didn't really accomplish a whole lot, but the truth is, we showed up very early, right at the beginning of the effort that's still going on. Much of what we had to say would come around again.

We returned home exhausted, but elated, and began to prepare for our July trip to Hawaii. Seven of Andy's friends and two of their moms were going along, and the kids were so excited. They were going to knock Hawaii on its ear.

Dr. Schlemmer gave us an all clear.

Andy showed the kids all the sights. They'd snorkel or surf or just get brown in the sun. We mothers followed along, trying to keep some kind of control; see that they ate, stuff like that. We were also conscious of the bars where call girls and drug dealers were soliciting trade. The kids had their eyes opened quickly, and they would laugh about their adventures as we cringed. The trip

Photo by Ron Bath. *Argus Courier*, Petaluma, CA.

Andy under the hood of his pickup after returning home from Washington, D.C., and his lobbying efforts.

was over far too soon for the kids, who were tan and happy, but not for the moms, who were exhausted.

We got home, as planned, in time for the county fair where Andy was going to show two of his beef cattle. He didn't place very high in his categories except for showmanship, in which he came in first. He'd known he wouldn't do so well in the judging for perfection of breed. The beef Andy had bought to enter in the fair were not exceptional.

But showmanship is judged on how well the person shows the animal. If the animal is clean, clipped properly, and stands and leads well, it gives evidence of effort and care. Andy was relaxed and smiling while his beef went through the routine. After years of dairy showmanship and stories of broken halters, jumping cows and other horror stories, he was thrilled to see all of his hard work pay off. Over the years, our kids bought what they could afford and tried their best, and many times it wasn't good enough to win. For our family, 4-H and FFA had been humbling experiences. But that afternoon, though, everything worked perfectly, and Andy held the trophy and grinned from ear to ear. Finally winning a class was sensational.

During the fair, a local newspaper published an article on Andy's lobbying efforts. The article was in the paper two days before Andy sold his beef at the auction, and it called him a hero. Then his beef sold at auction for the best price he'd ever received. He was grinning, embarrassed and thrilled, as the price kept climbing until he came close to the top price paid for beef that day. He knew the price didn't reflect the quality of his beef.

The auction was probably his first awareness of how deeply the local public supported his efforts. It was totally unexpected. He left the fair with almost four thousand dollars that year, the first time he'd made money on his fair project. This remarkable summer was still only half over. We had the Make-A-Wish trip to Alaska yet to come.

We packed different clothes, grabbed Simon, and Andy's best friend Frankie, and were on our way to Alaska. John would run the dairy while we were gone.

Simon was apprehensive about leaving the ranch and went purely for Andy's sake, not to mention the threat of what I might say if he even uttered a word about not going.

We began with a fishing trip, flown into a lake with no name (Lake 165 on the U.S.G.S. map), 150 miles southwest of Denali. We were going to spend five days there. It was green, beautiful and isolated, and when the plane left we were alone.

Wait a minute. *Did the bush pilot say what time he'd come back for us? What day is this? What day did he say he was coming back? What if he forgot? What if he crashed? Did anyone else know where we were? How far is it to civilization? Could we walk there if we had to?*

What was I in control of here?

There was no one to answer. We were all scared, not just me, though my fear had little hooks on it that attached to much larger, darker things inside.

Moose antlers found at our camp in Alaska, during Andy's Make-A-Wish trip in August 1989.

12

THE OTHER SHOE DROPS

ndy is cured. He doesn't have the cancer anymore. The fear in Alaska is from something else. It's just a reasonable fear about being in the wilderness, isolated, at the mercy of others. We feel small in the middle of nowhere.

Andy's fear seems physical. It seems he isn't breathing well, and when we talk about it, it's like he's not himself. He lacks his physical grace and easy presence. Fears interlock like puzzle pieces. *What if it's the cancer again? I brought him here. I brought him to a place where we can't even rely on Simon. There's nothing Simon can do. I may have made a mistake.* The sky goes over us in a huge, empty arc and we need someone in a tiny plane to take us through it. *I'm not allowed to make a mistake. I can't be a dumb little girl. Not anymore.*

The plane does come, of course, and we fly out safely. It was all just stupid. Andy still seems a little . . . I don't know . . . shaky perhaps. But that's just left over from being in the wilderness. First thing when we get back, we'll see the new doctor and start getting comfortable with him. He'll tell us what to do and we'll do it. It's over except for the healing routine. The wilderness was just a shock, the emptiness.

We get home and head down to the medical center early on the following gray day.

The new physician is Dr. Young. In the waiting room, we're unusually comfortable. Circumstances have changed. The nurses aren't as chatty as usual. *Our circumstances have changed and they don't feel they have to be chatty anymore.* That's what I think.

Dr. Young is a small woman with a beautiful smile. After Dr. Schlemmer, she seems positively radiant. Her black eyes sparkle and watch our faces carefully, processing all the time. We all talk about the Alaska trip and she seems interested and unhurried—kindly, gentle and relaxed. She puts up with all my local color. Andy sits on the exam table and I have a chair.

It was perfectly fine. The new doctor was better than the old and everything was falling into place. I could feel the air getting lighter as we talked. When the conversation was running out of topics and it seemed time to talk about treatment, I asked about the CAT scan and MRI. I wasn't pushy or changing the subject. I just said, "I guess the CAT scan and MRI were good."

But she paused before answering, and in that second or two the darkness rose up inside me again and stopped my breathing. I caught Andy's eye, and the color was draining from his face.

"Well," she said, "actually not. They weren't good at all."

"What?" I said. There was a fine edge of indignation in my fright. "What?"

"The scans show twenty to thirty tumors in Andy's lungs. They're mostly the size of quarters."

"What?"

She was a beautiful woman. She had no right to do this to us. We liked her. She was delicate. She was beautiful. She smiled beautifully.

"No," I said, "Andy was able to run ten miles. He'd been doing double football practices before we left. You don't do double football practices with tumors in your lungs. There's some mistake."

She looked at me intently, holding my eyes as she took the X rays out of their manila covers and put them side by side on the viewing screen. I looked first at the lower right corner where the name goes. Andy's name was on them. I looked at the X rays. Neither of us stood to move closer. There wasn't any need. The lungs were the usual, dark masses, but inside the dark—all over it—were white circles. Just like quarters. Just that size. Deathly white, clear-edged quarters.

Andy said nothing, but tears were rolling down his face. I'm sure my mouth was open. I turned to the X rays, then back to Andy. *My God, my God* I thought, and started to go to him. The seconds broke down into close-up stopwatch chunks as I had to get out of my chair and walk the ten steps to be with him. The room was stretched and the time with it. Under my feet was the wet cement of the nightmare escape, the soft, sucking, hindering ground.

They told us it was all right. They told us to go. They said it was all right and we went to Alaska and now there's this. His lungs weren't like that when we left.

I put my arms around Andy. "They told us to go," I said to Dr. Young.

The doctor cleared her throat. "I know," she said. "I guess it was a judgment call." I looked again at the X rays. A judgment call?

"I'm so sorry."

She started talking quickly. We'd need more tests before we went home, and there were more decisions to make. First, she had to research Andy's disease to see if there were any new options since the previous year. Medical treatment changes so rapidly that a year can be a vast period of time. She was hoping someone else had written about a success with clear cell sarcoma.

She left us to go set up the appointments. Alone in the room we held on to each other, crying. Andy looked great. His muscles felt strong. How could this be?

After what seemed a long time, we composed ourselves enough to walk out of the room and into the hallway. The receptionist looked up with tears in her eyes. This was why they hadn't been chatty. Everyone had known. I suddenly saw them all talking before we'd arrived, trying to decide what to do. Dr. Young had inherited the situation.

The communal atmosphere was sad understanding. They'd all known, and now they all knew more about what we had ahead of us than we did. Much more.

Dr. Young called our insurance company and, as we stood by, received immediate approval from the medical director for all the needed tests. We were to go for an MRI of Andy's brain right away and come down for the rest of the tests in the next couple of days.

We walked through it all, one foot in front of the other, in what felt like slow motion. We were numb. We were the undead. We went ahead with the scheduled tests. We started in the radiology department. While Andy was in there, I called Simon. The silence on the phone was terrible. "Well, come home now," he finally said.

It was late as we drove home. Conversation was sparse.

Andy said suddenly, "On our way down there we were talking about school and college. Now none of it seems important. I felt fine, then I come back and they say, 'Hey, it's still eating you.' This time I might die."

That's all I remember. The drive is about ninety miles, but that's all I remember. When we reached the road leading to the ranch and made the turn, Andy began to cry again. He said he wanted to live long enough to see his baby niece Stefanie grow up. He wanted her to remember him. He wanted her to know how much he loved her. He was afraid she wouldn't be able to remember him.

The words were tearing me up. I said, "Listen to me, Honey, we'll fight. We'll give it a hell of a fight. We'll beat it. It's just harder now. We'll do the chemotherapy, everything possible, and we'll beat it."

"Yeah."

It was after 11 P.M. when we arrived at home, and the whole family was there. Simon had called and all the kids had come. Alex was there, too. She'd been planning to stay overnight anyway so they could go to school together on the first day of their senior year. She'd walked in smiling, and they'd told her. She was wide-eyed and devastated as we came in the front door.

Stefanie was asleep on the sofa. Nick and Kerri sat by their mom, needing to be close. We all began to do what we needed to do to survive. We did it as a unit. There were hours, it seemed, of agony before someone said something funny—threw it out into a silence—and the tension broke. Andy laughed, and we all laughed.

Alex and Andy went out for a drive while the rest of us waited and talked. When they came back, the house was empty except for Simon and me. They hardly said anything—"Hi" maybe—and went into Andy's room and closed the door.

The house was dark except for the reading lamp next to the sofa and the light from the television. It muttered away to itself, turned down low and flickering. I looked at it. Johnny Carson was telling a joke. I could tell from the way he was moving. We were drained and uncaring and unseeing, and Johnny Carson meant nothing at all. Johnny Carson was a pointless, foolish man on a dark night.

The light from the lamp brought out the red in Simon's swollen eyes. We couldn't go to bed, but we couldn't do anything else. We watched the TV stupidly, waiting for something to happen, for someone to tell us what to do. Gradually, the murmurs from Andy's room died away. I turned off the television and we went resignedly to bed, up the stairs with effort.

The room was dark, but when I turned on the light it was much too bright. I turned it off again and we got into bed. We just held each other. There wasn't a thing to say. We couldn't tell ourselves that everything was going to be all right. We each needed someone stronger to hold onto. But it wasn't either of us.

Simon said, "What do we do now?"

"I don't know."

The moon, I remember, around the edges of the shade threw white lines across the bed, the floor and the wall. I watched them creeping with the clock. I listened for Simon to snore, to be asleep, but he didn't, and every once in a while his body would shake with a sob. When the sun came up, we got out of bed. It had been like a solitary confinement for two, and we arose to precisely the world we had left the night before. We had to start curing Andy.

I called the insurance company and Gary, our family doctor. His staff would have to start the paperwork. I called Michael, the doctor who had first diagnosed Andy, to let him know what was happening.

There were calls to the extended family and to the high school to tell them Andy wouldn't be there. The proposed speech to the new students was forgotten.

The insurance company said everything was set: just be sure to advise them of Andy's condition and his needs. But remember, do all that you can in Sonoma County.

The next call was to California Children's Service (C.C.S.). What if the insurance company won't pay for treatment at the medical center? Will they cover Andy? The answers were given in steps that I would need to follow:

1. Before C.C.S. could step in, we had to have prior authorization from the insurance company for all nonemergency scheduled procedures.
2. The doctors had to prove the need for each procedure.
3. If our insurance company denied something his doctor ordered, and it couldn't be done locally with the same results, then C.C.S. would cover the costs.
4. There had to be a dialogue between all the doctors, the insurance company and C.C.S. to make sure nothing was missed.
5. Remember to go through proper channels!

In an emergency, our case manager at C.C.S. said, just do whatever is needed to save Andy's life. Everything would probably be covered, unless it was really radical or experimental, and they would probably support the medical center's decisions for treatment. No matter what crisis developed in Andy's illness, the need to include both the insurance company and C.C.S. at each turn was overridingly important.

His situation was beginning to be known outside the family. That weekend an article in the sports section of the paper mentioned the return of Andy's cancer. Another article mentioned his lobbying in Washington, D.C., for children with cancer.

Barbara Boxer was quoted as to the impression Andy had made on her, and she noted that Andy's efforts had had a positive impact on the legislation then pending in the California Industrial Relations Committee. She said she'd appear at a fundraiser being set up for Andy by the Parents of Kids With Cancer Foundation. The funds were to be used to help cover any uninsured costs. These were costs we hadn't thought about at all: gasoline, food and lodging, any unapproved treatments, etc.

People started calling to see how they could help. Soon the downstairs office was converted into a bedroom for Andy, complete with new carpet, electric heater (the first in our 110-year-old house), a water bed and a small sofa, all donated by local businesses. People were wonderful. In an amazing outpouring of love, perfect strangers donated money and supplies.

Once people started showing up, their good feelings overpowered any discomfort we might have felt about opening our lives to strangers. They felt good helping and we, in turn, felt good receiving. It was such a boost of love and energy: dinners and boxes of cookies, calls to see if we needed anything in town.

Our whole family was being held in the hearts of strangers, and they were doing it with considerable tenderness.

On our return to the medical center for results of the last tests, the news was generally good: no metastasis to the brain, bone or abdomen. One test, though, the liver function study, was way out of whack. Liver cancer was suspected and blood was drawn again. If it was liver cancer, we weren't even going to have time to begin fighting. There were questions about Andy's habits.

Alcohol and tobacco weren't the culprits. What was? I asked about the amino acid muscle-building pills he bought at the health-food store to bulk up his muscles for football. The doctor thought they probably weren't the cause, but said to stop them anyway.

The radiology department had to do a biopsy of one of the lung tumors. Andy would be awake while the test was done with an iodine contrast. He walked stoically away with a resident.

The biopsy was to find out if the tumors were the same kind of cancer as his finger. If the biopsy turned out as expected, the test would prove metastasis.

I knew they'd be inserting a long needle through Andy's chest wall and hoped it wouldn't hurt too much. I'd told him he'd do fine, that they would make everything numb and we'd be waiting for him when he finished. Simon, Linda, Alex and I waited a long time, and when Andy came out on a stretcher, we followed him into the waiting area.

"Things are fine now," the doctor said, "but we had a little problem while the test was being administered. When they injected the dye into his vein, Andy immediately began to cough, sneeze and have difficulty breathing. He had an allergic reaction and we had to medicate him. He shouldn't have the dye injected again."

The journal was opened and the information noted. The

journal had become a very important part of Andy's care. All the problems, questions and concerns I couldn't keep in my head were written down. It had doctor, hospital and social worker's business cards stapled to the inside cover, and it contained notes from every doctor's visit and every telephone call to the health insurance company, the doctor or anyone else involved in Andy's care. It was becoming our memory. There were doodles, scratches and drawings highlighting the text. The pages were filling rapidly.

While all the new test results were being compiled, we went home. Andy and I went for an echocardiogram of his heart at the local hospital. He needed to have a baseline to compare any changes that chemotherapy might cause in his heart. A plain X ray of his chest was also needed.

On the ride home, Andy said he'd really hit the X-ray tech with an unthinking joke. He felt bad that he hadn't thought before he said it. I asked what he'd said.

"The tech was checking my X ray after it was taken, and he got really quiet. So I just blurted out, 'Kind of looks like a pepperoni pizza, doesn't it?' The guy looked at me with his face growing whiter and walked out of the room, not saying anything. I wish I'd gone after him and told him I was just making a joke."

I told Andy he could call the tech at the X-ray department and explain when we got home. I don't know if he ever did.

At home, we put the video of the echocardiogram in the VCR, and Cheryl sang an impromptu rap song to the beat, dancing around Andy on his bed while the rest of watched and laughed. It was a totally stupid song about Andy's heart, but we loved every minute of it.

It could have gone on forever.

13

*B*EWILDERMENT

*B*ack at the hospital for more scans. You know how some old people feel that the most important thing is to avoid going to the hospital? That the hospital seems to them to be the beginning of the road to death? I was beginning to understand.

In dreams, the hospital is a maze with a nightmare at the center. The white hallways go out in every direction and when you turn a corner, you may be anywhere. You may be somewhere impossible. You may be on a boat. You may be in a library. You may be in an operating room full of people whose faces change suddenly, people who aren't what they seem. And way at the center is a dark room around which all the other rooms are arranged chaotically.

But dreams are just dreams. The hospital is also our hope.

It was a confused place to be, a kind of hell where fear and hope lace together and tighten and flex around your head. We needed to start the chemo right away. We should have started the chemo weeks ago.

Nothing was clear. The biopsy was classified as a clear cell sarcoma by some of the pathologists and a melanoma by others. Dr. Young wanted us to think about dropping the soft tissue sarcoma protocol and going to a cookbook approach, permitting her to use different drugs that would change in relation to Andy's responses rather than research criteria.

First she had to tell us everything—all the statistics, all the possibilities. We'll sit in a room in a shifting/solid, dreamlike/matter-of-fact, threatening/reassuring building, and listen to a terrifying litany of facts and figures that really don't clarify much.

Andy's treatment was going to depend on what he decided after hearing everything. So we all drove down for the meeting, with Maureen coming from Sacramento. Maureen had already done a lot of research and pretty much knew what we were going to hear. She wasn't sharing it, and that was terrifying in itself.

Andy was quiet as we waited in the hall to meet the doctor. It was going to be an awful day. It was an awful day.

I couldn't bear Andy's pain. It didn't matter that I'd experienced the edge of death and found it to be comforting, almost radiant, because in terms of the real anguish, death isn't the issue. The issue is how my baby feels. The issue is physical pain. The issue is how it is inside his head when he wakes up in the night and remembers how things are, and that not being is coming toward him relentlessly.

I had my journal and the tape recorder had new batteries.

Dr. Young met us in a large conference room and began before we were all seated. Her voice was calm. She mentioned prestigious names. She put out a huge amount of information, all of it grim.

Andy was very quiet.

The central fact was that the pathologists were still uncertain what kind of cancer Andy had, and that we would have to decide which cancer diagnosis to address. It came down to our gut reaction and nothing else. The diagnosis was too close to call.

The vicious facts were these: If Andy's cancer were a melanoma, now that he'd had a recurrence, his survival time could be estimated at between six and eleven months, no matter what we did. His chance of survival with metastatic melanoma was around 1 percent.

With clear cell sarcoma the chances of survival were about 40 percent, even with the recurrence. So what choice was there?

The options were limited. Surgery to remove the lung tumors was not one of them. There were too many tumors. If the chemotherapy shrunk the number by two-thirds, then surgery would be a good option.

A lung transplant wasn't an option because lung transplant patients need to be cancer-free. Radiation therapy generally works well on soft tissue sarcomas, but the clear cell sarcoma results were unpredictable. With chemotherapy, clear cell sarcomas had a 30 to 40 percent response rate.

Response doesn't mean cure. It only means that the tumors shrink or don't grow during the chemotherapy. Once chemo stops, the tumors may grow again.

Andy spoke to ask the doctor what kind of cancer she thought he had. She told him she just didn't know.

Andy said, "Okay. This started as clear cell, so it might as well stay clear cell."

Dr. Young agreed. She would vary the chemo drugs every two months in the absence of a favorable response. This also meant we would have to sign him off the protocol study. We all agreed.

"There are two other options I have to present," she said.

There was general, expectant silence.

One, she said quietly, was to do nothing. We all looked at her aghast. Andy's voice broke when he said, "Nothing?"

She said it was a valid choice, and something to consider.

"I'm going to fight it," Andy said. The words hung there, and Andy dropped his head onto his arms.

The doctor touched his arm and explained that ethically she had to offer him that choice. He didn't look up.

"The other option is immunotherapy."

Andy raised his head and looked at her. His eyes were red-rimmed and swollen.

"Immunotherapy programs are experimental. They wouldn't be covered by your medical insurance, and you'd have to go with a melanoma diagnosis."

Andy seemed to have been driven into his chair by the accumulated weight of the data, and his face was becoming stony. He was overwhelmed and beginning to wall himself off. And now, here was the melanoma diagnosis again. He grew quiet, withdrawn and resistant. His answers became abrupt.

Dr. Young finally said she needed to talk to Andy alone, so we all filed out. No one said a word while we waited. When Andy came out, he was talking to her and seemed a bit more relaxed.

In the van on the long drive home, in the silence, Andy and Alex held each other tight. When Andy broke down and began to cry, it was agony. It was like we could see into the depth of his isolation. Hugging the fear away wasn't going to work.

At home that night, Andy and Alex spent hours alone while the rest of us listened to the taped conversation.

A football game was coming up on the weekend. Even with thirty tumors in his lungs and the specter of chemo in front of him, Andy really wanted to play. He wanted something normal.

The day of the game, Andy and Alex drove up with a group of their friends, and Simon and I drove with ours. Cheryl met us there.

God knows the team was on his side. These were kids who'd been together since grammar school. In the locker room, they were more subdued than usual. They were the visiting team and had been given the girls' lockers. The room felt strange in a lot of ways. It didn't even smell like a locker room. Not enough sweat, too clean. Maybe at halftime, their own sweat would soften it.

There were jokes about the girls who normally dressed there. Just the usual adolescent stuff—they're getting pumped up. They know each other so well that all the little individual requirements for preparation were honored and had a place.

Fred is quiet and smiling, not really there at all. Justin is quiet, with no smile. Dave and Erik talk compulsively about what they'll do when they get the ball, pure bravado. Brian and Brennan are in their first year of varsity and have an edge of uncertainty about them. They take a lot of ribbing from the seniors.

These are guys who share camping trips, fishing, drinking, cars, girls, clothes and family problems. They share Andy's sickness, too, and tonight they want to give him his chance. The cancer has brought them even closer.

Waiting for the game to start, we're all stretched nerves. I had pleaded with Andy: Be careful, don't push yourself too hard. Please don't get hurt.

He was going to play football with thirty tumors in his lungs, and there wasn't anything I could do about it. I wasn't there for fun. God, I was afraid.

My heart pounded all through the first JV game. At the start of halftime, Andy was called out on the field, and the opposing coach announced with a deep current of emotion in his voice that the games were being played in Andy's honor, as tribute to his strength and his courage. The opposing players came out and, one at a time, shook Andy's hand. We found out later that the coach's sister was battling cancer, too. It was a wonderful moment, but as Andy walked by on his way into the locker room to change, I was completely wrapped up in fear.

I did want him to have the chance. I didn't want to be over-bearing or too protective. I did want him to have the thrill of winning. Most of all, I wanted what he wanted: to be a good seventeen-year-old football player again.

But what might happen? What would I have to watch? What awful collision and slow recovery?

In the locker room, the guys were waiting around to go out on the field when Andy was still suiting up. His pants seemed harder to pull on, and lacing his cleats was taking a long time. When he stood up to put on his pads, he swayed. Shaking his head, he tried to get his jersey on. When it was over his face, he couldn't breathe anymore and he fell on the floor.

"Hey, Andy, you okay? Hey, Coach. Andy? What's the matter, man?" The guys helped him up and put him on the bench.

"I'm okay," he said, "it's okay. I don't need any help. Go ahead, I'll be right out."

"See you there, huh?"

"Yeah. I'm okay. I just got dizzy."

The coach sat with him. "You feel good enough to play?"

Silence.

"No, I don't think so."

"I need to go out with the team. You need a doc?"

"Nah, shit, I guess I just have the flu or something."

"We'll miss you out there."

"Yeah, thanks."

The coach left and Andy took off his uniform for the last time in the empty, strange, girls' locker room. In his street clothes, tears of frustration in his eyes, he wandered out to where the coaches were on the sidelines.

I had been watching the team come out of the locker room, waiting anxiously for his number 32. I hadn't been able to see him. Neither could Cheryl. I'd caught Simon's eye down on the sidelines, but he just shrugged and turned back to watch. The warm-ups had started, and there was still no sign of Andy.

When I finally spotted him, he was standing on the sidelines with the coaches, not looking at his dad or me.

He looked okay, but something must have happened. I stood and Simon looked at me, willing me to stay put. I couldn't, though. I went down to where Andy was and asked why he wasn't playing.

"I got dizzy when I was suiting up. I had to sit down," he said. His voice was pained and his eyes were filling with tears, so he looked away from me and I went back to my seat.

These are the emotions of desperate illness. Nothing is clean. Andy is heartbroken and so am I, for him, and yet I know I'll be easier with this, not having to watch him getting hit out there. And underneath (not so far underneath) a voice is saying, *He got dizzy? What is it? It's new. He got dizzy? He had to sit. What does* dizzy *mean? Oh, God.*

Andy's figure moved back and forth in my vision as I tried to act interested in the game. He was yelling encouragement to his teammates. He thrust his arms in the air as they scored and jumped to hug the ball carrier as he came to the sidelines.

I gave up on the game and watched him exclusively, until I started to cry anyway. You could see how he needed to be out there. The angles of his body, how he stood, how he turned to the coaches. I couldn't watch another minute. The pain was unbearable. I had prepared myself for the possibility of his getting hurt, but not for this. This was even worse. I asked Cheryl to drive me home, and I cried all the way.

It was the one thing he wanted: to do something in the teeth of reality; to kick off the fight of his life with a graceful, confident gesture.

Next morning, Andy said he felt okay but didn't act like it. He was quiet and withdrawn. He had no energy, no spark, as I watched him through the day.

His chemotherapy was scheduled for the following week, but something had to be done right away. He wasn't feeling any better. He became dizzy when he stood up. I called Dr. Young, and she told me to go to our family doctor for a checkup before coming in.

Gary examined Andy and said there was nothing really out of the ordinary, but his blood pressure was low. He said he might be dehydrated from all the tests and gave him a couple of bottles of IV fluids. They helped, and Andy felt a little better.

He spent that evening watching a movie with Alex. His dog, Spuds, was snuggled on top of them.

In the morning, he felt worse. Even so, we went to our

acupuncturist for his last scheduled treatment before the chemo. Both Andy and I had been seeing Bill for the last year—Andy, to help build up his immune system, and me, for stress management. When we arrived there, he was so weak he couldn't climb the stairs to Bill's office. I took him back to the van and went in to tell Bill that we'd have to cancel the appointment. Instead, Bill came out and climbed in the van to examine him.

While feeling Andy's pulse he said, "Boy, I wish I could see your heart." He said, "Good," when I told him about the echocardiogram we'd just had taken.

I thought nothing more about what he'd said.

Maybe I just couldn't fit it in.

14

*B*ATTLE *L*INES

I was changing. I can't remember now if I knew it or not. Certainly I knew I was becoming more efficient with the peripherals—the paperwork and the notifications and the logistics—but whether I felt myself moving away into the structured place where nothing existed but Andy, the cancer and my own will, I really couldn't say.

The changes come gradually, and all of them seem perfectly normal, perfectly useful. What happens is you have to be able to respond quickly and effectively. You know this. Your mind makes its adjustments. What seems extraneous starts to fade and becomes little more than ambiance. The world peripheral to the conflict washes out, slowly and imperceptibly, and what's left is an almost military cast of mind that makes its decisions on hard fact. I learned some of that from my father anyway. He was a tough thinker. But some of the change is coming from the process. To some degree, I'm becoming someone else. Is this good? I don't know at all.

It probably isn't for the people around me who have to deal with it. My new requirements are going to have less to do with the feelings of others. It only involves survival, and in that place there's no one but Andy, me, the cancer and a long row of medical foot soldiers.

If I don't tell them what to do, who will?

The feeling is barely noticeable at first, but it comes to take over your thinking and move you away from the people you love till you seem to be looking at them through the wrong end of a telescope. When it's over, when Andy and I are standing there, smiling and whole, then they can say what they want.

I work well on my own. I am the rock at the center of the storm. Don't ask me for answers you won't understand. Don't get in my way and, if you're in my way, don't expect me to slow up. I know all of what's going on, and you don't.

Leave me alone.

I don't know if anyone can tell I'm changing. Simon can, I'm sure of that. I think Andy, perhaps, is too isolated in his own apprehensions to notice. Given the circumstances, though, I'm getting better. I'm getting more efficient.

Where will I be when it's over?

I have no idea.

What if I fail?

We'd borrowed a motor home so we'd have a place to stay once Andy was in the hospital. Had there been fewer of us, we could have stayed at the Ronald McDonald House. Cheryl and Linda followed us in the car so they could take Simon home once the chemo was underway and things were going well.

Andy slept on the way down. When I woke him up to go into the clinic and register, he was so weak he couldn't stand. *Something isn't right. Something is out of sequence.* I went inside for a wheelchair. Andy was very weak, and we placed him in the chair with difficulty.

When the script isn't going the way it should, there's panic. I rushed Andy in and through the halls. No one seemed concerned, they'd all seen kids come in sicker. But this was my kid and things weren't going the way they were supposed to. I didn't know what was going on, and I needed to see Dr. Young. The admittance process was taking too long.

They don't hear me. Why don't they hear me?

Then there were blood tests and the wait for a room. By the time a room was available, Andy couldn't even sit.

We're in a hospital. This can't happen.

He was pale, groaning and could barely hold his head up.

Dr. Young finally said she needed more blood tests, an IV and a chest X ray. Andy had a large raw area on his tongue, but no one thought it was the problem. It had been there for about a week, not too sore, but definitely different.

Another doctor was called to help in the evaluation. No one had a clue.

After a conference, the doctors said that they thought Andy had an infection, but that they needed some answers before they'd admit him to the children's ward. He couldn't go when he might infect someone there.

We waited in the treatment area where Andy lay. The results were all negative.

We all trudged along behind Andy's gurney as they wheeled him to the children's ward. He was nauseated now. His color was dusky and his hands were cold. Was it fear?

When you're following the rules and doing things in order and you've learned everything you can learn, you feel like you're involved in a kind of magic, a don't-step-on-the-cracks kind of magic. When the enemy gets crazy and out-of-bounds, it's like the world is coming apart.

He was already terrified of the chemotherapy. If he felt this bad already, what would he feel like at the end of the week? We all tried to be strong for him, but he could sense the fear.

He was quiet and submissive (probably it was all he was capable of), and he seemed like he didn't care what was happening. He moved along in the process like a pawn across the board. I thought of how someone might be just before his execution.

When he was finally in bed, Dr. Young came by to see him again. She tried to calm him and explained what would happen with the chemo. Andy broke down then, sobbing in fear. She talked and talked to him, sitting on the bed patiently.

This is more like it. This is how things should be.

In the bed across from Andy's was a teenage boy. He was pissed off, and we could feel it clear across the room. His television was blasting, and he glared when asked to turn it down.

He waited a while then cranked it up again. I asked him to turn it down, too, and he yelled, "Just shut up!" at me.

The random again. The wild card.

I looked around the room at the other parents. They just shrugged.

I went out to get help, and a nurse came back with me and told him to turn it down. He stared at me as he did.

I pulled the curtain across the end of Andy's bed to block our view, but we couldn't block the other boy's voice and all through the night we had to hear him. He was loud. He swore at his visitors and yelled at his mom. He was hooked up to chemo and he must have been terrified.

We saw him leave, too, angry in his bulky, black leather jacket. Perhaps a bit less hostile, but still angry.

The other children on that first day were a different story. Diagonally from Andy's bed was a tiny girl with hardly any hair. She was wan and quiet and watched everything with huge eyes. She didn't play and she didn't talk. Her mom and dad stayed by her side.

Alongside Andy's bed was a young, dark-haired boy without any visitors. He was also receiving his chemo, sleeping quietly.

This was our common room. The yellow curtains between the beds provided the only privacy. Tables next to the beds held toys, books and medical supplies. And untouched food, brought by parents who were hoping for a sudden improvement in appetite.

Outside the door, kids walked by on their way to the game room, dragging their IV poles. One boy used the IV stand as a kind of scooter: he'd get a running start, hop on the metal legs of the stand and ride. A nurse caught him, but as soon as she was out of sight, the pole glided by again. The kids walking or gliding by didn't seem hindered by the lines running into their bodies. They were having fun with whatever was at hand. They could laugh, talk and smile. They even made me smile.

They talked to each other so knowledgeably. They talked about dosages, counts and treatments, matter-of-factly. They knew what neutrophils were, what they did in their bodies and when to expect them to go up or down. I was a nurse, but these kids knew things I didn't.

They lived their lives on the oncology floor. Blood cells, blood counts and chemotherapy protocols were the stuff of everyday conversation. The counts ruled treatments, meals, vacations and school. The counts rule your life when you're receiving chemo.

Dr. Young wasn't willing to start Andy's chemotherapy until she had a better idea of what was going on with him. So nothing was going to happen till the following day.

As the night wore on, the father of the little girl pulled out his folding bed and made it up, getting ready for sleep. A nurse brought linens for me.

Each child still had a schedule of medications, IVs or injections. They needed to go to the bathroom, they needed to be comforted. Some would be sick and start to cry. Mom or Dad tried to help. They'd clean up and call the nurse. Flashlight beams whipped around the room as the nurses looked in to check on the children and their fluid levels.

Andy slept in fits and starts. The newness of the situation, the fear of what might happen and the noise kept me alert all through the night. In the morning, the parents prepared for another day's battle. Me, too.

The medical team still hadn't figured out what Andy's problem was. His blood pressure was better, though still low, and he could stand up for a short time without passing out, but he was complaining now of rib pain on his right side. The doctor didn't know if it was the lung tumors or just being in bed.

Andy was still pale and still couldn't eat. His ears had developed a blue tinge. The doctor said she would wait another day before starting his chemo.

Our family came during the day. Linda brought Andy some animal crackers, and he ate a few. Alex and Lisa came down in the evening.

Lisa, a month younger than Andy, was his buddy. Her mom had been a friend of mine, and these last two children in our respective families had grown up together, attending all the same classes from preschool on. They loved each other without question. Their lives were intertwined.

Lisa was at the hospital because Andy needed her, and that's all that mattered. School could wait. I had been Lisa's mom's hospice nurse when she died of breast cancer. Lisa and Andy had been in the eighth grade then, and from that time on, Lisa had become part of our family. We all loved having her around. We still do.

Later that night Simon, Maureen, Cheryl and Linda left for home. Alex and Lisa stayed over and would leave for school in the morning. That was fine with me. I didn't want to be alone.

I am though.

That Saturday, there would be a fund-raiser for Andy in Tomales. Barbara Boxer would be there to speak. The girls were going, and Alex and Lisa, too.

The next morning, Andy's ribs were still hurting. The doctor said that if the pain were from his lung tumors, it was all the more reason to begin chemo as soon as possible. She was going to give Andy a three-day start to see how he handled the dosage. She thought we'd be home by the middle of the week.

She told us to contact a local surgeon so we could have a Port-A-Cath inserted. It would let Andy receive the drugs he needed through a tube in his chest and eliminate the need for the multiple needle pricks that go with the search for good veins.

We got a semiprivate room that day, a quieter room. Andy wanted a bath so we went down to the tub room, Andy in his wheelchair. He was able to climb in without much help, and he took a long, relaxing bath. He couldn't get out, though. He was dizzy and too weak.

When we finally managed to bring him back to bed, his lips, ears and fingertips were blue.

I called a nurse who came in, looked and left immediately.

A few minutes later a team of doctors and nurses streamed into the room. They were concerned and talked among themselves as though we weren't there. Andy was very scared. So was I. I held his hand and we waited like we had no business being there, like we were in the way.

They hooked an oxygen monitor to his finger, EKG leads to his chest and put an oxygen mask over his nose.

As they started to give him oxygen, the oxygen saturation level on the monitor registered at only 80 percent. With the oxygen going, he should have registered 90 to 100 percent. A blood gas was needed to evaluate the amount of oxygen in his blood, and a doctor started to draw the sample.

This is a simple but painful procedure. A needle is passed very close to a nerve in the wrist. It's the first place they try for arterial blood.

John, Paul and Toni arrived during all the confusion.

The doctor was trying to draw the blood in the now-silent room. He felt around with his finger and put the needle in over and over again. Still no arterial blood. Andy was grimacing with pain, and the tears were welling in his eyes. Finally, the doctor said he couldn't get the sample. Someone else would try. He left, and nobody said a word.

A nursing supervisor was next. Then two more doctors. Tears of frustration and pain were running down Andy's face.

I was holding his other hand and trying to talk him through another attempt when John exploded. He rushed up to the doctor, close, talking right into his face.

"If you don't get it this time, I'm going out to the car, get my bat and beat the shit out of you with it." The doctor looked at John, then Andy, then me. He put his equipment down and walked out of the room. We all gave a sigh of relief. Andy thanked John quietly. We knew it wasn't over, but at least he would get a break in the agony.

Finally, a young, sandy-haired doctor came in. He sat down next to Andy and started to talk to him. They talked about surfing. Then he explained what they were trying to do and why it hurt so much. He said they'd stick him one more time. If it didn't work, they'd do something else. Andy said "Okay, go ahead and try."

The doctor looked at both red, bruised and swollen wrists and said he was going to start. He worked the needle slowly, and it seemed to take hours. But he finally hit it and we had a sample. Andy smiled and wiped his eyes.

The sample was put on ice and whisked out the door.

Now the finger monitor was registering weird readings. The technician came back and adjusted the monitor. He said it was working fine. We all watched as the machine registered 80 percent oxygen, then 70 percent. The oxygen flow was turned up as the readings fell, but the level kept dropping. Andy's ears, lips and fingers were still blue. This was cyanosis.

When the lab results came back they showed 70 percent oxygen in his blood. The flow was turned up. They'd have to do another blood gas later.

While this was all going on, a nurse very quietly brought resuscitation equipment into the room. Andy didn't notice, but I did. They thought that he might die. They were getting prepared.

Andy braved the needles again. The result this time was 60 percent. It was still dropping, though he actually looked better than he had when he finished his bath.

The doctors and nurses were obviously anxious. They didn't talk to us at all. *Am I useless? Am I helpless?*

They talked about results, equipment and gases. They brought in another oxygen setup and put a re-breather mask on over the oxygen prongs, and turned that mask on, too.

Andy's eyes were moving around, looking in our faces as if something were there to read.

The consultation in the room continued. They were talking about transferring Andy to the intensive care unit. They discussed his condition technically, as if he didn't exist. There wasn't any human dimension at all. They started to get loud, and the situation moved inexorably toward Out of Control.

I went over to the knot of professionals and told them to stop it, that Andy needed to be treated with respect, not like a piece of meat. I told them to leave the room and have their discussion elsewhere. I told them that when they had finally figured out what they were doing, then they could send someone back to tell us. I told them to leave Andy alone, and they looked at each other, nodded and walked out.

The room was quiet.

What have I done? They're angry, they're pulling away. What is there left to do, what have I done to Andy, when does this end, who is there to help me? Help, what have I done to Andy?

It's so quiet.

15

Heavy Heart

A doctor did come back to explain their plan. Andy would stay there for the night and they'd see how things went. They wanted to assess his oxygen level, then just keep him quiet. Blood gases would be drawn again and then he could rest. If things were no better in the morning, he'd be transferred to intensive care.

After the last blood was drawn, the room grew quiet and Andy slept. We were all exhausted. Paul, John and Toni said hesitant good-byes and left for the long drive home. They didn't want to, but it was already late and they had to be at work in the morning. Simon would be coming back. John would take over the work at home.

I sat up that night, watching. I was vigilant for anything unusual. It was very quiet. I caressed him with my eyes while he slept, trying to put love and strength into his body.

There was a hole in the middle of everything. The worst was somewhere in Andy. His strength was draining away and I couldn't stop it, and everything I'd done so far had been for nothing. The magic wasn't working and the science wasn't working and the luck hadn't even showed up. I couldn't protect my baby. He was slipping away. Sleeping there, he was slipping away like the tide.

The nurses checked him often through the night. They were quiet and not much was said to me.

I shouldn't yell at the doctors.

They were in early to examine Andy. His oxygen saturation was down to 41 percent, with two oxygen setups going full-blast. He was really in trouble. At 41 percent he wasn't getting enough to keep alive, and his brain and tissues wouldn't last long with so little. Something was drastically wrong: This was not a fluke, this was big trouble.

Am I screaming?

Dr. Young said he'd be transferred to the ICU and that they would start the chemotherapy. She said they thought the lung tumors were blocking an artery and causing his oxygen levels to drop. The tumors needed to be shrunk if they were to relieve the pressure. I nodded as Andy watched with huge, scared eyes. Simon and Linda walked in with pale, drawn faces, and Andy cried when his Dad's huge frame bent to embrace him.

"It'll be okay, Andy," he said, tears rolling down his cheeks. Linda cried, too, and nestled into Andy's shoulder.

Dr. Young motioned to me that she wanted to talk to me outside.

Oh shit, what now?

She was intense. Her tone was different. Blindly and apprehensively, I followed her out into the sunshine. We settled ourselves on a bench without saying anything.

He's going to die, now; there's no more time.

"You are doing Andy *no good*," she said. She looked right at me and her eyes were intense and angry. "Your attitude works against him. It's a detriment and it's got to stop. It's got to stop *now*."

Me? What's she doing? Why is she doing this?

My mind was scrambling around for a place to stand.

"Andy could die at any minute. You removed the doctors from the room of a boy who was in crisis. You sent the doctors away when he could have died at any time without them. What are you *doing*?"

I sat there. I looked at the sky.

"He should have been moved immediately to the ICU. Do you know that? Your interference put him in jeopardy. You made a medical error when you thought he was better last night. He wasn't better; he was worse, much worse."

I knew I was crying. I was personally hurt. I was taking it personally. That wasn't right, either.

I was wrong again. I was stupid.

But I had to say something.

"I *wouldn't* hurt my child. And I'm not a child to be yelled at."

I glared at her. "You weren't even there. You don't know what they were doing. *My child is not a piece of meat.*"

You need control.

"I know about cyanosis. I didn't think he was better. How could you say that to me? It had nothing to do with my thinking he was better, it had to do with the staff treating him like a piece of meat. *He is going to be treated with kindness and respect.*"

We looked at each other from the ends of the bench. She was thinking. I was floundering.

"Okay. Let's say that's why you did what you did. It's still inappropriate. Understandable, but inappropriate. I need to be able to trust you in this. I won't have my patient threatened because medical personnel have been kicked out of his room by a relative."

"By a mother."

She gave a half-smile. "By the most difficult kind of relative."

Silence.

"We need to work in tandem."

She reached over and touched my arm gently.

"We have a huge fight ahead of us. I'm going to get another opinion this morning, then move Andy into the ICU. There's a possibility he could code."

Code is an emergency situation. The breathing stops, the heart stops.

"We can't deal with personalities and we can't deal with emotion. We have to be quick and right in everything we do."

She put her arms around me for a second. "We'll work together," she said.

We went back to Andy's room where Andy lay very quietly, responding only when necessary. It was taking all his strength just to breathe. Terror was visible in his eyes.

Despite our reassurances that we were there with him, his face said, "I'm in this alone." Telling him how much we loved him, we would get a murmur of "I know. Me, too."

Speaking was very difficult. The lack of oxygen was taking its toll. I wanted to be able to pick him up, run away and make everything normal again, but his only hope for life now was at this hospital, at this moment. There was no turning back.

I had always thought "heartbreak" was just a cliché. Then I felt it and knew that it meant something particular, a sinking and tearing in the chest that feels like nothing else. It's almost unbearable and there isn't any medicine that will reach that pain.

About noon, the ambulance transfer team came for Andy. Simon, Linda and I climbed in the ambulance and sat down. No one said we couldn't, so we did. Andy was scared and quiet.

We waited in the corridor while Andy was settled into the ICU. I knew the transfer added stress to his already weakened condition and that he didn't have anything extra to give.

He could die at any time.

The area was filled with other families waiting for news of loved ones in the ICU. The sofas and chairs were arranged in family groups. We found places and sat.

When a nurse came out and said one of us could go in, I jumped up. Simon and Linda both said, "You go."

Andy had IVs and lines attached to him everywhere. The nurse said his chemotherapy was running, and that he wasn't having any problem with it. She also said that his oxygen level was still dropping and they were going to try a pressure mask to force the oxygen into his lungs.

I leaned over to give him a kiss and he looked at me and shook his head, unable to express his fear or frustration. I told him to keep fighting, and that we were just outside the door, but only one person could come in at a time. He nodded in agreement, but his eyes were sad, almost resigned.

I told him how much we loved him and how proud we were of him. He knew I was telling him because I might not have another chance later. He knew he was deteriorating rapidly.

He was being forced to give up the hope of living. I kept talking. I told him how strong and powerful he was and that he would have to fight really hard so the chemo could get ahead of whatever was going on in his body. His eyes never left mine.

Linda, Simon and I traded off going in to be with him throughout the afternoon.

They tried the oxygen pressure mask, but his oxygen level kept dropping. The mask was very uncomfortable. In fact, the mask made breathing even more difficult. It panicked him. The nurse asked me to stay in the room and help him relax so the mask could work for him.

Simon and Linda were terrified. They became weak in the knees watching, and neither was able to tolerate being in the room for long. I stayed and talked to him quietly about places we'd been and things we'd seen and done. I wanted him to remember some of the peace we'd shared in the mountains and at the ocean. He listened intently, but didn't relax. The mask was terrible.

When his oxygen levels came back even lower, doctors decided to go back to the earlier prongs-and-mask method.

Throughout the night the nurses and doctors worked to stabilize Andy. Simon went back to the motor home to sleep. Linda and I took blankets and tried to sleep on the couches in the lobby. Every time one of us woke, we'd go back in to check on him.

In the middle of the night, another family moved into the waiting area. They found places for themselves. They were talking through their nervousness and we tried not to listen, hoping they'd quiet down soon. During the long hours I made a note to buy earplugs, and from that night on I always had a pair in my purse.

Early the next morning, I went back in. Andy was awake and waiting to see us. He was pale and had no strength. I took his hand and kissed it, and he gave me a weak smile. The nurse said his oxygen level had risen during the night. Maybe things were improving.

I went outside again, so Linda could have a chance to see him. Simon was waiting, too. They each went in for a few minutes. About an hour later, Andy's oxygen levels started to fall.

Two ICU nurses were with him, and the pressure in the room thickened as things deteriorated. Andy was falling in and out of consciousness. The doctors would come in for a few minutes, examine him and leave. Things were not going well.

Around 10 A.M., a doctor asked to talk to me outside. He said that Andy's respiratory status was so bad that they were going to intubate him and put him on a respirator, but that his condition was so fragile they couldn't use anesthesia for the intubation. They would have to do it cold. Would I explain it to Andy so he would cooperate?

When they want to hurt him, they come to me.

To intubate cold is awful. To watch is awful. The patient fights for air, body bucking as you try to force the tube down the airway.

I went in and told Andy that his breathing was worse. He nodded. I told him that they were going to put him on a respirator and would have to put a tube down his throat to his lungs. He nodded, and then grabbed my hand. I asked if he wanted me to stay and he nodded yes. As the doctors started the preparations, they looked at me and I said I'd be okay. "Just do it!"

The head of the bed was removed, the bed raised and the doctors took their positions. I stayed at Andy's side, wedged between his IVs and monitors. I was trying to stay out of the way and hold his hand at the same time.

They started and Andy started to buck. He jerked and kicked, his eyes wide open, frightened. The first try failed.

It should have been over in seconds. Andy was struggling to breathe. The alarms were sounding on his monitors, and he had to be held down. Finally I told them I was leaving. I couldn't take it, and I felt that I was making the doctor nervous. I turned and walked out.

I'm leaving to make things go better. Things will go better.

When the doctors were done, they called me back. Andy was calm, the respirator breathing for him. He could only respond by opening his eyes when I talked to him.

A young doctor I hadn't seen before asked me to agree to put a catheter in his heart. He thought it might show just what was going on. First he wanted to order an echocardiogram.

The echo was soon done and showed a huge mass in the right atrium. No wonder Andy had no oxygen in his blood: his heart chamber was blocked. The questions then were: Is the blockage old or new? Was the mass a tumor or a blood clot? Had something ruptured, or was it his cancer? They'd check his previous echo to see if anything had showed.

Linda called the family and told them things were much worse, and they better come down to the hospital quickly. I don't know how our grandchildren were cared for, but every single one of our children and their spouses arrived within a few hours.

Someone went off to call Alex's mom, Rebecca, and tell her she better bring Alex down. Andy may be dying, she was told. Rebecca rushed up to the high school for Alex.

We were in the waiting area, crying and talking, when a hospital volunteer came bustling up.

"You all need to quiet down! There's a young boy in there dying, and his family needs some quiet!"

We looked at her. The staff had been told Andy was dying. We hadn't been.

"We are his family," Cheryl said with a certain amount of savagery. The woman left white-faced.

After a while, she came back and took us to an alcove closer to the ICU.

Andy had gone downhill so fast none of us were prepared. We floundered and groped. Andy lay there, opening and closing his eyes.

The results came back. Andy had a huge tumor in his heart. The cardiac staff was sending someone over to evaluate him. They'd decide if they could operate.

Decide if they were going to operate? Decide?

Someone had to tell Andy, get his approval. Simon was crying and said he couldn't do it. How do you tell your son he's dying when he can't even answer, but just look at you helplessly? I didn't know if I could. I said I'd go talk to him.

I told him he was very, very sick and that he had a huge tumor in his heart and that the doctors were considering an operation to remove it. The operation would be very difficult and risky, but if they didn't remove the tumor he would die. Andy looked away. I felt he already knew, he just didn't want to hear it. He didn't look back at me. I asked if he understood. Finally, he turned, his eyes brimming with tears. I asked if he wanted me to explain it again. He nodded yes and I explained it again, more slowly.

I can't do this anymore.

I asked him if he wanted to have the operation.

He signaled with his hand.

"What?" I asked. He signaled again, like he was scribbling.

"Do you want to write?" He nodded.

I grabbed a piece of paper off the chart, then a pencil. I held the paper for him.

Concentrating, with extreme difficulty, Andy started to write.

"How much longer? It's hard to breathe," his hand slipped down the page as he wrote.

16

Miracles

*I*t's one thing for a patient to agree to surgery. It's quite another to find a surgeon who's willing to do it. And I'm so tired. The kind of tired that you know is going to require giving in and collapsing. I want to succumb and let somebody else do it. You know how it is when you're little and you're so tired you just swoon and you have to be carried? Well, that's what I want. Somebody has to pick me up.

The room has become a carpeted, upholstered prison. Andy wants surgery. Where's the surgeon? We sit there. I want to succumb. The light is creeping around the room. Medical personnel walk by the open door. Nobody stops. I can hear approaching footsteps as far away as the corridors go. I lift my head to the footsteps, they approach, the body goes by the door quickly, I look at the carpet.

I know that any doctor would want to help Andy. I know it. Down the corridor the elevator doors open and close and open and close. Sometimes steps come toward us. It's like a fairy-tale wait for the Knight Who Has Passed The Tests. Not that one. Not that one. There's a flower garden out the window. I watch the light creep there for a while.

The first three say, "No." This is almost surreal to me. My son is dying in the bed, and the only thing that could save him right now is surgery. Three doctors say, "No." What is it? Are they worried about their batting averages? Is it too much trouble? Do they care?

What are they thinking? Is it money? Do they think that our HMO won't pay? Or is it simpler than that—an engagement for lunch, a round of golf? This is the thing about illness. You can bring little or no pressure to bear when it comes down to the actual work being done. "At the mercy of" is a good phrase to describe it.

You can be in the best hospital on the planet, with the best staff and the biggest budget and best views and best reproductions in the hallways and the best coffee in the cafeteria, and none of it makes a bit of difference if there's no one willing to work for you. It's a hard notion to become used to. You have all these television ideas about doctors rushing through white hallways to perform impossible, life-saving surgery. And that's just for somebody else's kid.

This surgery is for *your* kid, but they're just standing there in the room looking at the charts and saying, "No, sorry, not today."

Andy has a low chance of survival. For the cardiology group, the stats—dead patients, live patients—are the same thing as money. Better stats, greater stature, more money. Andy's death will cost the surgeon money. Run away, run away. Don't touch him. He isn't worth the risk.

It's an accumulation of emotions you never thought you'd have to deal with that finally, imperceptibly, changes the way you think and the way you feel. Some is for the good and some is so bad you turn your eyes away from yourself, because you have to be open to all the possibilities all the time. Some of them are very bad, and just thinking them seems like a betrayal, like the source of the evil is you. (*What have I done?* When the wrong thought comes, this other thought always occurs.)

I'm living through-the-looking-glass and the Red Queen is dragging me by the hand toward Andy's inconsequential death. (*Who does his death matter to? Where have the three surgeons gone?* The chessboard stretches out in all directions.)

An anesthesiologist who wasn't directly involved in Andy's care came in to tell us that one more surgeon was on the way, someone who was more willing to operate in chancy situations. So surgery might still be an option. It's a simple thing he does, but it feels like an epic kindness.

And the fourth surgeon does come. It's like his presence reels me back into the room. Dr. Sullivan, blessed among surgeons.

He gave us his name and background. He told us that Andy would probably be a cardiac cripple after the surgery and never get off the respirator. His current understanding was that even if Andy didn't die on the table, the surgery would spread cancer cells throughout his body. He said Andy might be much worse after the surgery than he had been.

I told him we could handle the possibilities, but not quitting. I asked him what he would do if Andy were his son? He said it would depend on what his child knew. I told him that Andy knew everything. I showed him his note.

He looked around at the family, then said he'd give us an hour to think about it. John jumped up at him and said, "No, go now!"

He looked again and said "okay" calmly. He'd start setting things up. He told us to go say good-bye in case the surgery failed.

We screamed, jumped and hugged each other. We patted his back as he walked out the door.

Now everything was great.

Now we had to say good-bye to Andy.

You have to. What else can you do?

Simon knows everything will be fine and wants to tell Andy but, strangely, it isn't that easy to say. He can't say it, and he struggles. The pain in his eyes is terrible.

"It's going to be tough, Andy, but you can make it. I know you can. This is your chance, and I know you're going to make it."

He has his huge, work-hardened hand on top of Andy's.

"I'm proud of you, and I love you, and I know you'll do fine."

He hides the good-bye in a kiss and walks out the door.

Cheryl, Linda, Alex and I waited in the room as the staff untangled the IVs and readied him for surgery. A troop of doctors, nurses and residents pushed and pulled his bed out in the hall. Cardiac monitors were still attached, as were IV poles jammed with bags of fluids like bright fruits waiting to be picked. Face masks were already on.

(These are the trappings of salvation. They'll take him in another room and save him. The bright liquids; the clean, shiny metal; the eyes bright and big above the masks. *Please, God.*)

The family is lining the walls as Andy and the OR team pass

between us. It's a football rally. "Go for it, Andy!" Les yells. "You've got the ball, you're on the fifty-yard line and there's a hole opened in front of you. *Go for it!*"

We all cheer.

Andy raises his fist in a salute before he's quickly pushed through the double doors into the operating room. Arm upraised, he's still fighting. And he heard us. Not the usual entrance into the OR, but perfect in its own way. The doors close behind him, and it's very quiet.

Dr. Young stayed with us until we calmed down. Her real reason for coming over that afternoon was to convince us not to operate, and to be with us while Andy died. She had tried to secure an ambulance to take him home to die, and then realized that he never could have made the ride. He would have died before he arrived.

So she'd had a room set aside where we could go and be with Andy while he died. This changed, she changed, when she saw how hard we fought for the surgery. She said that after what she'd seen, she was encouraged. She said she could do nothing less than follow our lead.

She also said she would be honest with us. If Andy lived through the surgery and the cancer became uncontrollable anyway, she would let us know right away. She said she would rather not treat under those conditions, but preferred to give him a chance to have some quality of life.

She was pleased that he'd had a dose of chemo before surgery. The chemo would be working on the cells that would be manipulated during the operation. She stayed around for a while, and talked to each of us in turn. She told us to go eat some dinner, that the surgery would take a while. After giving me a hug, she walked away down the long hallway.

We got some dinner. Cheryl stayed behind.

As we walked back in and Cheryl saw us, she yelled.

"He's out! He's out of surgery and he's doing great and he's following commands and his oxygen levels are normal and everything is just fine!" This was yelled to us across the lobby. We ran up the stairs.

She told us that Dr. Sullivan had come out after forty-five minutes and it was so soon she was sure he was going to say that Andy had died. But the tumor had been intact and when he cut around it, the tumor had popped out in his hands in one piece. Andy had immediately pinked up with his oxygen saturation shooting up to 99 percent. They'd also closed a small hole in his heart that had been forced open by the increased pressure, and the operation was finished.

He was now in the cardiac intensive care unit on a respirator with his oxygen level completely normal. Everything was fine. He wasn't in a lot of pain, and we could see him in the morning!

The family moved over to the ICU waiting room to wait for word on Andy. Cheryl went off to find the surgeon so we could talk to him. When Dr. Sullivan finally came out to talk to us, he said that Andy had done great and the only problem he'd found was fluid in the sac around his heart. And it probably contained cancer cells. The fluid had spilled through his chest cavity during surgery, and the doctor was worried about a spread of cancer cells. He said, "I did the easy part. Andy will have the tough part."

This would be the last we saw of him till months later.

The next morning, when I went in to see Andy, the nurses had already hung his second dose of chemotherapy and he was tolerating it well. I kissed him and he smiled groggily. He looked so much more like his normal self that I just started to cry. I told him that he had done a great job and that everything would be fine. He nodded and smiled again before drifting back to sleep.

We all waited our turn to visit throughout the day. Five minutes every hour was set aside for visitors. Simon went in and returned white-faced but smiling. Alex was able to go in. Things improved so quickly that at 10 A.M. the respirator was discontinued, and at noon the breathing tube was removed. Andy could talk.

He said his throat was sore. This wasn't much of a complaint considering the surgery he'd just been through. He'd sleep and then wake for a few minutes throughout the day. When we were in the waiting room, we couldn't control our glee. The day was spent waiting and visiting with each other and the people who shared the small room with us. Everyone was there because a loved one had just completed heart or lung surgery, or a transplant.

One man, though, just sat there and watched as we talked among ourselves. He never joined in, never smiled, and you could almost see the cloud of fear and isolation around him like a smudge on the air.

When I came out of Andy's room, the man was crying. I sat down beside him and put my hand on his arm. "Don't give up hope," I said. "Yesterday they told us to let our son die, and today he's doing great." He didn't answer, though later that night he came over to thank me for being kind. He and his wife were from out of state. She just had a lung transplant and wasn't doing well. He was frightened and had no one to talk to. The only other places he'd been during her stay were an empty motel room and the cafeteria. He was exhausted and afraid, and I wondered how my optimism must have seemed to him.

All the people you pass in the hallways, each is facing

something unbearable. They can't communicate much with those who don't have the *trouble,* and the people who do have it understand without saying anything. The rooms are full of a tacit acknowledgment of the unbearable. The clichés, I guess, cover most of it—"Each has a cross to bear," "Cry and you cry alone"— but you wish for something else. You wish that human beings were made a little differently, that they didn't shy away instinctively from misery, that they didn't look on the afflicted as people who brought it on themselves.

The first day after surgery a nurse came in to tell me I had a call. I took it down the hall. It was Barbara Boxer calling from Washington to see how Andy was doing. I told her.

"Everyone on the Hill has been praying for him, Marilyn, and I'm going back to tell them now. Remember, we care, and call me if you need any help."

All these bits and pieces come back—phone calls and strangers and the odd moments when you're sitting somewhere and you suddenly realize that you'll never forget a particular moment again—a slant of light or a figure moving down the hall or a dreamlike snatch of overheard conversation.

Was I sane then? Perfectly. I was doing what I needed to do in that place at that time. Would I appear to be sane were I acting the same way now? Probably not.

The second day a nurse asked me on my way past her desk whether or not I was excited.

"What about?"

"Andy's visitor."

"What visitor?"

"Joe Montana is coming to see Andy this afternoon."

"Joe Montana?"

"The newspaper called."

"No one asked me if he could visit Andy."

"I guess they said someone in your family had asked him to visit."

"Well, it wasn't me or anyone else here with us. Andy's barely conscious. He wouldn't recognize Joe Montana."

"But it's all set."

"No, it isn't. You call them and tell them it's off."

I walked in to see Andy myself.

Joe Montana didn't visit.

17

REPRIEVE

We have all these sentimental ideas about children, about their helplessness and fragility. My experience is that children are much tougher than adults and much less prone to self-pity. They wake up in the mornings and face what the day has to offer. They may be worried, they may not want to go through with it, but they tend to do what they have to do and move on.

All those kids at the medical center. I think about them all the time, ranged up and down the scale of likely mortality, and almost all look right back at me with clear eyes. A lot of them are dead now. But the memory I have of them is of reasonably clear-headed children, dealing with the world as it comes.

We walk around complaining and bitching and there they sit, looking into the darkness without complaint. They shouldn't be sentimentalized; I've tried to avoid that. I don't know why it is we have to see them as little objects of nondescript pity. Maybe because that's the way we feel about ourselves, as adults, and like to think they're using the same sad tools of rationalization and resentment and self-pity.

They really don't seem to, though, and they approach death with more grace than would seem possible. Andy's story is the story of the strength of the children. I want to make that very clear. It's for all of them, waking up every day to face that day, that pain. You'll find more grace in a roomful of sick children than you'll find in any of our ceremonies, religious or otherwise.

Andy loved them all, too. He cared about them through his own fear and pain. What else is there in the world? What else is there to talk about when you want to talk about real things?

Paul, Brenda, John and Toni—all came down after work and were thrilled to see how good Andy looked. He was able to talk, even to laugh. The Andy we knew was back, one day after open-heart surgery. Day two after his surgery, his "re-birthday," as it came to be called, was purely wonderful. He was doing so well he was stepped-down from the CCU to the ICU. When he came down the hall in a wheelchair, I saw him as a hero. He had just climbed Mt. Everest.

Settling in his bed, he reached down and pulled up his blue blanket. We'd brought it down from his bed at home. It was a fuzzy blanket with a dairy scene of cows, barns and hills, and it was home and comfort to Andy as he slept with it tucked up around his neck. The dairy supply company dropped it off one winter day, and it had been his since he first saw it. No one else had a chance at claiming it. Possession was nine-tenths of the law, and the whole family quickly learned that the blanket was Andy's. These are the things that really break your heart: when a colored cow on a blanket suddenly appears in your head. It's the little things (though maybe they're not so little, the way even a child will pick out something for himself to symbolize permanence and home). In the clean strangeness of the hospital, teenage Andy was able to find comfort by pulling his dairyland blanket around him.

No one else was going to be in the room with us, and it made me nervous. No nurse unless we called for help or one came in on her rounds to check on him. The nurses in the CCU had been so supportive, one nurse for each patient. It wasn't like that anymore.

The new staff seemed so relaxed, and I wasn't sure they could be in the room quickly enough if needed. I watched Andy's monitor.

Later that day, Simon, Sharon and Linda left for home. Being at the hospital was especially hard for Simon. He had always hated them, had always lived outside institutions and bureaucracies, as best he could, anyway. There was always the county and state to deal with when you ran a dairy.

So his first instinct was to get away. He wasn't any less anxious or pained than the rest of us, it was just that he hated being there. When Simon was home, Andy filled his whole attention anyway. He'd stayed through the crisis and now that things had settled down he could go home, and could drive down each evening to visit after the cows were fed, after the familiar rituals had eased the threat of the deathly random. The drive would add four hours to his already long day, but for Simon it was the best solution.

Cheryl and Toni stayed with us and slept in a separate waiting room. They made their beds on the sofas. I was given a recliner in Andy's room so I could be there all the time. What a gift! No more five-minute visits and the pitiful effort to get natural and comfortable with the clock ticking. We could sit and be ourselves. The girls could visit one at a time or come together to give me a break.

He was calm now, and the chemotherapy hadn't made him sick. Things looked better and better. The oxygen monitor was off. The cardiac monitor was showing some irregularities that were making me nervous, but I was sensitized and raw; everything might be a threat, as I still viewed everything with fear. In spite of my worries, we made it through the night.

I know I've mentioned a few times the way the nights are. It isn't that I don't remember I've said these things, it's that the whole split between day and night is such a huge part of the nature of the world you move into that it comes up naturally. There's the day moving by itself, and there's the night hardly moving at all with your thoughts in a tight, choking circle. What if this, and if this that, and side thoughts you watch for where maybe you can sit down for a minute. I'd never been so aware of the split between night and day before. Three in the morning is different. It's an ungodly, comfortless time. The nights in the hospital aren't quite so bad, oddly. When you open your eyes in the dark, there are faint lights from under the door and the sense of other people awake, doing things, methodically fighting the whole idea of sickness.

As Andy improved, I began to relax. Sometimes the family forced me out of the room for a break. I didn't want to leave at all, but at times my presence would drive Andy or the girls nuts. They were right, and I was resistant. Forced out, I'd go down to the cafeteria or outside for a walk. That was if I felt secure enough to actually leave the building. The mind gets very odd and fragmented so that opening a door can seem like moving into another world.

Andy's third post-op day was even better. Another chemotherapy treatment was completed and, best of all, he stood up to walk. Not far, but he walked. A week before he couldn't even stand or breathe on his own!

That afternoon I asked him what he remembered about the past week. He said not much and asked what had happened. I told him his story. It was hard to do. I was surprised how hard it was. I told him we thought we might lose him and how we had to struggle for the operation, for his chance at life, even though we knew he might die on the operating table. I explained how we reached our decisions. I showed him his note.

He didn't remember it. I told him how hard he fought for a chance and how hard we fought to give it to him. He said he was sure the chemotherapy would work. He radiated confidence. He said he was strong enough for whatever he had to do. And he was. You could see it in his eyes.

Everyone came to visit the next day, and Andy showed off, walking across the room and down the hall. The ICU doctor told him he could go home soon if the pain stayed under control and he exercised. There was only one more test to check out the irregularities of his heartbeat. The test would take twenty-four hours of wearing a monitor. If there was no serious problem, he could go home.

Later that afternoon, we held a "re-birthday" party for Andy. Everyone brought presents. September 25 would become a day for the family to celebrate Andy's courage and strength.

He got a hat to cover his soon-to-be-bald head. He got sweatshirt-and-sweatpant sets, so he could dress easily. He got soft, warm slippers. The point behind each present was explained with jokes and gibes. We broke into a riotous "Happy Re-Birthday." It was a crescendo of emotion and must have traveled a good way through the halls. Whooping and clapping ended the party, and Andy lay back in his bed exhausted while the packages were put away. He drifted into an afternoon nap as the last of the chemo filtered into his body. The room became very quiet. It had been a great party, a shout of defiance.

The next morning Andy was in a lot of pain. Until this time, his pain control had been exceptional. He had been getting relief from the drugs he was given to ease the effects of the chemo. Now, with the chemo finished, the post heart surgery pain kicked in. The pain made him mad. We had to force him to walk, cough or use the tri-flow to expand his lungs. He resisted movement, and all he wanted was to be left alone. Andy hadn't expected the pain, and it felt as if he was being smashed back down after his recovery.

Maureen came to visit and told him that, from what she'd seen, he'd missed the worst part of the pain while he was on the chemo. She told him to hold on tight, things would improve quickly. Her years of experience in post-op cardiac surgery gave her the knowledge to explain things easily and clearly. Better yet, he believed her.

The pain did lessen the next morning. We all started thinking about going home, and how much that would mean to us, and how much it would help the healing to be back where our past and our hearts were. He tested himself, moving gingerly, smiling when there wasn't any pain. He was able to wash and get ready for the day.

Dr. Young was going to be off for the next week so she came in to say good-bye. She set up appointments for the following month. She told Andy that he had taught her a lot, and that she was proud of him and glad to be his doctor.

His blood counts were explained along with the problems to watch out for once we were home. Counts are what you live by after chemotherapy. I was given a formula to use to calculate Andy's absolute neutrophil count (ANC). I was also given the boundaries and probable problems for the platelet and the white blood counts. All this information was meant to teach me how to gauge the threat of infection. If Andy were to have a fever over 101.5 with low counts, he would be hospitalized immediately for IV antibiotics. The low counts would mean that his body wouldn't be able to resist an infection without the antibiotics. If a chemo patient were to develop an infection with a fever and not get treated, death could result.

I'd heard all of this before, but now that Andy's life depended on my accuracy, the words began to make sense. I wanted to be absolutely clear, and I had the doctor go over it again so I could be sure. Parents who weren't in the medical profession were able to handle this stuff, so it wouldn't really be a problem. But right then it panicked me.

Dr. Young wrote it all down, listing each step I was to take at home. Number six of the instructions was, "Try to relax. Andy will be fine." I knew I couldn't follow number six.

When she felt that I knew what I had to, she gave me the names and schedules of the doctors who were covering for her while she was away. They had been updated on Andy's condition so I would be able to have help quickly if I needed it.

Andy's last night in the hospital went by without a hitch. The monitor showed no dangerous irregularities, and the cardiologist felt that things would continue to improve.

By late the next afternoon, Andy was discharged and we were on our way.

Simon and I loaded all of our supplies: blankets, books, pillows, presents, medicine, syringes and instructions. Andy was waiting by the door in a wheelchair when we went to pick him up. He said his good-byes and was wheeled down the hall and out the door. He smiled. We weren't coming back to the cardiac floor. No way were we ever coming back.

We were about halfway home when I realized that Andy had been quiet for a long time. When I went back to check on him, he was in tears, sobbing quietly. I knelt by him and asked quietly what he was feeling. He sobbed that he didn't want to talk. In a flood of relief and grief, he cried his way back into his own life. He could be in control again, he could *do things*. He was going home.

It really was a homecoming. The way our house is—on a little hill in the wide, rolling green—it feels just perfect coming home. It feels a little removed from the world, like you've come to a place where the gentleness of the landscape is all gathered together.

Everyone was in our front yard. The sun was out. The back porch and the steps from the house were crowded with cheering people. The first thing Andy wanted to do once we all went inside was go for a ride with Matt and Alex.

"No." A ride in a car? "No." I was running the reasons for "no" through my brain when Cheryl and Linda said "Mom!" almost simultaneously. So I said, with some hesitation, "Okay." Andy, Alex and Matt grinned and headed for the door. This was the first of the many "Mom"s I would hear as my children tempered my decisions. I was an overprotective mother, I guess, but deep down I knew they were right.

But I was so afraid something would happen to him.

The hard lesson for me was that Andy was entitled to make his own decisions, even when they made me nervous. This would be a constant weight on me: having to temper the automatic "I don't think you should" into "Okay, Honey, just be careful."

After returning safely from his first move away from my control, Andy went to sleep on his water bed. Alex stayed with him, ready to help with anything he might need. His pain had come back, and Alex was just too tiny to be able to pull his huge body out of the water bed. I finally put a cot up along the other side of his bed so Alex and I were ready to help when he needed it. Working together, we were able to do it without hurting him too much.

We were really strong now. It was good because we were going to have to be ready for whatever monster might come lurching down the road.

18

*T*REMBLER

*E*very time I do something that causes Andy pain there's that terrible feeling of failure. That rotten, sinking, "I should be better."

If you're a mother, you may remember the feeling when you bring your baby home from the hospital and suddenly the fuss is over and you're left alone and it's just you and this little being and the wave of "Am I good enough to do what needs to be done for this helpless little creature?" comes over you, cold as ice.

Well, that feeling doesn't die, not really, because when your child is sick and you're expected to do things right—*to know and to do*—then it doesn't matter how old he is or whether or not you've been a nurse or how many people believe you can do it, there's still an icy wave that comes by and soaks you with fear. "What if I make a mistake? What about taking the blood? *What if I do something that kills him?*"

When Andy wakes up with a fever, I'm frantic. I call Gary, our local doctor, and he orders a blood test to be done at our local hospital. The results come back with an ANC of 378, a huge drop from 5,900 two days earlier. The medical center says to see if the fever goes up. If it does, he'll be going back for treatment.

By this time, the local newspapers are all over the story. They want telephone interviews with Andy and with me. They've been covering the story as it progressed, and now they seem to want to be on top of it day-to-day.

They've covered his lobbying efforts for Parents of Kids With Cancer. They've covered the football game he tried to play with thirty tumors in his lungs, Barbara Boxer's fund-raiser support and the catastrophic heart tumor. They've talked to Simon and John at home and Cheryl and Linda down at the hospital. Now they want our version. They'd even called Dr. Sullivan at the hospital for a quote. They'd quoted Andy's high school principal. They'd found out that Joe Montana had been scheduled to visit Andy, and that I had canceled the visit. I was amazed at the information they had.

This isn't a complaint. In general, they were respectful and caring. They weren't going to push for an interview if we didn't want to do it. They genuinely thought of Andy as a hero, and that's how they followed him. His courage was an offering that gave hope by example. We were getting cards from people who didn't even know him. People with cancer would write to thank him for giving them the strength to keep fighting. People who weren't sick wrote to say that they had learned just how much they loved their children from reading about Andy.

Listening to Andy during the phone interview, the depth of his understanding and compassion for those of us who had gone through the process with him astonishes me. His overall attitude is positive. He tells the reporter that he feels great, and though things have been hard since his rediagnosis, he's confident he'll beat the disease. He says he's going to the homecoming game and will dance with Alex.

It all made it into the paper, but none of it was to be.

The next day his fever rises again and his counts drop to an ANC of 97, and a white count of 0.7. A white blood count needs to be 1.0 even to begin to fight infection. A low white blood count (WBC) is called neutropenia. With a fever and an infection, neutropenia is life-threatening.

I call Gary early that morning. The decision is made to admit Andy to Memorial Hospital for antibiotics. A local oncologist will meet us there. It's so early in the chemo I really don't understand yet, I don't know the progressions and I can't read the signs. Andy's in the hospital and his temperature is up to 104. That's what I know. What if we were still at home?

If the fever is being caused by an infection, there's no way for Andy's body to fight it off without antibiotics. Andy is angry. He's only been home for two days. The homecoming game is two days off, and Alex is running for homecoming queen. He's already *done* the hospital, they've sent him home. The hospital means fear and pain and a step back. He's going to escort Alex out on the field in his football uniform, just like all the other guys.

But we have no choice, and we take him, crying, back to the

hospital. When we arrive, he becomes quiet. That's how he is when he's angry. As it turns out, he's very sick. The staff thinks the surgery site around his heart is infected.

But the tests show nothing. Many lab tests and antibiotics later, no reason for the fever has been found. A cardiologist is called in to consult, along with an infectious disease specialist. Even though nothing conclusive is found, it doesn't mean that every time Andy has fever and neutropenia after chemo they can be disregarded.

Two days later, Andy is almost asleep when we get the telephone call from Simon telling us that Alex has won the title of homecoming queen and that the football team is winning. Andy smiles, briefly. I ask him what he wants to do and he says, "There's not much I can do. I can't get out of here, can I?" The smile was very brief. His eyes are cold and there's something like an all-encompassing, abstract hatred in them. It isn't a face I'm used to.

We talk for a while and I try to defuse the anger. Finally, he comes back a little and I can tell when he says, "I think we should have roses for Alex when she comes to visit."

I go out and buy a beautiful bouquet of yellow roses at a small florist's not far from the hospital. Once we set the flowers on his bedside table, Andy cheers slightly.

Dinner is mystery meat, canned green beans and potatoes. Andy looks, then pushes it away. It does smell awful, so I tell him I'll get him a pizza.

Just then, we hear the tap-tap-tap of someone walking down the hall in high-heeled shoes. Alex comes in in a swish of taffeta, beautiful in her dark blue gown. Her dad is with her and she's carrying a huge spray of red roses. She has a glittering crown on her head.

"Surprise," she yells, and runs to Andy's bed to tell him she was homecoming queen and that Lisa had come in second. "I wanted to win for you. I wanted you to be there. And then all I wanted to do was get out of there to be with you."

Andy reaches over for his bouquet of yellow roses and hands them to Alex, and she squeals with delight. He grins. We need to give them some time alone, so Carlos and I go out for the pizza.

Later that evening, Simon comes in grinning and carrying a grocery bag as if it were delicate. He sets the bag down and tells Andy to reach inside. Andy does and pulls out a signed 49ers football. The coach of the 49ers, George Seifert, had given a friend of ours the ball to give to Andy at homecoming. The excitement grows in their eyes. Simon is as pleased as Andy.

Homecoming's gone and over, but the day is special anyway. When Alex and her dad leave, the guys get busy with their football. It was more than a gift, it was hope: hope that Andy would be able to finish his football career in high school and maybe, someday, be good enough to play for a professional team like the 49ers.

It wasn't a bad day, though there was still that gap, that all important Big Day that had never materialized. You have to be careful with these things, the anticipations and the expectations and the way dates and events turn into symbols of recovery. When they don't pan out, it's bleak. When they do, the joy is really way beyond the facts of the situation. But you have to have something. The mind needs to hold on to something, and little victories can be huge. A nondescript date on a calendar can loom in your head like a bright city at the end of the road.

The next morning we met Jules Jaffe, who was to become our local oncologist. First he became our doctor, and then our friend. His demeanor was kind, and I had the feeling that he was glad to meet Andy. That means a great deal, when you see more in a doctor's face than "Well, here's another one."

When Andy had first been diagnosed, I had called to investigate the services available in Sonoma County. I had been directed to the Hematology Oncology Group. In talking to the nurses involved with the oncologists, I got a pretty good picture of what they were like. That's how I was able to pick Jules. He was a perfect match.

Listening to Andy's heart and lungs that day, his head tilted up slightly in an effort to hear clearly, he caught sight of the 49ers football. His eyes would drift down to Andy then back up to the football as he listened. Over and over. Andy's eyes met mine and he smiled.

Andy knew what Jules was looking at. Finally, Jules couldn't stand it anymore and blurted out, "Where did you get that?" He was a dyed-in-the-wool 49ers fan and they had a wonderful time talking football as Jules turned the ball over and over in his hands, admiringly.

Jules answered our questions and explained the effects of the chemo and told us what to expect and eased our fear. He was clear and thoughtful and just what we needed. When he left, Andy gave a sigh of relief. Jules was already his friend.

Over the next few days, Andy's temperature decreased and his white count climbed. By week's end, he was able to go home. All the antibiotics, though, had ruined his veins, and his IV lines needed to be changed each time his veins gave out. There weren't many accessible veins left. The idea of having to find one filled me with dread. They needed to insert a semipermanent IV port, and now that his white count was up, it was time to do it.

There was a choice of catheters to use. When their differences were explained, Andy chose the Port-A-Cath because he wanted to be able to swim, surf and snorkel. You can't swim or surf with a port that comes through the skin, and being kept away from the ocean was not an option for him.

The real bonus with either catheter is that it eliminates a great deal of pain and suffering. There would be no more searching out veins on his already sore arms. The Port-A-Cath would be placed in his chest and the tube would go straight into his blood-stream. It was going to be inserted by a vascular surgeon in the outpatient surgery department. The appointment was set for October 17, 1989.

A nurse from the hospital had called the day after Andy's release to ask if she could take him, along with a couple of other local kids, down to the "Battle of the Bay," as the 1989 World Series was called. I told her Andy was an Athletics fan and would have loved to be able to go, but that the Port-A-Cath surgery would make the trip impossible. He'd have to watch it on tele-vision at home.

We were home early that afternoon, with Andy's new port successfully inserted.

Andy was in the recliner and Simon on the couch as they watched the crowd gathering at Candlestick Park. Simon took the Giants and Andy the A's and bet on them. Linda and Les had been able to buy tickets, so they were at the park. We were hop-ing to catch a glimpse of them in the crowd.

Then there was the sound of a locomotive and the house began to shake. I ran into the living room to scream "Earthquake!" It seemed like a reasonable thing to do, though I wasn't really bringing news. Simon helped Andy out of the chair, and we went to the doorway to stand under its lintel. The tremors rolled through our old wooden farmhouse like it was the train, rolling and swaying on an old track. As soon as the tremors stopped, Simon ran out the door to check on the animals and buildings. Andy gingerly returned to his chair.

We sat there for a very long time, mesmerized by the scenes of destruction as they scrolled by on the TV. The damage was severe in San Francisco and Oakland, and our children were down there in the midst of the panic. We didn't know where or how they were.

Later that evening, Andy's heart started beating irregularly. The beats made him panic. They made me panic. There was no telephone service at all. No 911, no way to reach the cardiologist. I felt his pulse. While the beats were irregular, his color was good and he wasn't showing any of the other signs of cardiac distress. I didn't know if it was an emergency. Even if it was, I didn't know if the roads were open or if the hospital still existed. Information was coming in from around the Bay slowly. Some of it was very bad.

I continued to monitor Andy. He could tell when the irregular beats were about to start. When local telephone service finally resumed late that night, I called the surgeon who put in the Port-A-Cath, but he was gone. Gary was not on call. Finally, a doctor called back and told me how to check Andy and talked me through it. She concluded that the extra beats were from the catheter insertion and the resulting irritation. She didn't want us to try to come in to the hospital during all the confusion. We had no way to know if we could get through anyway.

We spent the rest of the evening glued to the television watching the pictures of the freeway rescues, and the drama on the Bay Bridge. It was a long, hard night. Linda and Les finally returned, nine hours after walking out of Candlestick. They were full of stories.

Two days later, we drove through San Francisco to the hospital for Andy's second round of chemotherapy. The unknown results of the chest X ray absorbed us completely. We would now find out if the chemo worked.

Arriving early, we went to the clinic to wait. Dr. Young came by, chatted a bit and then went downstairs to view the X rays. A short time later she came back running. "The tumors aren't gone, but they're definitely smaller!" The chemo was working.

Andy was admitted into a four-bed ward with three other kids and was zonked out as soon as the chemo was started. His newly installed Port-A-Cath worked wonderfully.

I noticed on the last day of treatment that his hair was falling out all over his pillow. To me it meant that the chemo had really worked. (You find hope in the oddest places, the oddest events.) The hair-growing cells had been damaged. If these cells had been killed, maybe the cancer cells had been, too. After five days of chemo, we were able to go home.

The next day Andy felt much better and was able to go outside and work on his car with John. The only problems were at night. He couldn't sleep. He'd be wide awake—walking around, watching TV or just fidgeting. During the day he could direct his energy, but the nights were difficult. MTV kept him company during the long, dark hours when the rest of us slept.

On the second day home, I had to draw a blood sample from his port. This was something I had never done in my nursing career. The nurse had shown me how to do it, and while I had felt confident down at the hospital, at home I felt very insecure. I was sent home with the supplies, along with the schedule of draws I was supposed to make.

When I'd been working, drawing blood and starting IVs weren't difficult tasks. But this felt threatening. I'm bonkers with fear. We've taken him too far away from the hospital. We're out in the country. It's not the warm little gathered-in circle on the

hill anymore. It's an empty, threatening blank, miles from anywhere. If there's an emergency, I'll fail. I'll fail.

When I think about having to draw his blood, I shake. I can't
stop. I shake and shake and finally, I reread all the directions.
Shit, I think, *I'm a terrible nurse. I always have been. I got through
on luck and now I'm going to be exposed and Andy will pay for it.*

I wasn't sure how far to insert the needle, even though the
nurse said that I would feel the metal reservoir when I was deep
enough. I wanted help and felt too nervous to attempt the draw
alone. Andy is looking at me.

I called to ask Sharon to come out. I want her to double-
check, so I don't do anything wrong. While she was driving out,
I brought out the needles, swabs, tubes, tape and alcohol and
read over the directions again.

If something critical happens, I'm at the mercy of my fear.
Outside, the sun is shining and the wide, disinterested world is
taking care of its own business. When someone you love is in
crisis and you don't feel up to what's needed, you can almost feel
yourself as just a brain, a piece of thinking flesh in a bone prison.
All you've got is in there with you, and it isn't enough.

When Sharon arrived, we iced and disinfected Andy's skin, I put
on my sterile gloves and, as Andy watched intently, we joked about
my blood-drawing skill. I started, willing my hands not to shake.

As I plunged the needle through his skin and into the port,
Andy yelled "Ouch!" Sharon said quietly, "You're doing fine." I
was shaking so badly, I felt I was going to lose control. Oddly
enough, my hands weren't shaking at all. I drew back on the
plunger and no blood came.

Andy rolled his eyes quietly when I told him I'd missed. This
time he said nothing as I inserted the needle. I could feel the
bottom of the port with the tip and gingerly pulled back on the

plunger. We all watched the barrel of the syringe as the pressure increased and the blood appeared.

When the samples were safe in their capped tubes, I started to shake for real. My knees were weak. Andy said I did okay.

His counts kept dropping. On each alternate day, I would draw another sample and drive it ten miles to the hospital. He was coming through without the fever, and he didn't have to go back into the hospital.

By the end of that week, his counts had started to climb. The rest of his hair fell out. It fell out on the chair, on his pillow, in his bed and on his clothes. The worst part was that the loose hair was getting into his mouth, his eyes and his food. It didn't fall out evenly. There were clumps where it was totally gone, patches of completely normal-looking hair and sad, sparse little islands.

So I took out the clippers and cut it down as close to the scalp as I could go. Then I took the razor and shaved his head. When his hair was gone, Andy looked in the mirror. He rubbed his head and smiled. He was different without hair, but still handsome.

He looked adorable. He had a beautiful head.

It was the same shape as it had been when he was a newborn baby.

19

*D*UPLICITY

*H*is head was pale where it had been protected from the sun. Its only flaw was a bright scar. That was from the time I'd knocked a jar from an overhead cupboard and it had fallen on his head. His only complaint was that his head felt cold.

I looked at him sleeping with his bald head on the pillow and tried to see the baby head that used to be, as if it were in there somewhere. It's all so strange.

How did he really feel about it? It was an idiotic question. He felt bad about it. But in any nightmare, there are gradations of bad. I suppose the question really came down to, "How was he choosing to handle it?" Maybe that's *the* question. Maybe that's all we need to ask about ourselves.

Andy chose to leave that afternoon to show his friends his new "do." He called it his "chemo do," and his baldness would ever after be the object of his own jokes. Nobody else had a chance. He didn't seem to be feeling conspicuous and apparently didn't mind if someone came up and asked him why he had no hair. It was a different story, though, if someone stared at him. There were some he could feel judging him. For what? On what basis? It seemed he was being judged and classified as some kind of skinhead tough. It was true, he didn't look like someone who was sick or taking chemotherapy. When disturbed by staring, he'd sometimes blurt out "Chemo," and point to his head. Mostly, he kept it a joke.

Girls would ask if they could feel his "hair." Small children would gape and Andy would kneel down, answer their questions and offer to let them feel his head.

These are very gentle, tender memories. Sometimes I have to look at myself carefully and ask if I'm living in the past. I'm always able to say "No." I don't live in the past. I use it to provide that combination of understanding and continuity and occasional joy that permits me a useful life in the present.

I work with sick children. I can't live in the past because the present is right here, all the time, and sick children have the immediacy of an open wound. But apart from that, in spite of that, they have a grace that seems to spread backwards to alter the past a little bit at a time, infinitesimally, so that each time it's left with more meaning and less rage.

By the time our next visit to the doctor came around, I was back in the loop with the drunken monkeys. Maybe the chemo wasn't working. Maybe the tumors hadn't shrunk. Maybe this visit, this precise moment, would be the beginning of the end for Andy. No way out. This was the visit that would tell us, definitively, what was going on.

As it turned out, it would tell us something else, too—that when you're in a medical crisis, it doesn't pay to take anything at face value. Doctors have their own emotional flaws, and from megalomania to fear of confrontation, you're going to be at their mercy.

Andy went in for the whole set of tests necessary to have a clear picture of his progress. When he came out, he told me that he'd seen the chest X ray and that he thought the tumors were gone.

When I asked the technician for the tape of Andy's echo and his X rays to take to the hospital, she refused and said I could pick them up later. She said a doctor needed to look at them before I could have them. I got scared. Up-down, up-down, up-down. We had to wait three days till I got the call that I could pick up the results.

In the car in the parking lot with the X rays, I opened the package. First, I looked at the echo report. It said Andy's heart was stable and that any changes were probably related to the surgery. Then I took out the X rays. It looked as if only three tumors remained. One was large, about the size of a silver dollar. There were two smaller, one with a ring around it. The ring, I knew, probably meant it was shrinking. As I went through the complete set, I knew that Andy had been right. The tumors weren't all gone, but his lungs had responded to the chemo.

With easier hearts, Simon and I drove down with Andy for his next appointment. We were relaxed and confident, sure he'd get a good report.

Dr. Young came in and asked for the reports, and Andy said, "Things look much better."

"How do you know?"

"We looked."

"Well, let's hope you're right."

She headed downstairs to the viewing room. The wait was dreadful. She came back grinning and told Andy that he obviously knew how to read X rays because things really did look much better. Twenty-two of the tumors were gone. Only eight were left.

I suppose from the outside these wild, up-and-down swings seem unreal. The common, almost subliminal view of cancer is that "cancer equals death." As treatment keeps improving and success rates go up, the cancer equals death pairing will start to lose force. Maybe not. Something about cancer just strikes at people's deepest fears.

As with most deep, instinctive fears, it's different when you're inside. There's no sense of inevitability, and every movement along the way is a step up or a step down. Hope and loss of hope, elation and profound depression. And everything held together by the underlying fear—at any minute, from any direction—that the word may come that your child is being taken from you. We'd already traveled from Andy's finger and the hideous presentation of recovery statistics, to this moment of disappearing tumors. The statistics were of no importance anymore. Hope was in gear, and everything was new and unique and overwhelmingly positive. The tumors were disappearing.

We had weapons, and tumors were dying.

Dr. Young hadn't expected such a great response. Before we'd come in, she'd been downstairs researching new treatments. Now she wanted a couple of further rounds of chemo and, after that, surgery to remove any remaining tumors. The surgery would be done in two stages, and Andy could have both by the end of the year. Once the surgeries were done, Andy's chances would improve 1,000 percent.

It wouldn't mean he was cured, but he would be a lot closer to a cure. Dr. Young told us then that she'd be leaving at the end of the year and wanted us to think about transferring to a new hospital with her. She said she wanted us to know she had made a deep emotional and intellectual investment in Andy's treatment. Andy said we'd think about it and went in for another round of chemo that afternoon.

It was different. It seemed different. The ward was friendlier, the people happier. Maybe we were just elated. Maybe they all knew the results of the chemo. Everything went smoothly, and when Alex came down to visit she draped her long, black hair over Andy and told him he'd have just as much when the chemo was over. We told him we favored red and curly, and he laughed and said he didn't care what color it would be or even if he ever had any again.

At our next appointment, Andy was doing so well, we were told, that we'd be able to take his chemotherapy regime back to Sonoma County in the following month. Our pedi-oncologist would still direct his chemotherapy, but he'd be able to get everything at the local hospital instead of out of the area. Dr. Young said it was necessary to do this to appease the health insurance company and keep them on our side.

Can you see how everything seemed to be coming back and shrinking? From the tumors to the radius of our travel, it was all shrinking toward the way things had been before Andy ran into the kitchen with his swollen finger.

Dr. Young felt that there might be times when it would be

necessary for further treatments to be done out of our plan area, and she didn't want the insurance company to automatically deny our request. Her plan was for them to be billed only for what was absolutely necessary. She was sure that Dr. Jaffe would be able to handle everything. They had already talked and laid out their plans.

She moved on to her next topic. She wanted to know if we'd decided whether we were going to stay at the medical center with a new doctor or transfer with her?

For Andy and me, the memory of what had happened when Dr. Schlemmer left was the determining factor. Losing a doctor whom you have learned to trust was a lot more difficult than changing hospitals. Dr. Young said she wanted us to be sure because she had something else she wanted to bring up before she left. Andy said we were sure.

She told us she thought we were a good team, that Andy was courageous and that I was positive when she was negative. What's more, she said, we listened to each other and that made for a superb working arrangement. She felt we had a balanced team and that we trusted her.

Then she asked a question that had been bothering her.

"Why didn't you start chemo when there were only two tumors instead of waiting until there were thirty?"

We sat there blankly.

"What two tumors?" I said. I didn't understand.

"The tumors that were seen in April," she said.

"What?"

"There were two possible tumors in April. Five in May." She opened Andy's chart and showed us the CAT scan reports dated April and May.

We looked at them uncomprehendingly.

"Nobody told us there were tumors," Andy said. "Dr. Schlemmer never said anything about tumors."

"Why would he do that?" I asked.

"I don't know. But I've seen the reports he sent to two of our other doctors." This was very hard to get a hold on. We'd trusted him. If the tumors had been treated in April, Andy probably wouldn't have had thirty in his lungs. Or the heart tumor. What had he done? What kind of man was he to play God with Andy's life? How could he not tell a patient about tumors in his lungs?

What it came down to was that, without telling us, he'd come to a personal decision that Andy was sure to die and that chemo wasn't going to help. And he'd kept it quiet.

His solitary decision could have condemned Andy to death. *And it was wrong.* The chemo, as we knew now, worked. This was a prestigious teaching hospital and not only had our wishes been totally ignored, Andy's chances of beating the cancer had been diminished.

I asked again how a doctor could do such a thing. Dr. Young just shook her head.

"I don't know."

She said she'd wanted us to make up our minds about transferring before she asked about the April X rays. She hadn't wanted our anger to influence our decision.

"I was going through Andy's charts," she said, "when I found the results. I just couldn't understand why you hadn't started aggressive treatment early on. You'd been so aggressive about the surgery. It didn't make sense."

Andy was quiet as we left. In the car, he let his rage out.

"I guess I was just supposed to go to Hawaii and Alaska, then die, huh? Give the kid some scenery before he dies."

We talked furiously all the way home. I didn't know what we'd do with this information, but it wouldn't be forgotten.

I'd never forget.

About a week later, I called Dr. Schlemmer at the telephone number he'd given me when he left Stanford to go into research. His wife answered and was hesitant to give him the phone. When I told her I was the mother of a former patient in California, she asked, "What do you want?" I told her I wanted to update him on my son, and she finally gave him the phone.

"How are you?" he asked.

"Not very well right now; Andy's cancer is back."

"I thought it would be," he replied.

My voice shook with emotion and I demanded, "Why didn't you fight for Andy like you said you would, as we asked you to do?" I told him we knew about the two tumors in April and the five in May. I started to cry.

"You acted against our wishes and your oath as a doctor," I said, with as much strength as I could. I told him that Andy and our entire family would never forget his betrayal, or forgive him for his callous and heartless care of Andy.

"You condemned Andy to death," I said.

"I only tried to do what I thought was right!" he pleaded.

"You failed."

While I knew nothing would change because of my call, I was compelled to confront him. When I hung up, I didn't feel any better. That sickness in the pit of my stomach remained for days.

Andy and I made an appointment with a lawyer to see if we had any recourse. In his opinion, he thought we had a case, but it could be a long difficult process, and for us to go home and think about it. After much discussion, Andy said he didn't want to proceed, because he didn't want all those negative feelings intruding into his life when he needed to keep positive. We left it at that.

20

COMMON WEALTH

$\mathcal{W}$e finally were able to get a glimpse of Andy's impact on those around us. You get lost in your own head when you're fighting cancer. You see your friends, of course, and neighbors, and you know that everyone is aware—everyone in a small town is always aware—but you don't really know how other people are seeing you and how they're feeling. We found out, and the warmth from that communal heart will be with me always.

First, a group of alumni from our high school—as well as teachers who had taught Simon and me as well as our kids—planned a benefit for Andy: dinner, dance and auction. The dinner sold out. People who hadn't been able to buy tickets for dinner were lined up to pay at the door for the auction and dancing. It was a big night, and as Andy walked into the crowded room and was swarmed by friends and well-wishers, his strength and energy seemed to grow and be visible all around him like an aura. He was ready to celebrate. He had on a pink dress shirt, gray slacks, his Washington, D.C., shoes and a gray snap-brim hat with a small feather.

His heart surgery was six weeks in the past, and the chemo was working. Each day was an improvement, and the pain from the surgery was mostly gone. He was thrilled, but a little embarrassed by the speeches.

Late in the evening he danced with Alex, and while it didn't make up for missing homecoming, it came close. In the midst of everyone he knew, he danced hesitantly as his smile lit up the room. I thought of him two short months before, and gratitude was centered in me like an anchor, like an attachment to everything real. It was the best kind of love—for the evening, for the music, for the people.

What we hadn't seen before was that Andy had given a gift to the community. He had always been a hero in our eyes. Now we knew other people felt the same way.

About a week later, there was a small dinner party where the Alumni Committee presented us with a check for over twenty thousand dollars. The money was to be used for travel costs related to Andy's treatment—gas, food, lodging—everything that facilitated taking him where he needed to be. What a relief it was not to worry about how we were going to make our money stretch to cover the unexpected costs. What softness and comfort there were in the faces around us. Others in the wider community were supporting Andy, too. Local service clubs were planning fund-raisers, and the schools were starting benefits. A fifth-grade class at Two Rock Elementary School adopted Andy after following the newspaper accounts. He had been worked into their current events studies, and they sent him warm and sincere letters. They raised $131 on cupcake and cookie sales, then invited him to their class to present him with the coin-filled jar, a signed T-shirt and a party. Andy answered their serious, very good questions about cancer and what it felt like—surgery and having your hair fall out. A line of kids rubbed his chemo-smoothed head, while he grinned and joked with them. Andy was getting better.

Dr. Young called to say that after the next treatment, he'd be a candidate for surgery to remove the remaining tumors. We excitedly made the appointment to complete another round, this time at our local hospital.

This was our first serious introduction to the local oncology community. We met all the people I had talked to a year earlier. Part of our security had been the prestige of the teaching hospitals, and it was frightening to move back to a local setting, even though Dr. Young was still in charge.

We found our way to Dr. Jaffe's office in Santa Rosa with Dr. Young's orders for the chemotherapy and the latest test results. We were frightened, and our feelings of security had deserted us. Our worries, however, were unfounded. Dr. Jaffe's staff was friendly and knew who Andy was. The office was different, adult—no little chairs, no children, and no noise or commotion. It was sedate. People would smile tentatively when our eyes met, but that was all. Very polite. It felt strange.

I picked up a magazine so I could have something to look at, to keep from being caught searching people's faces. Andy seemed to adjust more easily. I relaxed as I watched him respond to the smiles and pats on the shoulder. A woman asked if he was the boy in the paper. He said "Yes," and they talked, and when we left the waiting room, we could hear her telling someone else about him. We were directed back to the lab to have blood drawn. The blood sample would determine if his system had recovered enough from the last round of chemo to have another. The nurses and the technicians who came to meet Andy were very pleasant as they introduced themselves, and soon our stress simply fell away. With promises from some of the staff to visit him when he was in the hospital, we went in to meet with Dr. Jaffe again. We were admiring the paintings and drawings on the walls when Jules entered. He told us that his wife Jennifer was the artist, and after some talk, we discovered that the black-and-white photographs in the hallway were his. Jules was a sensitive man, and it showed. He finished the exam and found no problems that would hold up the chemo. Andy's admission was scheduled for the following morning, and we left the office with a batch of new friends.

They showed up at the hospital during Andy's treatment and visited every time he was hospitalized. They became his cheering section. They loved him, and he loved the way they made him feel.

Throughout the local chemo treatments, Andy would almost always be given the same room. We'd put photographs and cards all over the walls, and his radio would play softly at the head of his bed. He had his blanket.

The room was large enough for all his friends and family to fit in easily. The staff felt it was important for friends to visit, and they went out of their way to make it easy for them. No one ever complained about our noise. Once, when Alex was visiting alone, a sign appeared on the door with a heart and big lips asking everyone to keep out unless absolutely necessary.

They found ways to give Andy control and honored his requests and decisions. If he wanted his door shut, the door was shut. If he wanted to watch a video, they tried not to disturb him until it had finished.

This was all new to us, and it felt wonderful. Someone from the dietary department came to talk about his food preferences and said that if he couldn't find what he wanted on the menu, to just write it in and they'd get it for him. He loved green salads, Mexican food and pizza. The kitchen staff became so attuned to his taste that they always kept a pizza in the freezer. They were absolutely great. After months of chemotherapy treatments, the food would become routine, but the staff always tried to give Andy what he liked.

I began cooking chocolate pudding at home and bringing in a supply for each admission, along with whatever juice he favored that week.

The first five-day chemo treatment was completed the day before Thanksgiving, and we were allowed to go home. It was our second Thanksgiving since the initial diagnosis, and Andy spent it watching television, eating turkey and feeling good. There was so much more to be thankful for this year, we could hardly believe it.

Thanksgiving became quite a raucous celebration, and as evening darkened the sky, no one was anxious to leave. We sat around, stretching out the day as best we could and enjoying being a family together.

Two days later, on my birthday, Andy and I hit bottom. He was in bed with a cold, headache and temperature.

I was worried.

The family came out to celebrate, but I floundered. I couldn't cut through my gloom. It was a stormy day and the electricity was out. The way the world looked seemed to reflect exactly how I felt and extended forever into the future: wet and gray and threatening. How does it happen? It's like the fear you've been carrying and keeping under control suddenly goes outside. It's in the air and it's forever. It can kill.

Maybe it was the outpouring from the community and the warmth and good feelings that had done it. Maybe, in some deep place, I felt that I'd let down my guard. I'd allowed myself to bask, and now I'd have to pay for it.

I didn't want to celebrate. I wanted to go to bed. My twin sister Maureen and her husband drove down from Sacramento to take us out for the evening, and I didn't want to go. Andy couldn't, so Jacob came over to stay with him. It was a long, hard evening, but looking back it was good for both Andy and me to have some time apart. We were getting locked in.

Through the next week, his temperature remained slightly elevated, and the symptoms of a sinus infection increased. His blood counts weren't critical, so we kept watch. X rays showed no pneumonia and, better yet, only three lung tumors. Dr. Jaffe wanted to put Andy in the hospital for antibiotics, but Andy pleaded to stay home. After a long debate, he was given a prescription and allowed to go home. In the next twenty-four hours, his condition improved greatly.

On the next visit with Dr. Young, the results showed the tumors hadn't shrunk much. She feared we were getting less response from the chemo, so now was the time to schedule surgery, at the end of the following week. Ten days after that would be a second thoracotomy to remove the last tumors from his left lung. He would be in the hospital for Christmas so we'd have it early at home, and go to the hospital on the nineteenth for the first surgery.

When we returned from the meeting with Dr. Young, there was a message from Gary, our family doctor. The last echo of Andy's heart had shown a thickening behind the tricuspid valve. He sent the results to Dr. Young, but when I called down to her office, she hadn't received them yet. It was the end of the day, and I was told she'd call as soon as possible. I cried throughout the late afternoon, and when no news came that evening I panicked and couldn't sleep.

The tumor was back. It had to be. If possible, I sank even further into the blackness. I just fell apart. I had no reserve, no strength to say, "It might be okay." The dismal skies were extending down the future like an exitless, blank hallway.

I didn't tell Andy about the phone calls. Simon only could say, "Don't worry, things will work out," which didn't help me at all. He coped by not thinking about what may lay ahead. It was all I could think about. He couldn't hold me because I'd cry and sob, and it drove him nuts. I'd turn away, miserable. He couldn't understand me, and since he could only block his own fear by not letting it come too close, we couldn't even meet halfway. Neither of us could get what we needed from the other. We pulled apart, confused and wretched. We knew we were united in our fight for Andy, but emotionally we were miles apart.

I called my sister and told her my fears while I cried. I tried to listen as she told me all the other things the thickening could be. "Try and relax," she said. "If no one called and the surgery was still scheduled, things had to be all right."

But I didn't relax. I waited in fear for the phone to ring. The telephone was an instrument of terror. I couldn't allow myself to get out of earshot, but every time it rang, my life ended. I'd race to pick up the receiver, afraid of the news I would hear. Finally, in a day or two, I calmed down. No word had come, and the surgery hadn't been canceled.

At no particular point did the relief come and the fear go away. There's a shift and that's that. Get on with it. We rushed to put the Christmas tree up. Andy and Alex took the Jeep to a Christmas-tree farm to pick one out. They had on Santa hats, Christmas music blasting as they left the driveway. They came back with two trees, though I knew they hadn't had enough money for two. The owner had recognized them and made a gift of the second. I decorated one that evening, and Andy and Alex delivered the other to Alex's family. They stopped along the way to pop in on friends, and they videotaped everything. Andy wanted to take the video to the hospital so he could watch it there.

Everything was put on tape. The jokes and gag gifts were duly recorded two nights later. Simon and I gave Andy new ski clothes, not only to replace the worn-out outfit he'd outgrown, but to send the message that he'd be skiing again, later that winter.

Late that evening, Andy's doctor called to say that everything was set for his surgery the next day. The echo of his heart appeared normal, and there was a complete go-ahead from everyone concerned.

I went across the room to Simon and whispered the news. He smiled.

"I knew that," he said.

We left early the next morning for the long drive to the medical center, stopping along the way to pick up Linda and the borrowed motor home. Cheryl followed in her car so we would have a vehicle to ferry people back. Alex came with us, too.

It took two hours to be admitted because I forgot to bring our health insurance company's approval sheet. By the time Andy was admitted, he was tense and exhausted.

The surgeon came in to explain the procedure and tell Andy outright that "This will be much worse than the heart surgery." As things were explained, Andy became more quiet and less responsive.

There was a Christmas party for all the kids on the ward that evening. Andy didn't want to go, but his nurse finally convinced him. Simon didn't want to stay, so he kissed Andy goodnight and went back to the motor home. Andy sat through the whole program, quiet and serious.

The other patients and their families sat around the playroom laughing and smiling at a magician and acrobat, but Andy wasn't involved. When the Christmas carols began, he started to cry and Alex held him.

The following morning, he didn't wake till 10 A.M. We were relieved that he wouldn't have a long time to wait before going into the OR, but as it turned out, the surgery was delayed and he didn't go in until two o'clock that afternoon. There wasn't much to say, and time dragged through us all like a heavy slow-moving chain. When the OR team came to pick Andy up, Simon and I went with him to wait till they took him into the surgical suite.

In what seemed a very short time, the surgeon was out with the news that six tumors had been removed. Three had been positive for cancer, but three were questionable. They had probably been killed by the chemo.

Andy's roommate in the pediatric ICU was a three-year-old boy who had been born with a huge heart defect and had already survived a transplant. He didn't look like he was doing well—listless, with poor color.

His father and mother were with him constantly, and I found out later his dad had learned Aikido while his son was hospitalized as a way of relieving stress. I'd see him early in the mornings in a quiet corner of the hospital, beautifully following his routine.

Watching him was soothing. It was like he was abstracting all our routines, all our tensions, all our fears. The slow, perfectly controlled movements were like a code for what we were all trying to do, for what we had to do.

Andy had a visitor.

"Hi, Andy, do you remember me?"

"No."

"I'm Dr. Sullivan. I hear you wanted me to stop by."

Andy beamed. "I wanted to meet you and thank you for saving my life." He took Dr. Sullivan's hand and shook it.

Dr. Sullivan said, "I want you to know that you taught me something."

"What's that?"

"You can't count anyone out. And I'm going to fight harder for my patients after your success."

"I can't thank you enough. I'm so glad to be alive."

Dr. Sullivan patted Andy's shoulder as he left. Andy lay back in bed and grinned.

Simon and I spent our thirty-first wedding anniversary in and out of the ICU. We didn't even know. One of the girls wished us a happy anniversary, and it was like we had to think about it for a second to respond to news from a different place.

21

*D*ESOLATION

*G*ood news/bad news. Life as it is. In the ordinary run of events, though, you have time to relax a bit, to pretend life is stable between the random body blows and windfalls. But you don't, when you're locked in a death struggle. There seems to be little or no time between. You know how a yo-yo sleeps, spinning at the end of the string between the down and up slides? Well, that's how the time-outs are. And even at the bottom of the string you have to keep spinning, because if you don't, you'll never make it back up.

It's as if you've come face-to-face with the nature of life. You can see that the ups and downs are what everyone goes through all the time. It's just that for you, they're so much closer together. A friend told me that in its terminal stages alcoholism mimics paranoid schizophrenia. Well, our struggle with cancer mimicked manic depression.

As it goes on, I really can't stand it; none of us can. But we do. Because Andy stands it. And because we're all he has.

Christmas Day was exciting, even if we were in the hospital. We went over early in the morning with the Christmas stockings. No matter how old our children were, Christmas stockings were always special. Presents were wrapped and hidden among the oranges, tape measures and assorted fillers. Andy's this year held a delicate glass ball with a snow scene inside. Simon got a new watch in his. They were watching when I went through mine, not expecting anything because I was the one who had filled the stockings. But there was a wrapped present for me, too. Andy scratched his bald head and looked slyly at Simon. I opened the wrappings and screamed. There was a diamond ring in my stocking! They both said "Merry Christmas" as I cried. I was overwhelmed with the sweetness of it. When your whole attention is stretched to the breaking point for months at a time, the simplest bit of affection can be a religious experience.

During the morning, Andy received presents. He also gave. He'd picked them out with a hospital volunteer while we'd been away. He gave Simon a manicure set and gave me a can of peanuts. When I opened the can, a cloth-covered coiled spring popped out, making me jump. Andy asked me if I knew why he picked the peanuts, and I said it reminded me of the description of how his heart tumor had popped out.

"That's right! Exactly," he said.

Two women came by pulling a wagon full of oranges. They had tinsel wrapped in their hair. They were going from room to room with oranges for every child. It was a sweet and tender morning, a morning almost out of time in its gentle spirit.

The nurse came in with reindeer antlers pinned to her hair.

Andy received permission to make a short trip out to the motor home. Waiting were John, Toni, Paul and four special guests. Andy's fox terrier, Spuds, had had puppies. Andy gingerly mounted the steps and smiled broadly when he saw the dogs. He sat down on the sofa and Spuds wiggled against him, watching closely while he picked up her puppies and looked at each.

He murmured, petted and snuggled with his dog. He talked to her about her puppies. They were in another world entirely. When Andy had gotten Spuds, she'd been small enough to fit in the palm of his hand. He'd wanted a small dog to take places with him. A dog who could sleep in his bed. The puppies were just as tiny now, like little black and white mice. He finally picked out one with a big black spot on her stomach and said she was the one he would keep.

"I'm going to name her Opu," he said. Opu means belly in Hawaiian. It was a perfect name. The others would be given away to the first on the long waiting list of his friends who wanted one. Andy sat there oblivious to everything but the new puppies. His visible scar was huge—long and tender.

He came home much sooner than I would have thought was possible. The pain wasn't completely gone, but medication let him spend time out with his friends and enjoy the break between surgeries.

Time is so valuable. We turn around and find ourselves somewhere else. The New Year came and with it another surgery. As we waited for admission, a friend of Andy's called the hospital to let us know that one of their buddies had just come down with chicken pox and that Andy had been exposed. That information stopped the admittance process cold. The doctors couldn't decide whether or not to isolate Andy. They were worried that if he came down with chicken pox, even though we told them Andy had already had them when he was little, he would expose all the other children in intensive care. Chicken pox, when a child's immune system is depressed, can be fatal.

A long, serious conference led to Andy being admitted anyway.

The second thoracotomy took longer than the first. This time they took out seventeen nodules. Only three had been positive for cancer, though. Fourteen were dead from the chemotherapy. The doctor was elated, because he knew now that the chemo was working. Out of all the tumors removed from both lungs, only six had been positive for cancer. Seventeen had been killed. It was a phenomenal success. Our spirits rose inexorably toward the next rickety crest.

Andy was transferred to the ICU for his recovery. This time we were more familiar and comfortable with the process. The epidural worked for his pain, and after twenty-four hours, Andy was transferred out to the step-down ICU. The hospital was very crowded, and as Andy started to improve there was talk of transferring him out of pediatrics to an adult floor. We were told that there was a large room and that we'd all be more comfortable.

He'd continue to be followed by the same respiratory and pain team, just at a different location. The move seemed like a good solution for our large family. It wasn't, though.

He was transferred to a large, quiet room, with two empty beds and one occupied. Andy was right across the room from a very sick, quiet man. As the day progressed we settled in, and I became more aware of the other patient. I could see he wasn't doing well. In the afternoon, when a team of doctors came in to talk to him, I knew I was right. They talked to him as if we weren't in the room. It was impossible to ignore their voices or what was being said. They told him coldly that he had liver cancer, only a few weeks to live, and that there was nothing anyone could do for him. I was horrified. We heard from behind our drawn curtain. Andy would glance at me as we were pulled into another world of pain. We heard no sympathy offered. The news was cut and dried.

What's the clinical value of emotional brutality?

Later, when I pulled back our curtain, his had been pulled closed. We heard no crying, but no one talking either. The man was alone, adjusting in a quiet way to a death sentence. I was angry at the callousness and at the violation of our world. The tone of the voices had drained the room of common humanity, and it was no place for Andy to hold on to positive results. I didn't want him unwillingly thrust into the misery of a man suffering through his last days without any support.

Andy and I were quiet as the afternoon faded from the room. The television droned away. Later that evening, a tough nurse came in and told me I had to leave. She said that Andy was on an adult floor. The rules were different and I couldn't stay. She assured me he'd be taken care of and nervously I kissed him goodnight. The bed across the room was still screened and silent.

In the morning I was up early, anxious to see Andy. When I entered his room, he began to cry. During the night, he hadn't been given his pain medication. When the respiratory therapist had come in that morning to give him his treatment, he'd refused to let her start. He hurt too much.

The therapist, furious that his pain had not been controlled, argued with the nurse in front of Andy. The nurse wanted to give oral medication when he needed IV. He was only two days post-op from his second surgery. He was in a great deal of pain.

The nurse refused to listen to him. He was out of ICU, he didn't need morphine and that was that. They had to fight for an hour to get the IV painkiller. He ended up missing two therapy treatments because of his pain. Both of his therapists came in early in the morning to apologize. They were still furious. They wanted me to complain to Andy's doctors and the director of nursing, which I agreed to do.

By the time Andy's surgeon came in for morning rounds, I was in tears. A morphine pump was suggested. That way, Andy could control his own medication and not have to wait for someone else to come to his aid.

While the doctors were there, I also complained about Andy having to listen to the cruel way his roommate was told he was going to die. The doctor said, "That's the adult floor for you," seeming to discount the point I was making.

When the morphine pump arrived and was hooked into his IV line, Andy was shown how to use it. The pump worked wonderfully, and he was soon up and walking the halls again.

He certainly didn't want to stay in the room. Andy's roommate's wife had come to be with her husband, and their quiet sobs seemed to fill the room. It was hard to listen to.

We spent the afternoon sitting in waiting areas, walking, playing games and going to the cafeteria. Andy's doctor saw us in the evening and asked if he wanted to move to another room. That night we gathered our belongings and moved into a small, crowded room. His new roommate was a school superintendent with a happy family around him. He had just been operated on for cancer, but he had a positive attitude. He talked to Andy as a comrade who had traveled a similar path. Both the families talked through the days we spent together, learning about each other and taking the edge off the hospital. Later that week, I heard that the man from the large room had died during the night.

Home again, feeling great. Preparing for another chemo session. The pedi-oncologist was thrilled. Tumor-free in three months was an eventuality she hadn't been prepared for. Andy was ready to return to school and his life.

On John's birthday, the thirteenth of January, Andy was admitted for a different kind of chemo.

Andy was zonked out quickly and the treatment started. Twenty hours later everything was finished, and we were ready to leave. What a difference a single dose of chemo made in our lives. It seemed that we were home in no time. Andy was tired for another day.

On the second day home, he was up and anxious to go back to school. He was able to do his homework and go out with his friends. When the period of neutropenia hit, his counts remained relatively high and he was able to ride through without being hospitalized.

His concentration had improved, school was more interesting and his life seemed back to normal. The soreness from the lung surgeries was subsiding. He was back working on his '50 Chevy pickup, tearing the motor apart and restoring it in tip-top shape. He and Alex wanted to take it to the senior prom in the spring. No limousine for these kids, they were going in style.

One morning Andy told me his left foot was tingling and his toes felt stiff. These could have been side effects we'd been told about from the new chemo, so I didn't think much about it. The next morning his foot was no better. In fact, his leg felt weak and he was unable to move his foot. I noticed his knee was hyper-extending a bit when he went off to school with Alex, saying that he thought his foot was better. (What else could he say? How else could he keep moving?)

I was nervous. (At this point, I was moving from *this* roomful of feelings to *that* roomful of feelings. Each room had the same furniture, all set up for efficiency. It's just that one room was darker than the other.)

He called later to say his foot felt much better. After school, the kids stopped by on their way to Alex's. As they left and walked across the yard, I watched Andy. He wasn't better at all. He was leaning on Alex as they walked. They were laughing as they waved good-bye and headed down the driveway toward the road. Alone in the house I called Dr. Young. When I told her what was happening she said, "Get seen fast. Don't come down here, just get to Jules fast and get this sorted out. It's not a nor-mal reaction."

I called Alex's house, but no one answered. I called Jules, who said to come to the office as quickly as possible. There was still no answer at Alex's. I called every three minutes until she answered the phone. It was 3:30 P.M. when I told Andy he needed to come home.

I waited for them alone in that special place where you sit on the edge of despair and have no control over anything. I didn't call anyone else. For what? A brain tumor would cause those symptoms, wouldn't it? The time in front of me was laid out simply. There was a car trip and a few deathly sentences. I kept it all to myself.

When Andy asked me what the rush was, I told him his doc-tors said we needed to check things out to make sure everything was okay. We were all quiet in the car. Alex was with us. I drove like the wind up the back roads to miss the traffic jam on the freeway.

Jules said "possible brain tumor." I hadn't said it. An MRI was scheduled later that same night. Alex and Andy both said they were sure the MRI would be clear. I knew the chances for a tumor far outweighed the chances for a negative report. We were all quiet.

When Jules was examining Andy's mouth, I'd seen a round raw spot on his tongue, just like he'd had before his heart surgery. Jules looked at it and thought nothing of it. But it made me terribly frightened, and it stayed in my head like an evil talisman. No one had paid much attention to the spots when they appeared, but this was the third time I'd seen it. The first time was when he had all the lung tumors. The second was when he'd had the heart tumor.

I was the weak link in the chain, I guess. I was the one who believed the spot meant trouble.

We waited quietly for the appointment at the hospital. The cold plastic benches did nothing to relieve our tension. Alex kept up a dialogue with Andy, trying to fill the void. When the X-ray tech came to get Andy, I was told that I could come along. So Alex kissed him good-bye, wished him luck, looked at me apprehensively and sat back down for her own lonely vigil.

Andy told the technician that he'd been through this twice before, and that they'd never found a brain tumor. "That's good," was the reply.

We were introduced to the doctor who would conduct the test and shown through a small room to the MRI machine, where Andy was positioned and made comfortable. I stood at Andy's head through the test, talking to him quietly throughout the two hours he was in the scanner. It was hard for him to lay perfectly still. To help, I took him on a guided-imagery backpacking trip to Spider Lake. I talked him through the trails and over boulders and around the lake. My voice sounded much calmer than I felt inside. The memories became hypnotic. Through my own voice, I heard others in the small-windowed room where the computer equipment was kept. I realized slowly that it was a phone conversation. The doctor came in to say he was going to pull Andy out of the machine for a few minutes, then do some more testing.

My apprehension increased while I waited. Andy went for a walk without me, and the doctor followed him out. I was sure he didn't want to stay in the room with me. I knew he already knew what was going on, he just hadn't told us. While everyone was out of the room, I moved over by the door and looked at the MRI screen. There was a white oval on the right side of the scan.

Hysteria can be like a fist to the back of your neck. I almost fell on the floor.

Andy came back in with Alex. She was holding Andy's hand. They talked together while I stood by in silent despair. When the last set of films had been made, they sat on the table and held each other.

Andy looked me square in the eyes and said, "What?"

"Honey," I said, "I think they found something."

I started to answer, but my voice cracked. The doctor came in and took us to the viewing screen. There was the oval the size of a golf ball, on the right side of Andy's brain.

We all seemed so quiet and calm.

22

THE VOID

The doctor gave Andy a slight hug, then one for me before we passed on our way to the door. He knew what he had just done to us.

I'm not going up and down, the world is going up and down. Did I say this before? When you're dealing with cancer you come to realize that the only difference between your world and the everyday world is that in yours, the shocks come closer together.

Terror again, terror again. Ring the bell and gather around

and see the zombies leave the hospital. No one cried, and I didn't call Simon or the kids. I just started the car and headed home. They'd all be there anyway. We'd walk in and everyone would be there, and we'd have to tell them and then there'd be that silence.

That's the way it was. The kids had waited for a phone call to let them know everything was all right. When there was silence, they knew we were in trouble.

As awful as it was to be at the hospital, waiting at home for hours without any word had to be worse. We pulled closer again and put up our communal barriers.

Jules called later that evening and talked to Andy and me. He offered hope, help, support and told us what to watch for.

In the morning I called Dr. Young, who was already working on consultations. She repeated much of what Jules had told us the night before. It was going to take a little time to set things in motion, but we would be moving soon. (Soon? Time? Time is a different thing now. Noncrisis blocks of time are like separators in a file cabinet.)

Jules called again to say he had already worked for hours reviewing Andy's options. I told him that Andy was very depressed and that his leg was noticeably worse.

The day dragged. Jules called back to tell us we had an appointment in San Francisco on Monday morning. It seemed that bad news always came on a Friday and we'd have to wait through the weekend for resolution. Both he and Dr. Young agreed that this was where we were going to have to start.

Monday would be Andy's eighteenth birthday. We looked at the clock. It was only 10:30 A.M., but the day had already been thousands of hours long.

Alex had just had her eighteenth birthday. We had planned a joint Super Bowl/birthday party. We talked about canceling it, but decided not to. (In front of us was Nothing. Waiting is just the kind of Nothing that hurts.) We'd be with friends and relatives. We'd have the party.

Then there was Andy's birthday present. That filled our minds for a while. We wanted to at least have something good, something positive. We would have given Andy anything he wanted, but that wasn't possible. There was no way to buy ourselves out of our situation. Not even money works.

Andy finally decided that he wanted a saltwater aquarium. The fish he'd seen while snorkeling in Hawaii would be swimming in his bedroom. We had a mission. We had something to do to fill the time.

We all piled in cars and drove to the store, about ten miles away. We spent hours selecting, and left with a complete setup for a seventy-five-gallon tank. Later that afternoon we'd go back to pick up seven Blue Damsel fish Andy had chosen.

We set up the stand and brought in the tank. It was huge in Andy's bedroom. The sand, rocks and shells my father had collected in the South Pacific went into the tank. It was very pretty.

Jacob came over to spend his birthday with Andy. His own came two days before Andy's, and the boys had always spent them together. I headed back to pick up the fish. I drove across the landscape like some lost, windup toy.

Once the fish were acclimated, Andy's room became a focus for visitors. The fish in the bubbling water were relaxing. The aquarium is still there. The sound has never stopped.

On the morning of Andy and Alex's birthday party, Andy arose with difficulty.

We were all down to Alex's parent's, Carlos and Rebecca's, by early afternoon, where we were served a wonderful dinner. Friends had helped make delicious dishes for the meal, and Alex had made and decorated a chocolate birthday cake covered with ribbons, candles, hearts and lovebirds. It was a wonderful meal, with lots of friends—on a sad and subdued and threatening day on the edge of a Monday that loomed like a huge darkness.

Early on Monday, we met with Jules before heading to San Francisco. Simon had been up and out the door long before the sun. But the crisp, cool morning did nothing to invigorate him, and he quietly (always quietly) endured the passing of the time. I wasn't doing much talking either.

The other kids had already arrived before Simon plodded back in for breakfast. What a birthday. Andy did tell us that the aquarium was the "best present ever."

When we met with Jules, he gave us the MRI films, a schedule for the day and directions on how to find the hospital. He gave Andy a hug, too. Simon, Cheryl, Alex and I headed for the city with Andy.

We were through signing in and waiting when the woman sitting across from us had a seizure and slipped from her chair to the floor, convulsing. Other people had problems of speech and mobility. Some showed surgical scars. I knew the others were watching us the same way. And that they would have easily picked out Andy as the patient.

His foot dragged on the floor as he walked, sheer willpower moving him along. It was an overwhelming experience just sitting in the waiting room.

The neurologist told us that Andy's case wasn't an emergency. (Emergency? No? What is it then? What's the time scale? How long did it take us to get here? Eternity. What would be going on in Andy's head while we waited? Eternity.)

We'd all thought Andy would be admitted immediately for surgery. We looked at them, shocked. "Andy's losing too much every day," I said. "Waiting for a week or two would cause irreparable damage."

The doctor said this was their procedure in nonemergency cases. We were told bluntly that Andy's cancer had metastasized and that removing the tumor wasn't going to cure him. It would only make it easier for him to walk. If we wanted something done sooner (what are these people talking about?), we needed to find someone closer to home who might have more time. He said Andy's surgery wasn't difficult, and any neurosurgeon would be capable of performing it.

He suggested that another MRI be done with dye to check for any other small tumors. Then he shook our hands, wished Andy luck and left. Andy had been dismissed as a patient for surgery, and we'd been told there might be more tumors.

It was a horrible day. We decided to go down to Fisherman's Wharf to try and salvage something of Andy's birthday. The walk was too difficult, though, and he really didn't want to eat. I remember arguing with Simon about food he bought at a stall along the wharf. I was mad at him, mad at the doctors, mad at myself. I let it all happen (another nosegay of responsibility to put among the souvenirs).

Whatever Simon ate was of no consequence. But he got the anger full-force anyway. The day stayed horrible. I knew I was immature and wrong. (So what?) We left the wharf in silence.

Andy was very depressed and cried all the way home. The day had no resolution. It was intolerable.

As soon as we were home, I called Jules and asked him to find a young, confident, aggressive neurosurgeon in Sonoma County who would be willing to see us quickly. He said he would call some doctors, talk to them and call me back.

Early the next morning, Jules called to say the doctors had all agreed that Andy could have his surgery done locally without losing anything at all. Another MRI was scheduled, as well as an appointment with the neurosurgeon for the following day.

When all the tests were done, the doctor told us there were no other tumors in his brain and some of the swelling had already decreased. This news was all we needed as a go-ahead.

We arrived for our appointment with the new neurosurgeon, Dr. Huntstock, with a certain degree of calmness. The horrific San Francisco experience had chastened us a bit. He showed us the MRI films and explained the situation, pointing out the tumor and which function was controlled in each of the surrounding areas of the brain. He said that some surgeons wouldn't consider operating because the tumor had metastasized. He didn't believe, though, that it was best to just let Andy die.

He said the tumor was removable and that Andy's speech, sight, memory and intellect wouldn't be affected by the surgery. There was a real possibility, though, that he could be paralyzed.

The doctor needed to know if Andy wanted surgery that might result in left-side paralysis.

The room was silent. I had always thought of his cancer battle as life or death, not as something that might leave him disabled and compromised.

"I have no other option," he said. "I'm going to live no matter how I come out." He then talked about his friend Jolene who had been paralyzed in a car accident when she was sixteen and how she'd gone on to college and managed to live her life.

He said, "If Jo Jo can do it, so can I."

Early the next morning, we received the telephone call that Andy's surgery had been scheduled. We were to have him at the hospital the next day so they could start the pre-op tests. We let everyone know what was happening, arranged for a motor home and found out where we could park. Alex and her mom were going to stay with Simon and I for the first night, while the kids would drive back and forth.

At the hospital, the nurse wouldn't let Andy use his Port-A-Cath, and she started a peripheral IV. He tried to convince her that the IV hampered his movement, hurt and wouldn't provide better access, but the nurse wouldn't change her mind. It was her territory. It wasn't a good beginning at all. Andy later named her "White Fang."

Andy stood up to walk when he could, and we followed him in a pack, out the door and around the hallway over and over again, looking in rooms as we passed. It wasn't comforting. People were yelling. Some were tied to their chairs or beds. It was a neuro floor, and there was a lot of disorientation.

One man passed pushing a walker. Half of his head was shaved. All our eyes followed as he walked away. I wondered how long it had been since his surgery. No one spoke.

He came around again on his second circuit. On his third time around, he looked at us, smiled and said, "Want to play poker?" while he kept moving. We made no response. The next time around he said, "You'll win if you play with me," and we all looked up at him as he smiled and passed us again. On his next circuit he stopped and said, "Hi, I'm Paul," and shook Andy's hand.

He pulled up a chair, and we hit him with an onslaught of questions. He'd been there five days; this was his second brain surgery. The surgery wasn't bad at all, he told Andy. Paul spent over an hour with us, calming us, making us laugh. Andy asked him about the nurse we'd been assigned and Paul told us she was tough, but not so bad. Paul left us after exchanging telephone numbers.

He was going home the next day but said he would call to

check up on Andy and maybe they could get together later. Paul helped us more than he ever knew.

That evening Carlos came to spend some time, and while he was there, the rest of us went out to dinner. He and Andy talked about death, disability, courage and strength. Carlos gave him a beaded warrior feather that a local craftsman had made, a feather that was earned by warriors through feats of strength and courage. When visiting hours were over, the family said goodnight and headed for the motor home. I stayed with Andy to calm him and be there to talk while he fell asleep. I wanted to be there in case he woke up afraid in the night.

The nurse came in and told me that visiting hours were over and I had to leave. I told her I wasn't going to leave, that I was staying with Andy till he was asleep. She threatened me with retribution. I told her I didn't care, I was staying. She left the room in anger, and I followed her. I told her how frightened Andy was. She didn't uncross her arms, she didn't soften. Neither did I. I told her that we had some relaxation and visualization to do, and I wasn't going to leave until Andy's Ativan had taken effect. With that, she told me she was going to call the nursing supervisor. I told her to go ahead.

Another nurse brought Andy's sleeping pill, and while he was becoming drowsy we visualized a successful operation. We visualized the mountains and snorkeling in Kealakakua Bay. I told him that no matter how the surgery came out, he would be safe through whatever lay ahead. When he fell asleep I just sat there, watching him breathe. At the motor home I took a sleeping pill to knock me out. At 7 A.M., Andy was taken down to the operating room. It turned out that a friend of mine from my days in the OR would be assisting. Andy remembered him, and I could see his tension decrease as the two of them talked. The anesthesiologist was also someone I had worked with, and he came out to talk. His parting words to me were, "If we get in trouble, I'll get you." Both of us knew that this meant that if Andy were to come close to dying, I would be able to be with him. It meant a great deal to me to have that reassurance.

The waiting room was full of our family and the friends who had come to support us. Annie Wells, the photographer, and the reporter from the newspaper were there, too. They had become so involved in our family that they felt they belonged. We did, too.

A nurse came out a couple of hours later and said Andy was just being draped and the surgery would start soon. She told me that she would come out periodically and let us know what was happening. I would be able to visualize the procedure and know where they were.

The television was on, and Simon watched without really seeing. He needed something to do. A clerk from the grocery store where I shopped came by with sandwiches for everyone. He wanted to help.

Around 1 P.M., the nurse came out and told us that the neurosurgeon had just reached the tumor and that Andy was doing well. They had to proceed very slowly through his brain in order to avoid damage. "Things will go more quickly now," she said. At the end of her shift, Andy was still in the OR. She told us they were finishing up and that Andy was well.

"Did they get all the tumor?" I asked.

"You'll have to ask the doctor about that, but things are going well," she replied. Fear and panic gripped me at the same time she was hugging me. "Take care of yourself," she said, and left. Everything crashed.

In a sudden outburst I said, "They didn't get it all!" Everyone was shocked at my reaction.

Cheryl said, "She just couldn't tell you, that's all."

But I knew she was wrong. I looked around the room. Simon's eyes were huge as he watched me. Sharon, Linda and Rebecca agreed with me, saying that the nurse's voice had seemed restrained. We sat there in a quiet panic until the neurosurgeon came out an hour and a half later. He told us the tumor was all out, and that Andy was talking and moving better than before the surgery.

I jumped up and hugged him. He appeared shocked. Everyone clapped and he grinned and told us Andy would be out of the recovery room in about an hour, and we would be able to see him then. He left the room a hero.

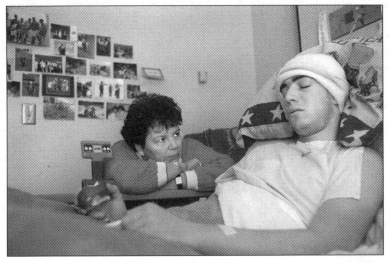

Photo by Annie Wells. ©*The Press Democrat,* Santa Rosa, CA.

Me at Andy's bedside on his first day out of intensive care after brain surgery on February 2, 1990.

We gathered up our things and were all waiting when Andy came out the double doors of the recovery room. It was obvious that he was doing better. He was alert and talking, moving his foot and hand. It appeared there would be no permanent paralysis from the surgery.

On the fifth post-op day, Dr. Huntstock came in and said that Andy was doing so well, he would be able to go home the next day. Andy said, "Too bad. I was ready to go today."

The doctor said without much hesitation that he couldn't think of any reason to keep him longer, and that he'd be back in the afternoon to take out the stitches. Then he could go home. The nurses came in with discharge orders, the physical therapist went over the exercises Andy was to do at home, and we packed up. Annie came by to take more pictures for the newspaper and was there when Dr. Huntstock came to remove the stitches. All was recorded, and Andy was given permission to leave.

Annie followed us home, where she recorded Andy's first steps back into the house and Spuds's welcome. Spuds was all over the place with excitement. When Andy settled in the lounge chair, she climbed up, licked his face and sniffed the bandage covering his head.

Annie took a great photograph of Andy's reaction to Spuds's wet kiss, his big wide grin with eyes squished shut.

(Pictures and charts and documents and newspapers. They're all over the place right now, at home, in Andy's room, on a Thursday in 1998, surrounding me as I remember the joy, the terror and the hope of that time.)

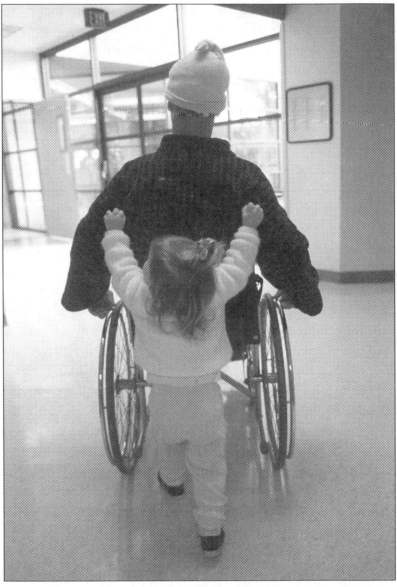

Photo by Annie Wells. ©*The Press Democrat,* Santa Rosa, CA.

Andy's fingers help his niece Stefanie push his wheelchair through the halls of the hospital on February 6, 1990.

Photo by Annie Wells. ©*The Press Democrat,* Santa Rosa, CA.

Andy's welcome home from Spuds on February 7, 1990, after brain surgery.

23

CRESTS AND VALLEYS

I know I've been dead. I was almost all the way there and I know it felt good and that there is no threat, there is no extinction. So why is the world the way it is now? Because I can't make anyone else know? Hardly. I never really thought I could. It isn't something you believe: it's something you feel, something you know in your whole being.

So why are things so grindingly difficult, so much like a battle with something evil?

Probably, because what I know about death doesn't matter to me when its other side is that Andy won't be with me anymore. Andy will be gone, and what will I do with the emptiness and the pain?

And because I don't really want to talk to Andy about death. It doesn't seem right. It would seem like a violation of everything he's done, all the strength he's brought to bear. I don't want to talk about death.

I want him here and he wants to be here, and the comfortable passages of death can wait. I'd die in his place in a minute. I've already had a life. Why is it different, that my death would be all right, but his would tear me apart? Because he's my son. In the far reaches of my emotions he's still a newborn infant, all eyes and tiny hands. He's everything in the world that matters and is beautiful, and nothing in heaven or on earth has any right to take him away.

The next report from pathology lists Andy's tumor as melanoma. That means less than a 1 percent chance of survival. After a lengthy discussion, things settled down a bit. When you are fighting cancer, you will inevitably find some way to look at the latest news, some stance to take that makes it bearable.

The pathology was really the same, there were just some confusing aspects. Melanoma does travel to the brain, but it doesn't usually respond so well to Ifosfomide and VP16, Andy's chemo. So his tumor hadn't really acted like melanoma. We were still where we were before, it was just a throwback to the early days when no one had been able to make an identification. The fact was, it had responded. And it was gone.

As a matter of fact, the doctor says that he thinks Andy has a

25 percent chance of a cure and that his positive attitude makes the odds even better. We're easing into our positions and getting our act back together.

Andy's first post-op examination showed him doing well. Radiation and chemo treatments were scheduled. They would continue to alternate the chemo between the melanoma and soft tissue sarcoma protocols. He'd have the melanoma chemo first.

I talked to Dr. Young that afternoon about stress, life, depression, fear, death, hope and the will to fight. She was most impressed with Andy's abilities in crisis. It was a good, honest conversation. She said she was sure Andy would relax with the chemo and radiation once they were started and things became familiar. The radiation would end in six weeks, but the chemo would go on for another eighteen to twenty-four months.

Photo by Annie Wells. ©*The Press Democrat,* Santa Rosa, CA.

February 8, 1990. Andy's friends visiting after his return home from his first brain surgery. His weak left leg is apparent here.

Andy spent the weekend with Alex and her family. He was home in time to go to the hospital. When we arrived there, we were told a scan had been ordered to check for bone tumors. He was quiet and nervous. At least he was back on the oncology floor.

We both watched the images on the screen. They looked good, but I wasn't sure. The scan is slow, and we waited for what seemed like hours. They *were* good. On the way back to his room, Andy told me he had been terrified.

He began going to radiation every day. First they marked his head up with red dots and lines to indicate the direction of the radiation. After that, it was over quickly.

At home that night several dams broke, and he cried and raged and asked what he had ever done to be given such a terrible cancer. It lacerated. I knew he couldn't always be positive, couldn't always be nice and courageous, but it still cut and tore. The next day Andy and Alex took a "mental health day." They went off by themselves hot-tubbing prior to his afternoon radiation treatment. When they returned that evening, Andy felt better again.

His condition was improving every day. He was able to go out with his friends. He started seeing the acupuncturist again, and the walker he'd been using was returned to the hospital. The hours spent with his "physical terrorist" had paid off. The only residual effect from the tumor was a slight clumsiness and drag of the left foot. He had come through the surgery almost without damage.

We were elated. The visits with the neurosurgeon confirmed Andy's return to health. His brain was recovering well from the surgery, and no new tumors were found.

I started talking with Dr. Young about alternative treatments. The problem with chemotherapy is that it is time-limited and can't be kept up indefinitely. The body grows tired from the assault, and the tumor becomes resistant to the medications.

Interleukin-2 (IL-2) was in clinical trials, and genetic therapy was just on the horizon as a possible effective treatment. I asked her about a bone marrow transplant. She said that while some hospitals were trying to treat melanoma with transplant, there hadn't been much success. The patient needed to be fairly healthy and responding to the chemo at the time of the transplant. If a transplant were offered early in the course of treatment, the odds of success went up. The problem there was that, in most programs, you needed a failure of the treatment to be considered.

In a bone marrow transplant, a huge dose of chemotherapy is given at a preterminal level before the bone marrow is infused. If the chemo hadn't been working, increasing the dosage to the preterminal level won't work. There will still be hidden cancer cells ready to grow just as soon as the effects of the chemo wear off.

For the time being, she told me, "We'll continue with the chemotherapy and see what develops." She suggested that Andy register at the local college and take some classes he liked. "We don't know where we'll be next fall, but that's no reason Andy can't start college and be with his friends."

We were talking in the kitchen one afternoon when I noticed the round spot on his tongue again. (*I don't want to say this. I*

don't want to tell him. I can't watch the reaction. I shouldn't be
required. Please help me, someone.)

We had an appointment with Jules the next day. Every time
the spot had appeared, it had signaled a new tumor. Jules
thought the spot was probably a virus caused by Andy's compromised immune system. (*Does he believe that? Listen very closely,*
study the face.)

Since Andy had a cold and other symptoms, he was given
antibiotics. A CAT scan of Andy's lungs was ordered. None had
been taken since before the brain surgery. It was time to check.
(No more, no more, we can't take any more.)

The next day Terror was in the car with us as we went for the
CAT scan. Both of Andy's doctors thought we had nothing to
worry about. Cheryl was worrying with me, but everyone else
tended to discount my fear.

The scan was done, and we took the films along with us. I'd
deliver them to Jules when we went to see him in a couple of days.

The knowledge that I had the answer in the car ate at me all
evening, and after Andy went to bed I took a flashlight out to the
garage. If ever anything threw the whole insanity of our situation
into clear view, it was that walk through the garage to the car, the
flashlight beam bouncing and the car just a series of gleams and
shadows wrapped around a manila envelope.

Interpreting the films wasn't difficult. I had seen so many
X rays and CTs of Andy that I could draw from memory his particular characteristics. I pulled the films out and went through
them in order. The spots were evident. I just sat there as if I were
waiting for someone to open the door for me.

When I finally went into the house and told Simon, he was
sure I didn't understand what I was looking at. He said to quit
worrying and not to make it so tough on myself. He just didn't

want me to be right. I knew that. Why say it? Fear clamped down on me. The night was unutterably lonely. The following day, though—out in reality—that was worse.

In the morning I vacuumed and shampooed the carpets, twice. I washed the walls. In the afternoon, at the appointment with the acupuncturist, I cried and told him.

At home was the message to call Dr. Jaffe. He'd have received the results. I called his office, but he was busy. So I sat down and waited for his call, which didn't come until early evening.

There were two new tumors, one in each lung. The right lung had a 3 cm tumor and the left lung a 7 cm. He and Dr. Young had talked, and she was checking out where we should go from here. (How about into despair?)

Jules told me he was going away for a conference and he might be able to come up with something while he was gone. His partners had been updated on Andy's status. They would do whatever was needed.

After I hung up, I called Dr. Young to see what she had planned. She thought it would be best to put Andy back on the first chemotherapy, since the tumors had grown through the newest treatment. She was checking out melanoma programs to see if Andy might qualify for any of them. They continued to present problems. Andy's diagnosis was complicated, and his age made his acceptance into any program difficult. Most would only accept adults. In the meantime she wanted more CAT scans, another brain MRI and a sonogram completed before his chemotherapy.

It was a rush to get to the hospital, and then an excruciatingly long wait as Andy completed all the needed tests so he could start his chemo on schedule. Then it seemed that no MRI of the brain had been ordered. I had to argue and get the tech to call the doctor to double-check. We had to wait till late that night to have it completed. The test had to be stopped and restarted, adding an additional hour to the process. Then Andy got sick on the table. The only good thing about the day was that all the scans were normal. The only tumors found were the ones that had already been found. He was sick again after we returned home. I don't know if it was the Demerol they used to calm him, or fear.

Andy was continually nauseated. When his neurosurgeon checked him out, I asked if the nausea could be caused by the Dilantin he'd been given to prevent possible seizures. The nausea had started right after Dilantin had been added to Andy's regime. He agreed that it might be the cause and changed to Phenobarbital.

Later in the day, I received a call from Dr. Young with word of an experimental IL-2 program for soft tissue sarcomas that might accept Andy.

In order for him to start, we needed to wait until the radiation was finished and for him to be off chemo for three weeks. He would also need a clean brain scan to qualify. She wasn't sure whether it would be better or not to bring Andy into the discussion. Some tough questions and hard decisions had to be made. Another study she was checking out was an autologous bone marrow transplant program. Autologous bone marrow donation meant he'd donate his own marrow, be hit hard with huge doses of chemotherapy and/or radiation and then have his marrow reinjected. It might work.

Of course, there was a 10 to 20 percent mortality rate and it might not be covered by insurance. Though bone marrow transplants had been proven successful with other cancers, Andy's was so rare that our insurance company could find all sorts of reasons to deny treatment. We'd have to cross that bridge when the time came. For now, we were going with the chemo as ordered.

The five-day chemotherapy regime went well. Andy was able to be awake for most of each day and go out for radiation without any problems. In the weeks between chemo treatments, Andy wanted only to go back to school and be with his friends. Spring was invigorating, and he wanted to fix his truck and be ready for the prom. The combination of chemo and radiation, though, had knocked his counts down dangerously low. He was told no lifting, no horsing around, no mechanics, nothing that could lead to bruising. His platelets were so low that he could start to bleed spontaneously.

His radiation treatments were stopped until his platelet counts started to climb. The break in the everyday trips to Santa Rosa was appreciated, and Andy was able to use the time to be with his friends. He was out the door like a shot.

And then came the next round of tests. And then, and then. Andy grew quiet as the time approached. I withdrew into myself. Simon again would say over and over, "Be positive." Andy's life would be determined by the test results we were going to receive. (The tests kind of narrow down, each series closer to a final pronouncement. And since all there is in your life is the hope and the sense of possibility, your life narrows, too.)

Andy and I headed up for the visit.

His platelets had started to climb, and his white count was rising, too. He might be able to go back to school after we analyzed the new films of his lungs. That was one possibility. When the MRI was completed, we were headed out the door with no indication how things might be, of which way things were going. No one said anything. I was too afraid to ask anything. Andy was silent, too.

When we returned to Jules's office two days later, he greeted us with a smile. The tumors were shrinking again. The MRI showed one shrinking markedly, the other smaller one shrinking a little.

"Go out and have a great weekend," Jules said. "Do whatever you want." Andy headed out to the high school and his buddies. He suited up and had a light baseball practice. He threw, caught and hit while the afternoon sun warmed his pale skin. He absolutely loved being there among his friends. The newspaper reporter followed him on his rounds, and Annie took pictures for the story.

The lead photo would be the picture of him receiving a radiation treatment, strapped to the table in his football jersey, baseball hat resting on his knees with his scarred head at the center of the image. When the picture came out, even though all we could see were his head, cheeks and nose, we could tell that he was grinning. It was a powerful photo, the huge machines on either side of a bare room and an athlete strapped to a table, hoping.

I can remember all the hope as if it were some foolish way we had of passing the time. It wasn't, of course. It kept us going, and if even a particle was justified, it was worth it.

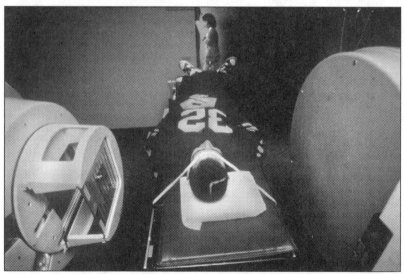

Photo by Annie Wells. ©*The Press Democrat*, Santa Rosa, CA.

Andy smiling during radiation treatment, March 5, 1990.

24

OVATIONS

January 29, 1998. Today would have been Andy's twenty-sixth birthday. His birthday every year remains a day of mourning for me. I guess by now there should be less grief right on the surface, less immediacy, but it just isn't that way and there doesn't seem to be much I can do about it. As you write something like this, the contradictions settle in like birds lighting on a field. Who do I feel bad for? What do I feel bad about? Why doesn't what I know more deeply affect how I feel?

It's the images, you know; his little bald head switching to his grown bald head, that symbol of pain and helplessness. This is a day of grief and always will be. I wish I could say to you, "It will fade," but I can't. What will happen is that you'll cease to feel it full-strength every day. But on the special days, there it is, here it is.

I hate January. I can feel it coming without any calendar. I don't have to look at the calendar. It's like the sky and the way I see it changes, the world and the business of living darken as the days go by. I grow sad and tired and depressed. My energy seeps away.

This morning, Cheryl called to say she had dreamed of Andy all night long.

"How was it?" I asked.

"It was harder this time. He was sick in the dream."

I gathered all my things together—my day pack, my flowers and my twenty-six paper sharks—and headed out to the ocean. Driving, I passed the rose garden where we'd held Andy's memorial service. The gates were locked. Last year, I'd thrown a rose and a paper shark over the fence, but this morning I didn't stop.

The ocean was fierce, breakers smashing halfway up the cliff and the rock we used to climb only showing through the surf once in a while.

I sat in the car and wrote twenty-six messages on twenty-six paper sharks. A rainbow arched over the northwest ocean. I tucked the sharks into my bouquet. There were too many to stay just in the branches, so the rest I tied by their tails to the ribbon on the rose stems.

I stepped out of the car and headed up toward Point Reyes and Bird Rock where the great white sharks are born. A couple was walking in front of me, and I couldn't pass. They'd speed up when I did. They went directly to my spot, the place I always go, and sat.

So I went by them and walked farther on.

Finally, I reached a spot where the ocean was directly under the cliff and the wind was blowing out to sea. I kissed the flowers and said, "I miss you, Honey," and tossed them into the wind. I didn't see them land. The seals were barking, and I climbed to the top of Bodega Head to sit for a while and listen. I hope Moho looks out for Andy.

This is how it is every year. How it will always be, probably.

The week the photo ran, his radiation treatments had finished. Chemo was scheduled for the beginning of the following week, and if the treatments ran a normal course, Andy would only be out of school for a few days.

Then it's the end of the month again and the apprehension takes over. End of the month and the time for scans and MRIs. The drunken monkeys whirled all night, but this time we were lucky. The brain was normal except for the area around the surgery, and that was getting smaller with each viewing. The lung scan still showed tumors, but they hadn't grown.

The small tumor wasn't there at all. Jules said that it might have disappeared or have been so small that it didn't show up. I was disappointed in the lack of dramatic change, but what it all meant was that the chemo was still working. If it weren't, the tumors would have grown.

When I returned home I wasn't able to relax, and I called the radiologist to ask about the missing tumor. He told me essentially the same things Jules had. The changes could be checked out with a plain X ray. It might even be more definitive. I told him I would ask Jules to order one when Andy went in for chemo.

When Andy was admitted again, a chest X ray was ordered. We went through the treatment with no news of the X-ray results, and I took him home to wait for the news there. I had a heavy heart. I was worn, worried and starting to have physical problems at the same time. A numbness had crept up my right arm, and a pain in my neck and back constantly nagged at me.

Andy was already back in school when Jules called to give me the X-ray results. It appeared the small tumor had grown. He was going to check with the radiologist to make sure, and another X ray would be taken in a week to double-check.

I hung up the phone as despair rose around me like a tide. I hadn't felt that much despair to this point. Terror and apprehension, but not despair.

I sat at the table crying, and when Andy came home that afternoon I told him what they had found and what we were going to do. He took it differently. He seemed certain that everything would turn out fine. He felt good and strong. He was sure things were improving.

I remained in an empty, stricken place by myself.

While we were waiting for the next X ray, I went to a nursing conference on childhood cancers. One of the speakers was from the University of Texas M.D. Anderson Cancer Center. I found her after the event and explained my situation, and she gave me names of two doctors who were doing research that might be applicable. She said she would find their telephone numbers and call me. It was something. I felt a glimmer of energy and hope.

When I went home, I listened to the message from Jules saying that the tumor changes had been a matter of magnification, that there was no growth and that the small tumor had calcified and died. I thought to myself that maybe now my physical pain and numbness would go away. It didn't.

At our next appointment, Andy had developed mouth sores from the chemo and his counts were very low again. His only concern was the senior prom, and I was in that rotten, voice-of-reason place. I wasn't sure he would be able to go. When we talked about it with Jules, he said, "If you won't let him go, I'll drive him myself." I wasn't sure how to take that. It was a relief, but I still didn't think it was a good idea. Everything was emotionally compromised. It makes you tense all over. It makes your head hurt, along with all the muscles that hold it up.

The Saturday of the prom, Annie was at our house early to take pictures of Andy and Alex as they dressed. When they were finally ready to leave, they were excited and beautiful. Andy hadn't been able to decide whether or not he wanted to wear a specially adapted baseball cap, or the top hat Cheryl had borrowed from the local college theater department. The top hat, with my father's silver cane, looked very dapper.

He took both and drove away with Alex in his shiny '50 Chevy truck for a dream evening. They headed down the bay to see Alex's parents and have portraits shot at a local artist's studio in the afternoon. They went to dinner before meeting their friends at the prom. The night was special, and they were crowned king and queen of the prom.

The final part of the evening was spent with friends at a party, and they came back to our house early in the morning to get some sleep. No staying out all night this time. Andy was tired, and the following day was Courageous Kids Day at Marriott's Great America. It was sponsored by the American Cancer Society and intended to honor children who were fighting cancer. Andy and Alex wanted to be there.

I was still hurting and numb, so I started going to physical therapy. The doctor gave me his best advice on stress reduction. The problem was, of course, that the logical premises of the

Photo by Annie Wells. ©*The Press Democrat,* Santa Rosa, CA.

Andy and Alex on his '50 Chevy pickup before their senior prom, on May 12, 1990.

stress reduction advice had little to do with the prevailing conditions on a runaway train.

I told him, yes, I'd try to control my panic. After all, what could be less productive than panic on a runaway train?

What could be less productive than serenity on a runaway train for that matter?

Graduation was approaching, and one more round of chemo was needed. We needed to keep it on track, but graduation was too important to Andy for him to miss it. If it was an option at all, he would be there.

On top of everything else, a speaking trip was scheduled right after graduation. He was going to Washington, D.C., to a National Candlelighters Foundation convention, a group for parents of children with cancer. The speech would be aimed at how health insurance companies treat children with cancer, and how their approach might be changed.

You try to hold conflicting information in your head, but you need compartments. In one compartment, my son has just been voted king of the prom, is graduating from high school and will be speaking, at age eighteen, to a large and serious audience. In the other, dark cartoons of blood counts, scans and phantom tumors hold their own demented prom.

With our heads so simultaneously overarranged and cluttered, everything had to be fitted in carefully. So it was decided that he would be admitted for his next round of chemo even though his counts were a bit low. The chemo would be given at a slightly lower dose in order to keep everything under control. At the hospital, Ron, one of the oncology nurses who had graduated with me, came bounding into Andy's room.

"I have good news," he said, and handed me the report. Andy's tumor had shrunk a half of a centimeter. There were no others found. As Andy woke up, I asked him if he understood what I was saying. He nodded as he drifted quietly back to sleep. He wouldn't remember, but it will be good news all over again when he wakes up.

The next day, a woman who worked for our health insurance company came by to bring flowers. I had spoken to her numerous times while trying to work out problems with our coverage, and she had always been supportive. She'd gone out of her way to make things work out well. It was nice to be able to put a face with the voice.

She said we had complete staff support and that they'd laugh or cry as the situation changed. She said she could tell us that the employees were 100 percent behind Andy.

When we arrived home, Andy was drugged and tired, but

determined to go back to school as soon as possible. He was hyped up from the drugs. He'd prowl around the house at night, then shuffle around the following day with his eyes at half-mast. His color was sallow, but as soon as he felt better, he returned to school.

Over the following weekend, he developed a temperature. Alex noticed it and told me. Back to the hospital, and Andy was quiet and withdrawn. He was only in for a few days, but his nervousness that it would drag on and he'd miss the last week of school and graduation, colored every minute of the stay.

We had made plans for a graduation party, but we weren't sure we'd be able to go through with it. As it turned out, everything was fine—better than fine.

Before he dressed for graduation, he and Cheryl had to finish up his bald head. He had wanted to paint it for graduation, so they gathered lipstick, eyeliner and a mirror and went to work. "C–YA," his head read. Cheryl painted it across the back of his head in true Tomales colors, red and black.

Alex and Andy headed off early to have pictures taken and distribute the Hawaiian leis we'd made for all his friends to wear. The rest of us picked up the food in town. Beer and soda were put on ice, and the tables were set. We didn't know how many people were going to show up. We had just sent out invitations to everyone who had been special to Andy. When everything was ready, we all went out to watch graduation.

We'd thought so many times that Andy would never make it to graduation, and the night was filled with a sense of his tenacious strength. The gymnasium filled up quickly. People gave us hugs. When I looked around, so many friends were there I couldn't believe it. There were even doctors, nurses and staff from both Jules's office and the hospital. Andy was grinning with embarrassment as he walked down the aisle with Fred to take their seats. As the other graduates filed in, our view of him was cut off, but when the national anthem was played and the boys took off their hats, Andy's tall bald head was a beacon for us. When the speeches were over and the diplomas were to be given out, Andy's was the first name called.

He stood and walked to the front of the gym and across the podium, a huge smile on his face. We started to clap, Cheryl yelling, "Yea, Andy," as the applause grew louder. Andy's grin broadened, and his classmates began to clap along. A nurse from the hospital who was alongside us stood, and then people all over the gym stood.

He received an extended standing ovation. We were all in tears—Simon, too. Annie caught that moment in a marvelous, tender picture of him. It was a wonderful night.

Fred and Andy were last to leave the stage. Their arms were around each other's shoulders as they made their way up the aisle. Andy's shiny head bobbed its cryptic "C–YA" message. It was all a great success. More than a hundred people crowded into our old farmhouse to celebrate. The rooms were filled, and people were spilling out onto the porch and into the yard.

Gary, our doctor, gave Andy binoculars and wrote a note to say that he was giving them because they brought clarity, much as Andy had brought clarity to Gary and the lives of everyone who knew him.

Andy was so happy, so touched, realizing that someone he respected thought so highly of him. Didn't he know?

I bring all these little things with me out to the cliffs every year and mix them with the big things and the bits of paper and roses swirling down in the wild air.

Oh, Andy, didn't you know?

Photo by Annie Wells. ©*The Press Democrat,* Santa Rosa, CA.

Emotion overwhelms Cheryl and Simon as Andy receives his high school diploma, June 14, 1990.

Photo by Annie Wells. ©*The Press Democrat,* Santa Rosa, CA.

Andy did not want to waste the space, so he left his graduation with this message as he walked out with Fred.

25

OPTIMISM

*T*he ocean will always be there. So will Andy, and so will I, and so will the particulars of that year and that world and that landscape and those people, those faces. Everything arranged vertically, layers and layers of time. You can't live in the past, not emotionally, but we all live in the past anyway. It's all around. It's my flowers drifting endlessly down to the water, endlessly wet and cold. It's the way things are. We're surrounded, and nothing dies. Who would have it any other way?

Our lives didn't change once school was out. Andy wouldn't

be able to make the move away from his family, not the way the others were. Alex was making plans. All his friends were making plans. He was an outsider. Disease will do that in a lot of ways.

The County All-Star Football Team was the culmination of high school careers for the Marin and Sonoma players. They all met in a last challenge, all the best players from each county. Andy didn't consider it an option. He'd missed so much football that no one had much of a chance to see him play. He was curious to see who the honor would go to, if anyone from Tomales would make it. One of the coaches called to ask if he could nominate him. The coach knew Andy couldn't play, but wanted to nominate him anyway. Would Andy have a problem with that, was all he wanted to know.

As it turned out, he and Fred would be the only representatives from Tomales High School. Andy loved being part of the team, and as soon as he left the doctor's office or the hospital, he'd head for practice.

He'd walk around among the team, encouraging. He tried to belong in the only way he could. He found that his opinion mattered. As the game approached, it looked like his chemo would make him miss it, as well as his speaking engagement in Washington. So he wrote his speech and gave a copy to another teen to read if he was unable to travel. He was willing to give up the speech if he had to. His feelings about the game were another matter.

At his next appointment with Jules, everything seemed to be orderly until Jules left the room to fetch the chest X-ray report. He came back white-faced. (Back and forth and back and forth. There's no place to stand still, and we slide endlessly on a lake of frozen possibilities.)

The tumor had increased two centimeters. Everything changed

again, and Andy sat there with the pale face of an unwilling saint as more plans were made for tests and surgery. There were scans of his chest, abdomen and pelvis, an MRI of his brain and a bone scan. Jules had to check it all out before scheduling surgery for the tumor.

I called Gary at his office. I wanted him to know that things had turned worse and wanted to know if I could see him. His secretary said she would spearhead the necessary paperwork for the insurance, so there wouldn't be a problem.

Gary spent some time with me. It was a horrifyingly intense dialogue, and when I left I didn't feel better, but just supported a bit. "Suspended" might be a better word.

At least there was nothing new in Andy's brain. What a terrible thing to have to say. Can you hear that, that hideous tone you have to become accustomed to? "Nothing new in his brain." I remember Andy's weak smile.

Simon was grief-stricken. Alex, too. Everyone. Andy would have surgery to remove the tumor as soon as possible—not only remove the tumor, but then to use the tissue to make a serum to combat the tumor.

The other kids were away waterskiing, so we had a ranger contact them. They called back to say they were packing up and heading home.

At the hospital, Jules had been trying to contact Dr. Young all morning. He was sure she wanted to see Andy and that the surgery would be done down there. Finally, he told us to just go ahead and drive down and he'd keep trying to contact her.

When we arrived and tried to contact Dr. Young, no one knew why we were there. No one knew anything about our being admitted. Finally, Dr. Young called, fuming. She didn't know why we were there; there was no appointment, no scheduled surgery.

She hadn't even talked to Jules. She said he hadn't even tried to contact her.

I told her I'd been there when he had called and that her staff had said she would call right back. What we were supposed to do? I had six months' worth of X rays, scans, MRIs and test results with us. Did she want me to leave them for her? She said, no, come on up.

She was pleased with how good Andy looked. She was very pleased at the absence of brain surgery residual. She couldn't hear any effects of the tumor in his lung. She gave us treatment options and explained the serum option and bone marrow transplants.

The serum was experimental. They'd take the tumor, try to grow cells from it and then see what would kill it. Whatever worked, they'd inject. The cells would theoretically find all of Andy's cancer cells and kill them. It could take three or six or even twelve months to accomplish.

The bone marrow program she described was autologous, but also risky. It sounded like jumping off a cliff and on the way down checking to see if anything was in the parachute pack. He would either live, be cured or die during the transplant process.

She needed more time. Andy had to eat as much as he could to gain strength for the surgeries and treatments that lay ahead. At the last moment, she checked his teeth. He needed to have his wisdom teeth pulled as soon as possible while his white counts were up. If Andy were to go into the experimental bone marrow program, the teeth could pose serious problems. An echo of his heart was the last requirement. Then we were out the door.

The echo showed the heart looking great. The stunning news was that the lung tumor was filled with fluid, which meant that it was most likely dying from the inside. The increase in size was probably just a matter of the increased volume of the fluid. I called Dr. Young and she yelled, "Great!" She said not to have Andy's teeth pulled because it would be better to start the chemo right away. She said to prehydrate Andy at home.

Jules called. "Great," he said. "How do you like that tumor?" His voice was thrilled as he asked if we could go to the hospital for chemo that evening.

"Sure," I said.

"We might still need the bone marrow transplant, but for now, let's see what happens."

I called everywhere to find Andy. Finally, he called back. He was with the football team at practice. I told him to wait there and I'd pick him up.

The whole team walked with Andy, giving him a cheer as he sat in the car.

The chemotherapy went well. There was talk of a bone marrow transplant, but Jules still wasn't sure. I asked if it would be covered by our insurance. Jules said they'd try to avoid paying, but we'd tackle that when the time came.

I told Jules that if the local insurance company wouldn't pay for it, then not to limit his search to local programs. He said he'd look everywhere. When we left the hospital, Jules gave Andy his tentative approval to travel to Washington, D.C.

The main problem Jules saw was the recirculated air in the plane. If Andy's counts were low, he could contract any number of infections by flying. We made an appointment for later in the week to check his counts and start antibiotics if necessary.

While we waited for the appointment, Andy went to football practice and rested. I called Dr. Young. She gave me the names and numbers of pedi-oncologists at the D.C. Children's Hospital. They could call her if they needed to. "Go and have a good time," she said.

The trip wasn't possible. The appointment showed his counts falling, and the choice was taken away from us. His speech would be read by someone else, and we would hear about it when they returned home.

But he wasn't going to miss the football game, no matter what. (Does that sound strange? Well, some pieces of emotion you have to honor. There's an attitude that needs to be sustained, and if it occasionally means taking a chance, so be it.)

Making practice the last two days before the game gave Andy a boost. They chose him captain of the team. The day of the game, as the sun was beginning to set, the Sonoma All-Stars ran out on the field, Andy in front in his number-32 jersey. There was no sign of a limp, nothing that said cancer, until he took off his cap for the national anthem. When the guys started warm-ups, Andy was in the middle cheering them on. When it was time for the coin toss, he was the team's representative.

When the story of the game ran in the newspaper, Andy was described as "the young man who displayed the most courage, the most strength and didn't make a game-saving tackle or run one hundred yards."

Fred was quoted as saying, "Every time I'm out there and I'm starting to feel tired, I just think of Andy and how much he would love to be playing." It was a sweet story, with a picture of Andy in line listening to the national anthem.

The excitement of the game was a great thing for him, but soon afterwards the neutropenia hit. It was really good that we had canceled the trip to Washington. He developed an infection in his jaw around his wisdom tooth and was admitted to the hospital for treatment. When it was over, Jules said that Andy definitely needed to have his teeth out. If he could get that sick from regular chemo, he certainly would have a problem during a transplant. Andy had his wisdom teeth pulled without any problem.

The talk of transplant became more frequent. I asked Andy how he felt about the possibility. He said he was excited and would talk to his friend who'd had one, once she returned home from D.C. The other topic was whether removing the tumor was going to be necessary.

Jules felt it would be good to leave the tumor in for a gauge during and after the transplant. Andy wanted it out. The thought of another thoracotomy didn't bother Andy, he just wanted it out. After a lengthy discussion, Jules convinced Andy that one way to find out what was going on without surgery would be to do a needle-aspiration biopsy of the tumor. It would be easy, and there wouldn't be the risk associated with surgery. If the cells were dead, we had nothing to worry about.

The biopsy was set up so we could have the results before the next day's scheduled chemotherapy. The news was that the cells were identical to all of Andy's other tumors, and that they weren't all dead. Maybe, just maybe, the wall was scar tissue that the chemo had a difficult time penetrating. That afternoon, Andy was admitted for one more round. His attitude was down. He had a cold, and his disappointment that the tumor wasn't dead was intense.

Jules talked to an oncologist at the Dana-Farber Cancer Institute in Boston, and he was told they might accept Andy for the transplant. Someone would be calling in the morning to give him the specifics. The news was great. There might be something we could do other than chemotherapy. Andy was excited.

I shifted into high gear that week. I was amazed I still had a high gear. I took out all the research Maureen and I had pulled off the computers and reread it.

We'd put on white medical coats and bluff our way into the UC Med Center Library to sit at adjacent computers and work. We searched over twelve hundred articles in two days. When we were through, we copied fourteen articles that could be useful. We searched out new treatment programs. Bone marrow transplant looked the most positive. But if we were to go ahead with something experimental, I had to know what the odds were.

It would be up to me to explain the pros and cons to Andy. Chemotherapy typically loses its effectiveness after a year to two of treatment. If we went ahead with a transplant, it was necessary to do it while Andy was still responsive to the chemo. We had already been at this for a year.

The more I read, the more the field narrowed. Interleukin-2 and bone marrow transplantation were the only programs that had shown any success at all. What success there was wasn't much, but it looked like the right direction nevertheless.

Jules told us that the doctor in Boston thought Andy sounded like a good candidate, and that we needed to go for a consultation. I made travel arrangements for a trip to Boston in three weeks. By that time, Andy would be coming out of his neutropenia and we wouldn't have to worry about the air travel.

Jules fielded the calls between the doctors and the hospitals, getting all the latest reports and MRIs in one place so we could take them with us. I called our health insurance company and talked to the woman who had brought us the flowers, telling her what we hoped. I asked her to please push for an authorization to pay for the consultation. She said she would do all that she could, but the decision wouldn't be hers.

I called C.C.S. and explained the situation to them. The nurse told me that they would need a written report with reasons that we had to go to Boston. She also said that C.C.S. usually approved bone marrow transplants for kids who were in good shape, not at the end of their ropes.

In the week that followed, Andy talked to everyone and finally came to the conclusion that a bone marrow transplant was his only hope. He might be doing well with the chemo, but that would end soon. If he didn't think ahead, he was going to run out of options. His only fear was that if the cancer came back after the transplant, there were no other treatment options.

Dr. Young said Dana-Farber was the mecca of hematology/oncology. She felt confident that Jules would get all the arrangements in order. Her only addition was to have Andy's blood checked for CMV (cytomegalo virus) before we left. That way there would be no mistakes if he was negative, which indeed he turned out to be. Being CMV-negative meant that he could not have blood from someone exposed to the virus. This limits blood products capable of being drawn on since the majority of the American public is CMV-positive.

At one week before our consultation, we still hadn't heard anything from the insurance company. Jules said he would double-check to see what was going on. He told us that no matter what, we were going. Once we arrived there, if the doctors said "Stay," we were to stay. He said not to worry about the money, to just do it. He didn't really have to say that about the money. There wasn't any way we would worry about that. He also told Andy to work on his tan and wear his letterman jacket.

I called the health insurer and told our friend there that nothing had come through yet. They were stalling again. Finally, the day before we were to leave, the consultation was approved, but just the consultation—no tests, no surgeries, no transplant.

But at least we could work from there.

26

HARBINGER OF HOPE

*T*he day finally came, and Simon, Andy and I were off for the Dana-Farber Cancer Institute loaded down with an art portfolio filled with X rays, scans and reports. I was so afraid that they would be lost that I refused to send them with our baggage. When the stewardess asked me why I wouldn't store them, I told her they were my son's life and that they weren't leaving my sight. If I had to, I would have stood holding them all the way.

We walked down the hill to the Dana-Farber Cancer Institute, passing Beth Israel, Brigham and Women's and Children's Hospitals on our way. We were in the heart of Harvard's medical community. The trees were lovely, and the walk through the Brookline neighborhood was comforting.

Once the details surrounding payment for the consultation were settled, we were led to our appointment. There were a lot of patients around, but the place seemed calm and people smiled as they passed. The feeling I had was one of peace. No frantic hustle and bustle, just people on their way.

After Andy's examination, we all went to the consultation room where the doctor and his associate were ready to give us the hard facts. I turned on my tape recorder and we began.

The first point the doctor made was how surprised he was that Andy looked so well. When he'd read Andy's history, he'd been sure Andy would never be able to withstand the treatment, and he'd almost called to cancel the consultation. Now he was glad he hadn't. Then came the real discussion.

The program was experimental. The insurance company had already sent a letter saying they wouldn't pay for the bone marrow transplant. Though the program had had some success, the odds weren't good. The successes, as a matter of fact, hadn't always led to a cure. More often, they'd ended in a regression. Success at this level was qualified as any positive reversal of disease, not a cure.

He explained the whole eight-week process beginning with the tests that led up to acceptance in the program. He went through all the hazards. By the time we had listened to all his information, we were stupefied. The bottom line was that this was still an experimental program.

He wanted most of all to make sure that Andy still wanted to be a part of the program. So what were the inducements? Out of all the patients treated so far, only one had gone on to a long-term remission, and there still wasn't a certainty of cure. "Was it better to give Andy a good quality of life for as long as we could, or should he enter a program that hadn't yet provided much success?" was how he put it. Sarcomas and melanomas can come back after years and years—even twenty years.

After the first bone marrow transplant, there wouldn't be another. At that time, they hadn't yet figured out how to be able to do more than one per patient. If they had been able to, the chance of cure would have increased.

The cost of the transplant would be between $55,000 and $110,000, depending on what problems Andy might have. The program would involve both Dana-Farber and Beth Israel. They wouldn't know which hospital until the time came and a bed was available. His marrow donation would be at Beth Israel for sure. The doctor said he didn't want us selling our home to finance Andy's treatment. He said we might end up with no cure and no place to live. Andy paled.

They'd had only ten sarcomas in the program so far, but 70 percent had shown a 50 percent or more decrease in the size of the tumor. All in all, he felt it was worth doing since we'd be treating any micrometastases at the same time. Perhaps what we needed right now was the knockout punch. The transplant might provide it.

We told him we weren't shocked by the cost. It seemed cheap, in fact. In California the cost had climbed to over $200,000. We would find the money. Andy asked if he could take the tumor out. The doctor said that as long as we're making a commitment to high-dose chemotherapy, we should wait. There was always a chance that the tumor would disappear completely. Andy could always have it taken out later.

Andy would come to Boston, meet with all the experts for tests, see a social worker and a dentist, and get set at the blood bank. Once this last line of hurdles was crossed, we could begin. He'd go in for the bone marrow harvest at Beth Israel, stay over one night and then come home. He'd be stiff and sore for about a day.

He could stay home (we'd need an apartment) for the first week, and receive daily shots to increase his stem-cell production. Once the stem cells were harvested, he'd go into the hospital for four days of high-dose chemotherapy. All his organ systems would be maintained and treated as needed.

Andy would have his stem cells reinfused in the hospital to help increase the bone marrow production. At about nineteen days his body should start to regrow marrow. During this time, things would be rough. The first four days he'd be in a daze, but after that he would be awake. The days till nineteen or twenty would be the hardest. He'd need antibiotics and blood.

The average stay in the hospital was twenty-four days. During that time, Andy would be in strict reverse solation. No fresh fruit, fresh vegetables or fresh flowers. Everyone touching him would wear gloves.

Once he was able to go back to California he should be out of the woods, and there wouldn't be any problem living on the ranch.

You listen to enough information like this and a sense of unreality begins to take hold. They could be Tinker-toy specialists, Erector-set wizards. "Then we'll do this and then we'll do that and maybe this will happen or maybe not." Your life becomes a matter of theory. Your son sits in the middle of it, dying.

The doctor said other programs might help, and he didn't want Andy to jump into this without thinking about the alternatives. (Oh good, alternatives.) There was the Tumor Necrosis Factor or the IL-2, either of which might be effective without the bone marrow suppression factor.

As we were leaving the doctor said to Andy, "If you don't think this is something to do, then it isn't for you. You don't want to put yourself through a regime that may not work. You'll come out feeling lousy, and it will take a while to build up your strength. Go home and think about it."

You understand there's no coldness here. We're all pros now. We talk matter-of-factly, no matter what's going on inside. He wanted to keep all the scans and MRIs to go over, then he'd mail them back.

Overloaded with information, we headed back to our hotel. I couldn't remember a thing that had been said, and I held on to my tape recorder tightly. Andy was very quiet.

Back home, our first mission was to see Jules. We told him how it had gone. Jules seemed optimistic, too, especially after talking to Dana-Farber. On the other hand, he was very angry that our insurer had sent a letter denying any services before our visit to Dana-Farber. They had prejudiced the doctors against accepting Andy before they even had a chance to examine him.

Jules gave me a copy of their letter. It said they wouldn't pay for any new form of treatment for Andy. They sent it before the fact to try and have him turned down so we wouldn't have any reason to fight the decision. What kind of people are they? Do they sit down in a boardroom and say, "Look, the kid is going to cost us money if he lives. Cut him off." Well, yes they do. Whether or not those are the words they use (probably not, we're dealing with masters of euphemism), that's the way the decisions are made.

I was in a deep rage. The probable reason it had taken so long to approve the consultation was that the insurance company needed the time to plan out their moves before we were seen.

I asked Jules if he thought there was any chance the insurance company might change their mind after the consultation. He said he doubted it, but we'd proceed positively anyway and see what happened. If they denied, we'd go public with their denial. Jules was sure the community would support us. I told him we already had about forty thousand dollars saved from the donations to Andy's nonprofit account with Parents of Kids With Cancer. We would need about sixty-six thousand dollars more.

I seemed to remember a dim past when the idea of having insurance was simply that the company agreed to provide for certain eventualities, if you continued to pay the premium. Were they hurting for money? Was the insurance industry on the rocks? Or were we dealing with a time in which lives had indeed become beans to be counted on a desktop?

We planned our strategy for application to the insurance company. Our request would center around two facts. First, Andy's drugs were standard for his disease. Even though the dose would be five times higher than normal, the treatment drugs couldn't be considered experimental. Second, the cost was cheap.

The cost of the treatment was less than ten standard chemotherapy treatments. It balanced out, and the cost of the bone marrow transplant would be more effective against the cost of Andy's long-term care. The final point we wanted to make was that no matter what the statistics said, Andy had proven exceptional in beating all the odds. He might be the one person in one hundred thousand to beat his cancer and pave the way for others. We would finish off the request for services with the news that we'd go public with the denial if it came to that. (Now why should the industry fear publicity? Strangely enough, they do. It must be the unreasonable, negative PR value of a dead child. The public is so sentimental.)

Jules said he would write the letter and send it over to the insurance company that afternoon.

When we returned home, I called my friend from Parents of Kids With Cancer and updated her. She said we would have the money no matter what. What she was planning to do was hope for the best and plan for the worst. We couldn't go to C.C.S. until we had a denial in writing. Then she would check out other possible funding sources.

The next day, I received a telephone call from our friend at the insurance company, telling us the company was going to deny Andy's treatment. I cried and so did she. I thanked her and hung up. About half an hour later, I called her back to thank her again and ask how one would go about an appeal process. She said she would find out and call back.

By that afternoon, when I had no word, I called the woman in charge of Andy's case, and she told me that she was typing up the letter of denial at that moment. She explained the appeal process. I asked if there were any oncologists on the appeal board. She said there weren't, and that we might want to bring Jules to the hearing.

(A decision is to be made about a child's treatment for cancer, and there's no oncologist on the review board. Probably they couldn't find one venal or brutal enough.)

I read her my letter. Our conversation ended with her assurance that the denial letter would be in my hands by the end of the week. It didn't arrive over the weekend.

We went to the hospital for chemo. Andy was very positive,

telling the nurse that he was going to go to Boston for a bone marrow transplant.

As soon as he was settled in and receiving his chemo, I called to find out where the letter was. No one knew, but I should have it soon. The following day was the first anniversary of Andy's heart surgery. Andy was too zonked out from his chemo to know, but the family talked for a long time about how far we'd come since that day.

We knew that we were in for a fight on at least two fronts. One was his cure and the other was the insurance company. We prepared. We wouldn't only be fighting for a beloved child, but for a boy who was willing to fight for other children who were too ill to fight for themselves. He was fighting for everyone who would have to fight their health insurance carriers for the treatment necessary to stay alive.

We talked about the strategy we'd use after the denial came. Simon was uncomfortable with going public, but there was no other way. We had no money in the bank. The money we had to fight with came from others. (Thanks again.)

The next day I called the insurance company again to ask about the letter. I told the woman that we needed it to proceed with C.C.S. and other possible funding. This time she said she was meeting with the medical director and someone else to review it, but that surely I would have it that day. She said she would call later with a status report.

By late afternoon, when I hadn't heard anything, I called again. The same woman answered, saying the letter was on the medical director's desk. She said she'd walk over, check and call me back. She didn't. (Some kinds of rudeness verge on brutality. You know how many people had to make monthly insurance payments for years in order to create the insurance monster? The same number, aroused, could bring the monster to its knees.)

That evening I talked with the head of Parents of Kids With Cancer. She would write a letter to our insurance company stating that it was unbelievable that they had no oncologists on their review board. She had already talked about it with several state agencies and suggested I call Barbara Boxer.

Next morning I made the call, and Senator Boxer's office said they'd get the information to her. They were sure she would act quickly. I also called Dr. Young, who also said she would write and call. She told me the insurance company was playing with Andy's life and putting it in jeopardy. They needed to know that we knew and that we weren't going to be quiet about it.

Later that morning, I called the insurance company. The woman was furious. She said she didn't appreciate my calls and that the insurance company had thirty days to issue a denial. I told her they had already issued the denial verbally. I wanted it in writing. She said she had tried to talk to the medical director that morning, but he was in a meeting, and that I needed to understand that she was doing all that she could for me. She would call me later, she said.

By early afternoon, I hadn't heard. I called Jules, who hadn't heard anything either. He would call the medical director himself and see what was going on.

When Jules came in the next morning, he said the insurance company would be sending another denial letter. I told him I'd had enough and that I was going to call the newspaper and start that process. After he left, I wondered if calling a lawyer would help. My heart sank at the thought. That's what they count on—that your heart and energy and money will all sink.

27

$\mathcal{M}$ANY HANDS

I don't like being angry. I especially don't like it when I am supposed to be functioning in a clear and thoughtful manner. I don't like the way it eats into me and pulls every bit of negativity into it like a magnet. I've seen these issues debated on television and it's always the same: the industry representatives are smooth and smiling, their opponents frazzled and a little inarticulate. It's a no-win situation, going into a contest with a hired gun who's willing to say anything at all just to take up the time, just to make sure that what is said will be limited by the time available.

The condescension shines off the faces of the company shills, and it accomplishes what it's supposed to accomplish. It makes us angry and we grow inarticulate and use our time badly.

So I don't like being angry because it makes me sick inside and because, in the case of the corporate power structure, it works to their advantage.

My kids said I needed help. Isn't that nice? What else am I doing wrong?

They don't think I'm handling things well? Things may be going out of control, but I'm the only one who has the right to say so. Help? From who? Divine intervention is what I need. I'm ready to fight, twenty-four hours a day. I am. Twenty-four hours a day, I'm in battle mode. And these slimy bastards are in the way, a battalion of them with briefcases and condescending smiles.

I scheduled my first appointment with Kathy, a therapist. I couldn't keep going without help. Kathy was someone Cheryl and Linda had met at a cancer workshop for families, while we were in Boston. The girls were sure she was just the therapist for me. They thought I'd trust her and that was the whole deal, really. They were right.

(There's enough anger washing around in me to float an armada. They're right. I seethe a lot.)

I was edgy, but it didn't take long for me to relax a little. Kathy was there to help me, nothing else. I told her my story, and we formed a union in pain. I talked about how hard it was to stay strong, how hard it was to even appear strong. And I had to, because it was expected. I was in the center, and everyone's fears washed up at my feet.

I was the only one who had read all the information and knew how bleak the future really looked. Everyone in the house wanted me to be positive with them. I had to support their fantasy structures, as well as keeping my own hope alive. I needed to support them.

Is that true? Why did they tell me I needed help? They noticed, I didn't. What don't I see? Is there anything about Andy I don't see? God help me.

She made a safe place for me. Sometimes I'd spend the whole appointment crying. I don't know how I would have made it through without her. She gave me permission to feel. It wasn't Simon's fault that I had no outlet. It wasn't that he wanted me to be solitary and crazy with fear and anger. It was just that he couldn't do anything. It wasn't in his experience to talk about his grief. He didn't know how.

I would see Kathy once or twice each week. She made it possible for me to survive, and she became my friend.

The story hit the papers the week I started therapy. Andy had a chance for a cure, and the health insurance company had denied payment. We asked the people who had helped already to help again with the money for the treatment.

The story was in four papers and was broadcast over the radio. Andy's account number was listed at a local bank and we waited. We still had a month before Andy was scheduled to leave for Boston, but I wasn't sure we had enough time.

The denial letter that we finally received was typed three days after the first article was printed in the newspaper. I immediately requested an appeal hearing. About this time, we were given our own private caseworker. I'm sure it was done to deflect some of the pressure off the woman I'd been hounding.

They told me that our caseworker was there to help us in any way she could. We now wouldn't need to call the insurance company for approval of doctor visits, admissions or tests. Our caseworker could handle everything for us. "It would all be so much easier on us," I was told.

In fact, the caseworker did help. She eliminated some of the drawn-out time needed to make decisions. She came to our home and to the hospital to oversee Andy's care. I was told that this was a service that the insurance company had just begun to help with the more difficult and time-consuming cases. I wondered why we hadn't been offered this service earlier.

Photo by Ron Bath. *Argus Courier*, Petaluma, CA.

October 1990. Andy being honored at a Petaluma High School fund-raiser, shaking hands with Matt Eldridge and Brian Flom.

Once the story hit, the donations, help and telephone calls started coming in. Fund-raisers sprang up everywhere. Tomales High School had a walk-a-thon, and during its homecoming week, raffle tickets were sold to benefit Andy. Subscriptions in the homecoming program were also sold. A local Tomales restaurant had a dinner and auction, and a Tomales art gallery donated all their October profits to Andy. The local 4-H Club sent a donation. Outside of Tomales, the cause swelled. Healdsburg filled lunch boxes all over town with the simple slogan, "Help us get Andy to Boston by November 1st." In Petaluma, Santa Rosa and Sebastapol, fund-raisers were ongoing. A Petaluma High School football game was dedicated to Andy, and a portion of each ticket was donated to his fund. He was called out onto the field during halftime as the team shook his hand, wished him well and gave him a signed game ball. A crescendo rose from the stands of "Andy, Andy, Andy." There was a drag race at the race track, a ski night with a Warren Miller film. Hamburger Heaven supported Andy for a full month. Service organizations collected money. A thirteen-year-old boy sold his winning turkey at the Harvest Fair for one thousand dollars to help Andy. He told the paper, "I had the money, why not donate it? It might save his life."

Jules headed an effort in a one-hundred-mile bike race to raise money, and a local clothing store donated the shirts the riders would wear during the race. They said "Riding for Andy" across the back. We headed out to watch the race that day, and Linda, Toni, Howard, Lisa, Cheryl, Matt, Alan and Alex all rode a thirty-mile portion. Andy and I followed in his Jeep. His shirt said "I'm Andy" on the front.

The bank kept a running tally of the money collected and the cards sent to Andy. I would go in weekly to pick up the information and began writing letters to thank each and every donor. Most of the donations were small, in five-, ten- and twenty-dollar amounts. An especially poignant letter came from a woman who sent her donation along with a three-dollar donation from her dad. He was on a limited income and had three dollars left over each month.

A local woman named Nancy came to help us then. She would come out to the house and help do whatever it was that needed doing. She'd show up early in the morning and say "Okay, what do you need now?" and head off to get it.

In less than one week, over $48,000 was raised; in two weeks, the total was $128,000. A woman sent $5,000 in memory of her son who had died fighting cancer. She sent his picture, too. Others sent money in memory of their loved ones, and to give thanks for their healthy children and in the hope that Andy would win.

An eighty-four-year-old man came out personally to give Andy the one-hundred-dollar bill he had earned thirty years earlier, baling hay for a full summer. Andy never put the bill in the bank. He kept it pinned to his bulletin board. He'd take it down, read the note and shake his head. (Have I mentioned what a remarkable boy Andy was, and how he could make me cry?) After Andy died, we called that man's teen-aged granddaughter and gave her the money and note. It meant a lot to her since he had recently died.

We knew, finally, that it didn't matter if the insurance company paid. We had the money to go to Boston anyway. I'd go first with Andy and Simon, and Cheryl would follow in time for his transplant. The other kids would come after Simon and Cheryl returned. Andy and I would fly to Boston on the first of November, see the dentist, blood bank, and social worker, and have tests done over the following two days. He'd be admitted on the sixth, have the bone marrow harvest on the seventh, and be discharged the next day.

During the subsequent week, I would give him injections of GMCSF twice each day to increase his stem cells. By the seventeenth, he would be ready for the high-dose chemotherapy, but that date depended on the lady who was in his hospital bed. As soon as she was discharged, Andy would be admitted. On November 17, Andy would start four days of chemotherapy and have three days' rest. On November 24, day zero of the program, Andy would receive his bone marrow transplant and stem cells. After that, days zero to ten would be rough, then things would begin to improve.

There would be a support group for me each week, and by day ten, Andy would need some stimulation, some contact. This was going to be the time for friends to send what they had to help—videos, tapes, messages, whatever they had.

I knew that 5 to 10 percent of the patients die during treatment.

Andy and Alex planned some time away alone before we'd have to leave. They wanted to take the Skunk Train over the coastal mountains to Fort Bragg. They wouldn't have a car once they were there, so I called Sena, the woman whose dad had sent the three dollars. I didn't know if they could travel around without a car once they were there.

I knew she would help. She said a car would be necessary and called back the next day with plans for a wonderful weekend.

The people of Fort Bragg had donated nights in bed-and-breakfasts, dinners, lunches and breakfasts. Someone had donated bicycles for them to use and a picnic to take along.

Once Thursday arrived, we would be on our way. I used the time to pack, get organized and show Cheryl what had to be done with the business, payroll and taxes while we were gone.

Andy and Alex were still in Fort Bragg when Jules called to report a problem with the last chest X ray. The tumor had increased slightly in size. What was worse was that another possible tumor had been found in the right lung. The question was, was this an old tumor that had been missed?

Jules said that in April, numerous small lesions had disappeared. This could be one of them. The large tumor's growth could have been from the biopsy. Now we had to double-check. He'd talk to Boston and call us back.

For now, we would go ahead with the plans to leave on the first. I cried through the weekend, had an emergency visit with Kathy on Monday, and was ready when Andy and Alex were due home. Everyone was worried, but still hopeful that we would be able to leave on time.

Boston called Jules to suggest postponing the transplant until things stabilized. I was devastated (and all the things that means: fearful, heartbroken, angry, helpless, ready to scream, ready to die). I tried to tell Andy in a way that wouldn't kill his hope.

Andy took the news calmly, and when Jules suggested taking out the large tumor, he agreed readily. Jules felt that with surgery and a round of new chemotherapy, Andy would be well enough to go to Boston in January.

On the morning of the surgery, Andy woke up with a headache. We figured it was just nerves and headed for the hospital anyway. Around noon, Andy was taken to the OR, and we settled down to wait.

The surgeon came out after about four hours. The tumor was actually two tumors encapsulated in scar tissue in the pleura, not in the lung itself. He had taken out a rib to enter and only had to do a wedge resection. While operating, he'd looked at the other lung and found no tumors. He felt that seeds must have spilled during the previous lung surgery and the two tumors had grown from them. The chemotherapy hadn't been able to punch through the scar tissue to reach the tumors.

Andy recovered for a few days before his new chemotherapy regime started.

Simon came in with the mail one morning to show me a letter from our insurance company saying their quality assurance committee would be meeting in six weeks. It was necessary for me to let them know within two weeks if I planned to attend, since they needed time to prepare for my appeal. It sounded like more of a scam and a snow job, but I immediately wrote them that I would be there.

Jules came by to say Andy should be able to go to Boston before January. We brought Andy home, and his pain lessened day by day. One morning, though, he tripped coming up the back steps and hurt the surgical incision. We increased his pain medication and went up to see Jules, but he could find no damage and said Andy would recover.

Jules contacted Boston, and once Andy's counts climbed back to normal, it was agreed to do a second round of chemotherapy. A CAT scan of Andy's lungs was taken. Andy asked the tech what it showed, explaining why he wanted to know. She said that as far as she could see, things looked the same. Andy left the hospital in a good mood. Jules called to say "Get out the bubbly." The results showed no tumor growth. One additional chemotherapy treatment, then Boston.

While we were waiting, Andy and I went to see a lawyer. He wanted to take a look at Andy's charts, our insurance policy and our correspondence with the company. He'd let us know if he thought there might be something he could do to help.

The appeal day for the health insurance decision finally came.

They called me several times beforehand. There were "helpful" calls to let me know that they didn't want me to be intimidated at the appeal hearing. There would be so many people there for the insurance company, they were worried about my composure, wispy little housewife that I was. I assured them that I wouldn't be intimidated. I was told to come alone, that I would be met in the lobby and led to the conference room. (*Who in God's name do these people think they are?*) I told them that since there were no oncologists on the board I would be bringing Jules with me, and if they didn't agree, I'd bring a newspaper reporter instead.

We met early in the morning for the hearing. Jules was prepared, I was prepared. I had a speech, copies of my letters from Barbara Boxer and my complete research papers. I knew the end was foregone, but there was no way I wasn't going to fight. And my fight might make it easier on someone down the road.

The room was full of consultants and lawyers. They weren't intimidating. We were asked to speak and then several proceeded to tear my position apart. They badgered, they pressured, they condemned. They belittled me. Essentially, they tried to break me down. Understand, that this is a roomful of highly paid professionals working as hard as they can to deny a boy life-prolonging cancer treatments. Understand, that this wasn't charity, that we had paid the premiums for years. Understand, I guess, that shame has become hopelessly out-of-date. There is nothing a corporate person won't do for the company. I knew that our position was futile, but they wanted to pound me down with their power and I wouldn't let that happen. We left the "meeting" on our feet. The insurance company would send its decision by mail.

The appeal was denied, and I was accused of "histrionics." I guess that's the politically correct word for describing the behavior of a mother with a son dying of cancer. What would be the words to describe their behavior: "Disingenuous?" "Cheap, stupid and vicious?"

They denied any part in delaying Andy's treatment since we had been able to raise the charitable funds to proceed. It stated over and over that the bone marrow transplant was experimental and, as such, could not be paid for. There was nothing in it I hadn't expected.

About a month later, they called me to say that because of my persistence, they had now instituted a bone marrow transplant committee to review all cases. I was told that even though I wasn't able to change the company's mind about Andy, they wanted me to know that I had been a help to others that would follow. They were protecting themselves. Treatments, including bone marrow transplants, were becoming more common.

Meanwhile, Andy's progress continued to improve and no new tumor growth occurred. I wasn't doing so well. The drunken monkeys kept me awake at night. The holiday season came, and on Christmas Eve, Andy and I drove down to the medical center with presents for each child on the oncology floor, Andy again wearing his Santa hat. Andy would go in and give a child a present and talk a few minutes. One teenage boy wasn't willing to talk. He finally told Andy that he didn't want to be there for surgery, he wanted to be home. Andy told him, "Well, look at me. Last year, I was in for two surgeries over the holidays, and now I'm doing great." I left the room while they talked.

After Christmas, I took Andy and a group of his friends skiing. He wanted to learn to snowboard. I didn't even want to ski. I just wanted to watch from the bottom and keep my eye on him.

He came down the hill on the snowboard, falling. He popped up and then fell, fell and fell again, grinning and yelling the whole day. I was exhausted watching him. I didn't know if all the falling was normal or a result of his surgery, but it didn't matter to Andy. He had fun. All the kids had fun.

(Have I mentioned what a remarkable boy he was?)

28

*H*ALCYON *D*AYS

*O*n our next visit with Jules, we were told that an admit date had been scheduled for two weeks away. Things were looking fine, and another set of scans was all we would need.

Andy hadn't missed his window of opportunity! There was room for him in the program and we had the money. Now all we had to do was organize the family.

This time, Alex thought she might be able to come to Boston during a school break. Andy was thrilled. I called the apartment complex we had reserved previously and started things going again. The tickets were ready, we were set.

A second CAT scan of Andy's lung was done in preparation for the trip. The doctors in Boston questioned a spot in the left lung. The radiologist at the hospital thought it was nothing to worry about, probably a hematoma (a blood blister), from the surgery or Andy's fall on the steps. Jules said he was inclined to agree but, "We've been here before and though it isn't easy, we need to wait." The radiologist couldn't see anything on the scan, so he called Boston to find out where he should be looking. He said he'd know by noon, so Andy and I went home to wait. He called back on time. Boston wanted the area biopsied. It would be done the following morning. The biopsy took hours. Andy was awake through it. He was given Novocaine, but said the needle still hurt. It was the same place he had hurt falling. We hoped that was a good sign. None of the other tumors had hurt at all. We went home to wait.

It was a long, hard night. The bone marrow transplant hinged on the results of the biopsy. If the area was a new tumor, it would prove that the chemo hadn't worked.

Jules called in the morning. The biopsy was positive. Andy's cancer had spread. My eyes went blank, and the phone felt like a dead thing in my hand. Jules said he'd call Boston and see what they said.

Andy was standing next to me. I watched his face redden then pale as he interpreted my responses. His eyes were defeated, and that was the worst thing. That was like being kicked in the stomach. I'd never seen those eyes before. Not through the whole thing.

I was still on the phone so I couldn't reach to touch him. The door slammed. When I finally hung up the phone and went outside, he was gone.

The radiologist called shortly after to lend his support. It was a wonderful gesture, but I couldn't think of a thing he could help with.

"Are you sure you looked at Andy's biopsy?"

He assured me it had been Andy's.

I called Dr. Young to tell her the news. At the moment of my call, she had been reading the reports that said everything was clear. She said she would talk to Jules, then call us back.

Boston called Jules to say that we might want to consider doing nothing more. Jules called us. Andy could have a good life until his symptoms increased. There was a resounding no from Jules, Dr. Young, Andy, Simon and me. We weren't going to quit.

Complete, silent terror. Things were said, but they seemed to be coming from a distance and the responses took a little too long to begin. *Shit, shit, shit.*

Andy left the house again. He and Howard worked on the truck. Andy could be as he wanted with Howard. They'd met at the fair, but had not become good friends until after Andy's brain tumor. Then Howard had started coming over to visit, and their friendship grew. He and his family meant a great deal to Andy.

There wasn't a clear direction anymore. (Had there ever been?) The doctors conferred and scheduled another round of chemo. The doctors at Dana-Farber reconsidered Andy's options. In the meantime, Dr. Young began looking at other programs. There had been recent advances in IL-2 and monoclonal antibody studies. Andy said he didn't want to switch to another program, if the bone marrow transplant was still an option. Jules told him it just didn't look good. Kathy was a great help to me, but I think in the deepest sense that it was Andy's strength that held me together.

Jules said they hated to be yanking him around, but at this

point we had to look at the options again. Dr. Young requested a full set of CAT scans, MRIs and lab tests before we came for a visit that following week. As usual, swallowing the CAT scan contrast was the biggest problem. It was decided to give Andy Compazine at home the night before the test and start the contrast then. In the morning, we were to repeat the process. The Compazine helped. It also made Andy sleepy, and that didn't hurt either. He managed to swallow the contrast without too much difficulty. It wasn't great, but it was much better than it had ever been.

Dr. Young went over each and every option. To continue with chemotherapy and watch for tumor progression or regression. To wait for Boston. To go ahead and try for the IL-2 or monoclonal programs.

She was distressed that the last tumor had been removed at the local hospital. If it had been removed at the medical center, it could have already been sent for monoclonal antibodies. If Andy were to get another tumor, he was to definitely come down to have it removed. The monoclonal antibodies could be used alone or in conjunction with the IL-2 program.

Since Andy had relapsed on the chemotherapy, he was eligible for the IL-2 program. The problem was that many of the studies were already closing. There was one starting in three or four months, but it wanted only melanoma patients.

We still didn't know what Andy's tumor really was.

Before we left, Dr. Young sent out a directive for all X rays and CAT scans to be done on the same machine. Some of the confusion may have come about due to the variances in the different machines used to comply with the directives of the health insurance company. We needed to know that every film was consistent with every other.

Andy was quiet and didn't ask many questions. He still felt his best shot was with the bone marrow transplant, but agreed to go for the IL-2 consultation. We gathered the new set of X rays, picked up the tissue samples and drove down to give them to Dr. Young. When we walked into her office, she was on the phone and motioned for us to be seated. We listened while she frostily ended an argument.

When she put down the phone, she was fuming. She'd been talking with our insurance company and with Andy's caseworker. The caseworker had been schmoozing her, telling her that while they didn't have a good working relationship with some of Andy's other doctors, they were sure they could have one with her.

(Our insurance company was trying to subvert our relationship with Andy's doctor. Charming, isn't it?)

She told us what she'd said.

"I'm a doctor, and I don't ask insurance companies for permission to treat a patient correctly. We are going for a cure, and you will be responsible for paying for it.

"We can keep Andy alive for another year with palliative care at ten thousand dollars a treatment, but we aren't going to do that, and you had better understand that we're working for Andy and that your money isn't our issue."

She said the caseworker grew silent, then finally said that the news wasn't all bad because after Andy's case, the company had formed a bone marrow transplant committee to review treatment needs.

"Not all bad." That's what she said.

We had hope again. (I can't stand this anymore.) Maybe the IL-2 program was the answer. For the present, we were to go back to the original chemo. In preparation for the next round,

Andy underwent another set of X rays and an MRI. The results of the MRI showed the brain clear. They would be forwarded to the various hospitals and doctors. The radiologist grinned and said he was sure Andy would have no recurrence.

During that five-day chemo treatment, I was visited by our health-insurance caseworker. She introduced me to someone else who was now assigned to Andy's case. They spent the morning talking about all they were trying to do for him, and the benefits that he had initiated in their group. I told them exactly what I thought, very clearly. Not with hostility, just clearly. They still had complete control over Andy's care, and I couldn't afford to alienate them. They thought I might be interested in accepting an advisory role with the company. I wasn't.

(Fail with the patient's doctor? Buy off his mother.)

They reiterated that their purpose was to make sure that what we went through wouldn't happen again. I'm sure they left feeling that they had improved the situation. But I didn't trust them. I never did. I never will.

Jules called shortly afterwards with more bad news. The CAT scan had shown tumor growth in his right lung and a questionable area in his left pleura. He asked if I would go over and pick up the reports and bring them to his office, so we could both go over them. Jules had an important observation to make. "Maybe people are missing things because they all want Andy to do well."

I left at once to collect the scans, and I swore out loud and cried all the way across town. In Jules's office, I was able to spot the right lung tumor easily. The other area was more diffuse and difficult.

We needed to wait another three weeks to see what this dose of chemo had accomplished.

Andy started looking around for a psychologist with whom he

could feel comfortable. During an office visit, Andy and Jules had a chance to talk for about an hour. He felt better after the visit and didn't tell me what they'd talked about.

He was making his own arrangements. He was moving away to his own acceptance. Where was I?

During the latest period of neutropenia, Andy developed a rash around the last surgical site. He had been hot-tubbing. Jules figured he might have picked up a staph infection. Back to the hospital.

Andy picked a psychologist and started to see him.

For Simon's birthday, we received the best news. No new tumors, and the one in the right lung had shrunk. The other hadn't grown. Simon and I cried with relief, and the birthday celebration was rowdy, crazy and full of fun. Everyone had a great time.

While arranging for the next chemo, Jules told us there was a new drug that had just been released by the FDA. Neupogen was a colony-stimulating factor that had been produced by a brand-new technology. It would make it possible to keep Andy's chemo on the optimum schedule by reducing the period of neutropenia. It would now be possible to hit his cancer cells on the prescribed days in order to do the most damage. It was something that had long been sought, and was a major breakthrough in cancer treatment.

The drawback was that the drug could act as a growth factor in myeloid malignancies. Even with the risk that Andy's cancer wasn't clearly defined as a clear-cell sarcoma, it was decided that Andy would start on Neupogen after the next chemotherapy treatment. A melanoma is classified as a myeloid tumor. It was a risk.

One night, when everyone was out to the ranch for dinner, Andy felt a lump in his abdomen. Maureen and I immediately checked it. It was a hard, round lump.

At Andy's appointment, his counts were too low to be admitted for chemo. This was exactly what the Neupogen would help prevent. While we were there, Andy showed Jules the lump and Jules ordered an immediate CAT scan.

That evening, the radiologist told us it was either a hematoma from the chest surgery or a new tumor. He suggested an excisional biopsy. I told him that I would call Jules to talk over our options. I didn't want to waste the tumor, if it was one. Its cells could be used to make serum to treat Andy's cancer.

Jules talked with Dr. Young and they decided to do the biopsy at the medical center so the tissue could be saved. The biopsy was done, and the lump was indeed a tumor. But it was necrotic. The tissue was saved for the serum, and Jules called Boston with the results.

The doctor in Boston said that the new tumor hadn't changed things. One more good CT and Andy would be admitted for the bone marrow transplant. He was still a little tender where the tumor had been removed but it didn't slow him down, and as soon as we got home, he headed off with his friends.

That evening, Andy felt well enough to go out to the movies with Matt. They came back late and went to bed. All I heard was Andy's usual, "Mom, I'm home."

When I woke in the morning, I was hearing a strange noise. As my head cleared, I thought it was Matt having a nightmare and yelling in his sleep. I tore out of bed and ran downstairs. It wasn't Matt, it was Andy.

He was lying on his right side and yelling, just noise. He didn't seem to be able to speak. He couldn't move, either, and the panic in his eyes was terrible. I rushed to his bed. He kept trying to talk but he couldn't form the words, and tears were streaming down his face.

I ran to the door and screamed for Simon before climbing on Andy's bed to talk to him to try and calm him. His left hand grabbed my arm in a powerful, terrified grip.

Simon hadn't come so I ran to the foot of the stairs and screamed for him again. I went back to Andy and called 911.

I told them I thought Andy had suffered a stroke. Paul drove up so I ran to the door and yelled to him. He and Simon got to Andy's room at the same time.

Paul called the other kids, and Alex, while Simon rushed upstairs to get dressed. When he returned and could hold Andy, I rushed upstairs to do the same. When I came back, I called Jules to tell him that we would be coming to the hospital by ambulance and to meet us.

The paramedics examined Andy, started an IV and loaded him into the ambulance. I rode in the front with the driver, while Simon and the kids followed in the car. Matt stayed to lock up the house, then went home. When we arrived at the hospital, Jules and Jennifer were already there waiting for us.

Andy's face was a study in terror as they wheeled him into the emergency room. When his condition didn't change, he was taken for an MRI. We all had accepted the fact that something had happened in his brain. We were all sitting together, each isolated. He'd either had a stroke, or a hemorrhage had caused a loss of function. He couldn't move his right side at all, or talk.

The MRI made it all very clear. There were five tiny tumors, each the circumference of a pencil lead, and one huge blood clot on the left side. The tumors were scattered all over his brain. One was in the area of the bleed and had most likely caused it. One was in the front of his brain, one in the rear and two around the site of the first brain tumor.

They were still tiny, and look what they'd already done.

29

GALLANTRY

The damage had been done in the first thirty seconds. Andy was admitted to the oncology floor and settled into his bed. He couldn't move himself at all. He was angry, helpless and unable to communicate what he needed. We tried having Andy nod yes and shake his head no, but that didn't work well. I could see his fear and his rage building as we tried unsuccessfully to communicate. We floundered.

Paul worked out flash cards: pain, Mom, Dad, move up or down, back and forth, itch, drink, hungry. We tried using the cards. None of them elicited a response until finally Andy gritted his teeth and contorted his face with the effort and said "Pee!" We took care of that and then let the elation set in. He'd spoken. He grinned at us, but that was it.

When the neurosurgeon came, he explained that the medications had probably already decreased the swelling around the bleed. He expected things to improve once all the medication took effect.

He showed us the MRI. The area where Andy's brain had been damaged was clearly evident. He pointed out the five tiny tumors, explaining that they were so small they wouldn't have shown up on any previous test. There were some serious considerations we needed to think about.

There were no guarantees that everything would go well or that anything would go well at all. It was just too soon to tell. If Andy were to decline, what was his code status? Did he want to be resuscitated? He would need to consider the possibility of living out the remainder of his life unable to walk or talk. Did he want to continue on with his chemotherapy? The bone marrow transplant was out of the question. The program wouldn't take anyone with brain problems. That hope was gone forever.

Hope is getting to be like the thinning surface on an expanding bubble of despair. Harsh thoughts and harsher words filled my head. The insurance company had stalled us past the time when the transplant would have been optimal. Glorified actuaries had taken away an opportunity.

It was very clear now that damage was going to be permanent. Some of the family stayed at the screen as he pointed out which areas controlled which senses.

I turned to go back to Andy and tell him what was going on. I wanted it to be quiet and just between us. When I walked into the room, Andy was crying. He had heard every word of what we'd been saying. Everyone came back in the room, and we did our best to give him some comfort.

When we were able to continue talking, Andy clearly said no, he didn't want to be coded if his situation deteriorated. It was easy for him to come to a clear decision. All the possibilities had been discussed before.

When things had seemed to stabilize a little, the kids drifted home. Simon stayed. He knew that if things took a turn for the worse, he might not have time to come back.

He slept on the floor that night, while I slept in the chair. Hospital rooms at night are a limbo. It's never really sleep time, it's just a nondescript layering of pale shadows with nurses passing quietly in the hall and all the small noises of a twenty-four-hour-a-day operation. Simon managed to sleep in fits and starts.

There was no change in the next twenty-four hours. Another twenty-four hours without change, and surgery would become the preferred treatment. Andy smiled at first when he was told that. When they told him the rest, he stopped.

The surgery wouldn't be removing the tumors, just the hemorrhage. Removing the tumors would cause irreparable damage and the loss of more function. Andy watched the neurosurgeon talking, his face stony. There wasn't any way to take the tumors out, and if the chemo didn't work, they'd keep growing. There weren't many options.

(We're going to reach a place where there aren't any at all. The bubble is going to break and there'll be no containment, there'll be nothing where something was. There'll be Simon and me and an empty bedroom. I know this and I don't know it. I'm probably thinking with two heads.)

This was probably the beginning of the end. My head, the

bones of my head, felt like a clamp around my brain. I was never going to escape again. What did Andy feel, clamped-down, silent, unable to move?

(What I feel is nothing. What I feel is just a portion of Andy's fear. I'm locked in a little room and over there my baby is scared beyond thought.)

The doctor left, and Simon stroked Andy's arm while I held his hand.

Removing the clot would improve some of his lost functions. He might not be able to walk again, but would probably regain speech. Andy wanted the surgery.

It was a difficult afternoon. (Compared to what? Yesterday? The day before? We're on a huge staircase, going down, the stairs behind us vanishing as we descend.)

During the next day, Andy had lots of company. Bits of speech were coming back as the Decadron worked. His vocabulary now included, "yes," "no," "pee," "itch," "no itch."

When Dr. Young called, he was able to say "yes" four times. She was thrilled with his effort. He was incredibly strong, she said, and she'd never give up on him. Surgery was scheduled for the next morning.

The surgery took five and a half hours. They hadn't been able to find the tumor that had caused the bleeding. They'd spent an hour looking for it. If it was in the clot that had gone to pathology, they'd find it in the lab.

The ICU nurse let us go in, quietly. Two by two, family members, Alex and Andy's friends were let in to give him a kiss, a touch or a smile.

Later, when I was sure Andy was safe for the night, I went back to his room on the oncology floor and slept there. Someone would come for me if I were needed. The bare walls and the passing light and the gleam of the stainless steel and the soft nurse treads and the faint bells, up and down the hall. *This is my world forever,* I thought.

In the morning Andy looked much better. His head ached, but other than that he didn't have much pain. When Fred came by, Andy managed an extraordinary effort. At first he wrote "FETER BETT, G" then changed paper and wrote, "FRED, I? FEEL BETTER," shakily, holding the pen in his left hand. In a matter of minutes he had been able to clear his confusion and express himself.

My worry was that Andy wouldn't be able to regain his speech. That I would have to take him home to die unable to communicate, adding insult to the already-intolerable situation. But he could communicate with his good hand, nodding, using his eyes and the ever-increasing pile of flash cards. One morning, while Cheryl, Howard and I were there, Andy was hungry. I was pushing the oatmeal off his tray for him to eat. He shook his head in a clear NO! I started with "Honey, it's good for you and it will be easy to swallow." He glared at me, the frustration building on his face with the effort to speak. Finally, in a powerful burst of determination, out popped "YOU EAT IT THEN!" A direct order! He spoke! We clapped, we laughed, and we hugged Andy, congratulating him on his first words. He said no more that morning, and with another round of hand signals, we finally remembered he wanted to eat. Cheryl ran downstairs and got fresh, hot scrambled eggs, which he ate with delight.

By the next day, he was able to sit up in a chair. His speech improved so dramatically that by the second day, he was talking in sentences.

Then his foot moved, then his leg. He was standing next to his "physical terrorist" when that happened. We not only had a team of "physical terrorists," we had a "speech terrorist" and an "occupational terrorist" as well.

His right arm and hand, though, weren't improving. He had to learn to use his left. The most astounding thing was the way he worked back into his writing and reading. He had to go back through all the spelling mistakes and backward letters he'd corrected in kindergarten and the primary grades. The move through reversed Bs, Ds and Fs only took an afternoon. His brain was tracking through stored information, routing it in new ways. It was absolutely amazing to watch. Within a week, his reading was back to normal. The writing was harder and took longer.

Chemotherapy was started on his fourth post-op day. During the seven days of treatment, Andy's physical condition continued to improve. He was able to bend his leg and could move from the bed to the chair and back with a walker. He did so well that the speech therapist discontinued her training, though she would occasionally stop by to talk and keep in touch. The occupational therapist taught Andy how to use implements in his daily life, and with the physical therapist, continued to improve his skills.

Then we were home again. Andy was walking and talking. He could walk across the room with a walker and a bit of help. The strain was clear when the sweat would break out on his forehead as he tried to make his body work for him. It didn't stop him, though. Nothing did. I'd only seen the defeat in his eyes that once. I never wanted to again.

Everything he did drew applause. A trip to the bathroom, hoots and hollering. A trip to the front room, "Wow, did you see that?" He was able to sleep in his water bed; it felt great. It was difficult to lift him up, but someone was always ready to help amid laughs, fumbling and Andy's urging to "Hurry up," so he could get to the bathroom. It was wonderful; it was great.

He went from walking with difficulty, to walking with a single-handed walker, and then with no assistance as the physical therapy continued at home. Within three days, he was able to walk unassisted for short distances. Occupational therapy continued at the kitchen table.

One morning he contracted his hand, then moved it up and out. It took practice and more practice to make his arm respond. The movement wasn't much, but there was a slight improvement each day. The useless arm and a continual cough were the only problems that nagged him.

Andy would cough with such intensity that it would take him a while to recover. He didn't have a cold, and in the back of my head was the terrible memory of how I'd felt when we'd taken him to the hospital, paralyzed and speechless.

I'd thought then it was the beginning of the end, sudden, out of nowhere. He'd wakened in the morning and there it was. It makes you feel unfaithful to think about stuff like that. But it doesn't go away. Threat never goes away.

We kept talking about alternative treatments. One program that seemed promising was radioactive tagging with monoclonal antibodies. We could move quickly into that program, even before the next scheduled chemo, but again we'd need permission from the insurance company just to have a consultation and evaluation. I called our caseworker.

We had a long discussion about whether the health insurance company would, should or could pay for the Neupogen, the new colony-stimulating factor we were using for Andy. I was very calm and polite. The drug was expensive and they initially denied payment, then reconsidered and reversed themselves, even though we weren't covered for drugs. The permission to seek further treatment was left hanging.

During the time of Andy's new recovery, a strain developed in his relationship with Alex. Throughout the year, there had been constant stress and strain. College was important to her. Meeting new friends and being with them was important, too. Andy couldn't participate in many of the things that mattered to her. They'd set a date and, most often, he'd be sick, hospitalized or recovering. Andy's cancer didn't lend itself to the free spirit she needed to bring to her school experience.

She tried to maintain her life as a college student and as Andy's girlfriend. She tried to be supportive and available whenever she could, but the strain took a huge toll on their relationship. Andy's birthday in January had been strained. The Gulf War created another, unexpected tension when Alex and Simon disagreed about U.S. involvement. It was painful for me to watch. I knew how much Andy loved her, and I began to wonder if Alex only came around because of Andy's illness. Maybe they would naturally have drifted apart after high school and the cancer had pulled them together in a terrible way, with a terrible responsibility for Alex.

Over the last six months, there had been serious discussions and long telephone calls, at home and at the hospital. When the time finally came, there was no avoiding it. Andy talked to me, his therapist and his brothers and sisters. He wanted to make sure he was thinking clearly.

(That's not an easy judgment to make when you're shuttled in and out of hospitals and pumped full of drugs on a regular basis.)

He had to know because he couldn't stand the pain anymore. He couldn't stand the confrontations and the horrible sense of loss. He'd lost enough already.

Andy told me they were going to talk. They did. I didn't want to be any more involved than I had to be.

They were in Andy's room, and I could hear the mumblings and crying through the wall. I went outside in the garden, in the sunlight. I couldn't leave in case Andy needed help, but I didn't want to hear.

They were in there for hours. Later in the afternoon, I was up in my room trying to ignore the whole situation when Andy called me. He said his heart felt funny.

I ran to his room. His pulse was so fast that I couldn't even count the beats. I called Jules who had us come right to his office.

Andy cried all the way to Jules's office. He'd broken up with Alex, and it was much worse than he had ever thought possible. Heart trouble now would be like a cruel parody of what he felt already.

His EKG was normal except for 166 heart beats per minute. The other blood tests were normal, too. Jules made an appointment for an echocardiogram along with a chest X ray.

(More tests and what will they find? A demon. A horde of demons? A black, thick clot of death?)

The echo showed two bright white spots in his heart. The chest X ray showed that the tumors had doubled in size.

We took the news in the kitchen.

(Where Andy came with his finger, in the morning. "Mom! Look at my finger!" Where are we now? The tumors come and go like dreams. They're phantoms, shifting and moving and getting fat on our terror.)

Jules saw the X ray and called to say the lung tumors had doubled in size. One was pushing on Andy's heart and causing the increased beats. The other tumor was constricting his left bronchus and making him cough.

(Pushing on his heart. I really can't take anymore, not any. These shifting things in my son's body. It's like they're bubble shapes slipping from one spot to another. Press on the lump by the heart and it moves like a squeezed bubble. "Look, I'm over here." This all came from his finger. How fast do they move? How do they know where to go? They're not even evil. They don't care enough to be evil.)

Jules said things weren't good. I asked about the brain tumors, and he said, "The brain tumors won't get him, this will." I cried as we talked about hemorrhages, comfort and what was best for the family. It was a terrible conversation.

It all came down to comfort. It came down to Andy being home to die. I said goodnight to Jules and felt like I had walked out into the dark.

He wanted us to see a heart specialist the next day.

Simon was standing by my side now, crying. We held each other and waited like zombies for Andy to come home with Howard and Matt. They'd gone out to get away.

When he came in with Matt and Howard, he asked if Jules had called. I told him he had, and asked if he wanted to wait to talk about it. He said, "No, Howard and Matt can hear whatever it is." I gave him the news. He got very quiet, saying "I knew," as he walked away.

He didn't come close to me, and I didn't go to hug him as he walked to his room with the boys. They stayed in there for quite a while. When they left, Andy called Alex and explained what had happened. Simon and I sat and waited, not knowing what else to do.

When Andy hung up the phone, he came out and asked for some pain pills. He said his back hurt. He was still quiet with me. I asked if he wanted me to stay with him, and he said "No," and went to bed silently.

30

*P*LUMMETING *I*LLUSIONS

I sat up that night, watching the room and the creep of the moonlight through the window. When your mind has something that has to be dealt with but it can't do it—it can't even begin—a merciful stupidity comes over you. Sit me in a corner and I'll watch paint dry.

I had to wake Andy for his occupational therapy. (I wake him all the time for painful things. That's my job. Let's get him out of restful sleep and back on the schedules and in pain.) As he ate breakfast, we talked about monoclonal antibodies and what I knew. I told him that Jules was trying to figure everything out. We just had to wait. (Let me get you out of bed so you can remember the situation. Then I'll tell you again, we have to wait.)

And then things turn again. It never stops. (If it did stop, what?)

The heart specialist begins with a second EKG, then tries to change Andy's heart rhythm with drugs and carotid massage. It doesn't work, though the beats per minute slow somewhat. The white spots in the echo, he says, are sutures from the surgery. He feels they aren't anything to worry about. He says the echo showed that the tumor pushing on Andy's heart is cystic. Cystic? Both Andy and I jump at him. Does he know that a tumor had grown in July and become cystic as it died? Could this be what was happening? He pulls out the echo and shows us the tumor. It was next to the left ventricle, and it definitely looks fluid-filled. There's only a thin wall surrounding the mass. Good news! We were out of control again. We headed home.

Jules called later. He was thrilled. He asked me if I was sure it was fluid-filled? I told him we both were. I asked if we could get a needle aspiration of the tumor to see if it was all necrotic. Jules said the procedure would be extremely difficult, but we could check into that later if we had to. He wanted to make some phone calls and have us come up in the morning. Then we could talk.

(You notice how the victories move farther and farther away from the root of the problem? The layers of effects on the body get more and more complex, and the elation that comes may be celebrating a victory on the outer edges of the disease. It doesn't matter. You take what you can get.)

Simon went to the appointment with us. Jules had talked with the radiologist and cardiologist and they felt that since this tumor was necrotic, the others probably were, too. The consensus was, we were winning this round. (How many rounds are scheduled?)

I asked Jules if we could do another MRI of the brain to check the development of those tumors. If they were gone or had stopped growing, we would know the chemo was working in his brain as well. Jules thought it was a good idea and scheduled the MRI for that evening. He said that if the news was good, we should go ahead with more chemo.

After the MRI, Howard was waiting for us and stood by as the radiologist told us Andy's tumors hadn't grown. With huge grins, the boys headed off for an evening of fun before the next morning's chemo.

1991. Three shiny orbs: Andy,
Pippin apple, and Howard in our
kitchen.

From the depths of despair, up and soaring again.

We went directly to the hospital for chemo. We were mounting a full-blown assault on Andy's tumors, so the chemo dosage would be increased.

Before Andy slept, his radiation oncologist stopped by to say that if the chemo failed, there was always isotope implantation. The tumors were close to the periphery of Andy's brain, so the placement wouldn't be too difficult. It was something to think about at a later stage.

The chemo was exceptionally difficult for Andy. With the increased dosage, came the increase in side effects. We had problems with nausea and vomiting, and with controlling Andy's fluids. When his intake exceeded his output, Lasix was added to help eliminate the excess. He was restless and uncomfortable, complaining of dizziness when he stood up. I wanted to use a condom catheter so he wouldn't need to stand so often, but Andy would have no part of it. He was up often, and so was I. Lasix made his kidneys work overtime night and day.

Groggy, tired and weak, Andy left for home smiling. No matter how crummy he felt, home was always better than the hospital. He did well for a few days. (It gets so you hate to write these phrases, these sad, shorthand, one-time prayers. "For a couple of days." We thought of forever for a couple of days.)

One morning, he asked me to take his temperature. He had a slight fever and asked me to try the oral thermometer instead of the electronic, hoping it would be lower. It wasn't. We tried Tylenol and watched with blank apprehension as the temperature climbed throughout the day.

By that afternoon, I had to call Jules. Andy was angry. He said he wished he'd never asked me. His eyes were on my back as I went to the phone. He was seething, I could feel it, as he heard the conversation take the turn he hated.

On the way back to the hospital, he cried, saying he'd taken too much chemo. He repeated the line to the admissions clerk and to the nurse who showed him to his room. He said that none of this would have happened if he had stayed at the regular dosage. The situation was unjust. There had to be an injustice somewhere.

The blood was drawn and when the tests came back, everything was out of whack from the chemo, but nothing serious had developed, yet. He was still very angry. His anger hurt, but we knew what it was. He was pissed. He didn't want to be in the hospital, and didn't care what anyone thought. His fever continued. He began to cough.

By the next day, his counts were worse. The infectious disease specialist could find no reason for the fever. There was nothing in the blood tests. His platelet count was dropping through the floor (thrombocytopenia), and we were all sent for blood tests to see who matched Andy. We weren't just looking for compatible blood, we needed to check CMV status. His CMV-negative status had become a huge hindrance. If he got CMV-positive blood, he'd get deathly ill. Simon was the only one in the family who was also CMV-negative, and his blood was compatible. We sent word out for all our relatives to come in and be checked. As his platelets dropped, the need for blood was going to be critical.

Thrombocytopenia is a decrease in number of the circulating platelets in the blood. Platelets are necessary to keep a person from bleeding. The normal platelet count is between 150,000 and 350,000. When it drops below 50,000, the bleeding risk is significant. Razors and toothbrushes are no longer used and anything that causes tissue stress is curtailed, even tight clothes.

Little dots of red, called petechiae, may appear on the skin after a blood pressure cuff or elastic band is removed. At 20,000, hospitalization is necessary and platelet transfusions are begun. The patient is cautioned to not even boost himself up in bed.

As Andy's platelets dropped and his coughing continued, things became more serious. Simon went in to donate blood so his would be available. Andy's mood continued on a downward cycle. He hated the hospital, he hated the nurses and he hated me.

(This was coming. I knew it was. I am not just the messenger with the bad news, I'm the keeper of the bad news and the one who dials the numbers for more pain and more grief.)

I began to cry. Howard came in as my replacement.

When I returned late that afternoon, Andy's mood had improved. During his occupational therapy, his nose had bled but it was easily stopped. Later that evening, his test results came back and he was anemic. Worse than that, his platelet count was 16,000. Blood and Simon's platelets were immediately given. In the morning, we'd know if they had helped.

In spite of medication, Andy continued to cough throughout the night. When he woke up, I thought we might have made it past the worst danger. I was wrong. (Always, always.)

A tiny cough turned into a nosebleed that wouldn't quit, and I held his nose as I raised the bed and called the nurse. She came running with a cold pack, but it didn't help. Nothing worked. Blood was pouring from Andy's nose and mouth. All over him. All over the bed. He was bleeding to death. Andy's life was running out and over my hands. His eyes were panicked as he watched the volume of the blood. Jules came running and tried everything that should have worked. An ear, nose and throat specialist was called. Morphine was given to ease the pain, and medication to shrink the vessels in his nose, before the doctor packed his nasal passage with gauze.

It took what seemed like hours, but the procedure finally stopped the bleeding and saved Andy's life. He was wiped out, had a headache and felt like his ears were full of water. But he wasn't bleeding.

Later that day, Andy's counts had come back to 27,000—not nearly good enough. Simon's platelets weren't helping.

Over the next few days, there were more blood transfusions and platelet transfusions. Andy was lethargic and his hip hurt. His counts hovered in the twenties.

The chest X rays came back reporting a reduction in the sizes of all the lung tumors. Everyone was elated, and when it came time for Andy's next platelet transfusion he was ready. He figured this one would do it! He visualized it working as it went in. He rubbed his eyes and said his mouth itched, so the nurse gave him Benadryl and he drifted off to sleep.

Through the remaining week, his counts rose slowly. It had taken two weeks and one day to get his platelets back to normal, and no infection had ever been found. When Jules said Andy could leave, we were out of there in a flash, all the nurses grinning down the hallways.

On the way home, Andy said that no matter what, he wouldn't take that large a dose again. When I tried to point out how well the tumors had responded, he said, "Look Mom, I almost bled to death in there. If I have to die, I don't want to do it there. I want to be home." He said he'd do chemo again, but not in that dosage. "Maybe they can give it to me over seven days instead of five, that might make a difference." I told him I didn't know, but Jules would work it out.

At home, a new physical therapist wanted Andy to do some kneeling exercises, but he couldn't. She lectured him about prioritizing her visits and making the most of what he had going for him. Andy became sullen. I became angry.

Did she have the slightest idea what strength he'd brought to bear already? If he couldn't do the exercises, there was a good reason he couldn't. I told her not to come back. She coldly asked to use the phone, called her boss and left. Before leaving she said to me, "If what you're saying is true, you better check out his hip." (She hit me with that. It was a slap.)

The next day's occupational and physical therapy sessions were done at the rehab center. Andy liked the people and they encouraged him to work hard, but stopped when he complained of pain in his hip. *What, what, what, what? What now, God?* (It widens and widens and our space gets smaller and smaller.)

We went to see Jules. Andy told him about his hip, and Jules gave him an anti-inflammatory drug to ease the pain. We went to the hospital, too, for a follow-up chest X ray. That evening the radiologist called to say the tumors had grown by 50 percent. This was the same machine, and there was no question of differing measurements. He had already talked to Jules. Another MRI of his brain and a CAT scan of his hip were ordered for the weekend.

Jules called and talked to both Andy and me, saying there were still things we could do. "Let's see what the tests show tomorrow." (This is like being permanently concussed. As soon as your head starts to clear, they hit you again in the back of the head.)

The MRI and CAT scans took hours. Andy's hip and back hurt and he couldn't lie still. The tests took twice as long as normal, with Andy needing to be pulled out and given IV pain medications. The radiologist found the trouble spot on the CAT scan. He said there was a large hematoma under Andy's hamstring. The MRI, he said, didn't look much different. No new tumors were found but, nonetheless, it was a long and horrible day, and we went home afraid and exhausted. (That could be stamped on our foreheads. "Afraid and Exhausted.")

The next morning, Andy had trouble walking. When we left in the afternoon, he needed to use a wheelchair to go out to the car. We were barely hanging on until we saw Jules the next day, going through the motions. We were terrified and very, very sad. (That's an odd combination, and not one I'd recommend to anyone.) I dropped Andy off at Howard's and went to town for groceries.

The trees go by on the side of the road and the ground goes up and down like always. In town there's the store and all the cutesy displays, and I push the basket around like always, dropping in the bright packages.

When I returned home, Simon was upstairs crying. Simon is never upstairs crying. Every certainty is slipping away. A bag full of bright boxes and Simon crying and the inside of the house where we've always been and the outside. Which will always be different now, too. Everything is different.

Jules, of course, had called when I was gone and rolling the smooth wheels of the cart through the aisles where all the other normal people were shopping. All the people outside who were All Right. Jules had wanted to tell us to do something for Andy before we came back in the morning.

I knew. I knew, he didn't have to tell me (don't).

Simon held me, crying. We had to tell Andy that all the tumors had grown. There wasn't anything else to do. It was all gone.

The spot on his hip that was causing such pain was a new huge tumor. He suspected there were more.

I didn't rant or rave. There was just a very heavy sadness that formed around my heart and stayed there, like the center around which I was organized. We were helpless now, and all the plans and the fighting and the tenacity and the hope were perfectly dead on the floor. "Tell your son he's going to die and you can't do anything about it."

Simon said, "We've got to tell him now."

I said, "Let's do it now, there's no use waiting. He'll know when he sees us. He'll know anyway."

I took a breath, grabbed Simon's hand and we walked down the stairs.

Andy was sitting in his chair watching television when we came into the room.

I knelt down on the floor next to his chair and put my arms around him.

When he turned to look at us, Simon let out a terrible sound of pain and bent to hold him.

"Oh, Andy," was all he said.

Andy watched us.

I told him, "Andy, honey, Jules called today and the tumors have all grown and the pain in your hip is from a new one."

He watched me.

He looked at Simon.

Silent tears came down his cheeks.

Then I told him the other news.

"Sweetheart, Jules says there is nothing more to do."

"Am I going to die?"

The moment is branded on my heart.

"Yes."

He grabbed my arm and held on. "There must be something! There must be *something*. I won't quit. I don't want to die." He grabbed tighter with his left hand, his right lifeless in his lap.

"Mom," he yelled it, *"I don't want to die!"*

"I don't know what to do. I know, Honey. We can't stop this thing. I know. I know."

"Then help me. Help me find something. I don't care if I can't walk, I don't care if I can't use my hand. But I don't want to die."

"The tumors, Honey. He called about the tumors. They're ahead of us. They're beating us. Jules has looked at everything already."

"I know," he said softly. Like the end of the world was in knowing. Like that's what knowing meant—defeat.

We stayed there holding each other for what seemed like hours.

We called the kids. Cheryl came first and took Andy for a drive. The others arrived soon after. When the kids went home, the real night started. When Andy went to bed, I asked if he wanted me to stay with him and he grabbed my hand and said, "Please."

I gave him a sleeping pill, then Simon helped Andy to the bath. While he was bathing, Simon and I had a few minutes to talk.

Jules had told Simon that Andy had between two and eight weeks to live. He suspected more tumors and that his cancer was so smart and so resistant that when we'd hit it with a huge dose, it had refortified itself and come on stronger. It wasn't going to let the chemo kill it.

It sounded like some third-rate science fiction movie, where a blob oozes under doors and over people.

No other programs would consider Andy. What we needed to do was give him the best, the most pain-free weeks we could.

I asked if Jules had said how much pain Andy might have. He hadn't.

When we put Andy in bed, I climbed in, too, and layed there

holding him. He said he wasn't afraid to die, "But Mom, I am really afraid I'm going to miss you guys. I don't want to be lonely, Mom."

We talked for hours. About death and spiritual beliefs, and about how much we loved each other. Long after midnight, I said to Andy, "This isn't what most nineteen-year-olds think about when they think of a girl in their beds."

"It's not so bad," he said as he drifted off to sleep.

31

A Time for Letting Go

*S*imon had to keep going. It was late spring and the crops were almost ready to harvest. How did he do it? How did we do it? We all go around in our day-to-day lives passing judgments, complaining and generally taking the world of small, passing irritations very seriously indeed. It's not good, but there doesn't seem to be any way out of it—unless real pain of the world rises up, a lot more than irritation and just a little less than madness.

I try to remember now that most of what passes for difficulty is nothing at all. When your child is dying, nothing else gets in. Nothing else matters.

But with the dairy, whether it mattered or not, things had to be done. (The mind is incredible. The mind can hold three or four different views of the universe and act on them all.) The cows had to be milked and bedded down. They had to be watched to see when breeding was necessary. When they calved, the calves needed to be cared for. (Children need to be cared for.) To produce either calves or milk, every animal had to be fed. In order to do that, the crops needed to be harvested.

Harvesting is a big production on our place. Equipment breaks and needs to be repaired, as quickly as possible, to keep everything running. Extra men are hired, and I feed them at noon. This act necessitates long hours of cooking and planning. Since I'm the "gofer," I make a lot of runs to town. I didn't think I could do it. (There isn't anything I can't do. Not anymore.)

The weather warmed, moving the time for harvest closer. Simon said, "Don't worry. Somehow, we'll get it done."

Then our neighbors called, in the midst of harvest season. George and Neil and their sons were finishing their crops and would come over and do ours, too. (Was I ever irritated at other people, at little things?)

Their chopper arrived the next day in the midst of the dust and silage trucks. Friends put in days of hard, hot, dusty labor to finish our crop, then headed off to work for people who would pay them to harvest. I didn't have to cook, I didn't run for parts.

Our crops were in. The silage pits were covered with plastic tarps to seal them. No bill ever arrived.

That's how the neighbors were. They came, did the work and said, "Don't worry about it," when they left.

In my spare time, I worked in my garden planting flowers. I planted roses, Andy's favorite, and forget-me-nots, my grandmother's. I planted furiously, then planted some more. I needed to make something live.

One morning, I made an appointment with Jules alone. I needed to talk, and I didn't want to have to worry about Andy hearing. I wanted to ask medical questions, so I'd be prepared. (I really don't want to know.)

Jules loved Andy, too, and was grieving when we met. I talked about controlling Andy's pain and making sure he wouldn't suffer. I told Jules that no matter what, I did not want Andy to die in uncontrollable pain. If controlling the pain meant shortening his life, that's how it would have to be.

We talked about medications and about keeping Andy at home. We were pretty much together as to the direction Andy's care would take. Jules's love for Andy rode home with me in the car.

The newspapers were carrying stories about Andy's lost fight. The cards, letters, phone calls and visitors were increasing. Our therapy sessions were now held at home. Andy's therapist and mine sometimes met at our house. Once we held our meeting together, and Simon, Cheryl and Linda joined us. We heard Simon's feelings—a remarkably graceful surprise. He opened up the closed-off emotions and explored his heart with us.

A huge number of things happened in a few short weeks. People Andy wanted to say good-bye to were called. His soccer coaches came. Andy wanted to tell them how important they'd been, and he did. He said he'd learned from them never to give up and never to leave the field feeling that you gave the game away.

Most of his nurses gathered one afternoon so Andy could tell them how much their care had meant to him. His physical and occupational therapists came for an evening. Janie, the phlebotomist from Jules's office, came with her husband. Janie was someone Andy had instantly fallen in love with on his first visit. He would look for her every time we went to the office.

An old friend from soccer days drove up one rainy afternoon on his motorcycle. He'd traveled six hundred miles to tell Andy good-bye.

There were school friends every day. Some came by at night to play games and just sit around with him. One friend came by only to have Andy read him the riot act. He was failing classes and goofing around, and Andy lectured him about not wasting his life. I was a bit shocked. Andy said, "Well, someone needed to tell him, and he isn't going to get mad at me. He's a great guy. I'd give anything to be in his place."

Andy had no trouble giving advice. In his last year of high school, he had sought out a girl who was contemplating suicide and spent hours talking to her. She sent a letter thanking Andy for taking time with someone who had been an outsider. She said his effort had changed her life.

People from the hospital wrote. People who were fighting cancer, people who had fought cancer or relatives of people who had died of cancer wrote. People wrote to thank Andy for going through his battle so publicly, and for giving them a broader view to life. Old people wrote, young people wrote. Many sent poems, tokens of love to help ease our pain.

There were disadvantages to the publicity, too. People who didn't know us would call to let Andy know there was still a way to cure him, if he only believed. If he'd do what they said, he'd be cured. If he saw some guru, or had the correct attitude, he'd be saved. I tried to take these messages in the spirit they were given. (In some way the people who send these messages just don't know. They've become abstract in their heads and their emotional violence isn't clear to them.) I explained that we appreciated the efforts, but that our belief system was different. Some actually drove to our home. We'd find them waiting for us.

An older couple waited in our yard for hours one afternoon. When Simon told them we wouldn't be home until late, they said that it was okay, they'd wait. When we arrived, they met us in the driveway. The man had made something for Andy.

We asked them in to the kitchen and the man opened the paper bag he was carrying. Inside, a newspaper wrapped a carving he'd made. On one side it spelled JESUS, on the other, SMILE. We thanked them. Andy kept the SMILE side facing him from the top of his television.

Some we didn't let in at all. It depended on how I felt and how they presented themselves. Nearer the end, there was a woman who came back time and time again to say good-bye. I thanked her and said I'd give Andy the message, but that wasn't good enough. She wanted to see him herself. She never understood when I told her that Andy wasn't in any condition to meet someone new.

One thing Andy did want to do before he died was go to the beach. We called Howard, Cheryl, Linda and Stefanie and loaded up the car. The lunch basket held all the unhealthy beach food we no longer ate.

At this point Andy could hardly walk, so we chose our spot carefully and parked as close to the sand as possible. We unloaded baskets, beach blankets and toys, and set up chairs. Opu was there without her leash. Cheryl and Howard, each taking a side, helped Andy walk down a slope to the sand.

Stefanie's clothes came off, and she and Opu headed for the

freezing-cold ocean. Andy watched from his chair laughing as Howard and Linda followed Stef and the dog. We ate sandwiches with sand in them, and laughed and talked. The sun came out and warmed our backs and even our hearts, for a few moments.

I was a little afraid that being at the beach and not able to go into the water would be depressing for Andy, but it wasn't. (Depressing? *What an odd thing my mind is,* I think.) He had a grand time though, and when we left it was too soon.

The next day, Andy wanted to go back. Kathy and Andy's therapists were coming that day, so I called and told them to wear beach clothes. We'd all go. When we got there, Andy was in too much pain to walk from the car. We waited, but finally he said he wanted to go home. We all ended up sitting around in the living room.

Cheryl moved back home. She told her boss that she needed a day off to help me take Andy to the doctors. When we tried to move him, it was so difficult that she knew we needed more help, so she called her boss and took an indefinite leave. She was home to stay, for as long as Andy needed her.

It was more difficult for the other kids with their spouses and children, but Paul and Brenda and their kids and Linda and Les and Stef would stay over whenever they could. Paul and Brenda had just bought their first home and were preparing to move. They stopped in midstream to be with Andy. Lisa and Howard were out of school, so they spent almost all their time with us. Lisa slept in the living room, and Howard stayed over whenever he could.

There wasn't a single night when Andy had to sleep alone. One after the other, the kids would take turns sleeping with Andy, sharing quiet times and giving him comfort. On a night when he didn't want anyone to sleep with him, Opu would be there.

I spent my days cleaning and working the garden in a fury. I dug and planted, then came in to wash walls or carpets. It didn't keep my mind quiet, but it used up energy so I could sleep at night. That and Ativan. I'd work until I dropped, either emotionally or physically, and then I'd take a pill. No dreams, no wakefulness until my eyes snapped open early the next morning ready to see and care for Andy. (This isn't a good thing. I need real sleep, but there isn't anything else I can do.)

I felt like a soldier in battle. (It's getting mechanical. The cancer does that.) I couldn't let down until Andy was ready.

Nancy became Andy's spiritual advisor and would come out and spend time talking with Andy about what was happening. She talked about healing sometimes, not meaning a cure but acceptance.

Nancy's visits began to include others of us. Simon joined in, not really in tune, but doing it because Andy asked him to. Andy's personal beliefs differed from his dad's, but Simon respected them completely. He listened and heard what was important.

Andy wanted to give Howard his great white shark's tooth as a reminder of their friendship and the bond they shared. One afternoon, feeling very comfortable with the decision, Andy gave the tooth to Howard. That night, though, it was a different story.

His hand kept feeling for the amulet around his neck, but it wasn't there. He tried to adjust for a couple of days, but couldn't. Watching him tore me apart and I wanted to call Howard and tell him to bring back the shark's tooth, but I knew it wasn't my place. One morning, Andy said, "Mom, would you call Howard and ask him if I can borrow my shark's tooth? I don't think I can make it without it."

Howard came right over and put the tooth back in its rightful place. It stayed there until Andy died.

Jules and Jennifer were going away on vacation, and Andy wanted to spend time with them before they left. He thanked Jules, telling him how much he appreciated all he had done for him. To top it off, Andy wanted to give him something. From behind his chair, Andy pulled out a brown paper bag. Inside was his prized 49ers football. Jules knew how much it meant to Andy.

Before they left, Jules gave me the number where he could be reached. He told me he would call to check on Andy, but wanted me to have the number in case I needed it.

Andy had thought about his college funds, and he wanted his money divided between his brothers and sisters. He wanted Nick, Kerri and Stefanie to each have a thousand dollars. Then he told us something else.

"Mom, I want you and Dad to use the rest of the money to help buy the ranch for John. I want to know that after you die, John will still be here." I told him we'd do that. (There isn't anything I wouldn't do.) We wanted him to know we'd always be where he could remember us, and that we wanted always to be where we could remember him in every rock, hill and tree.

He gave away his cars and trucks then. Howard got his hot rod, Paul got his '50 Chevy and we got the Jeep.

He was still able to sit in his chair, but each movement was more difficult. We needed two people now to help move him. His inability to make his body work wasn't the only problem. His pain was increasing. (No, no, no, no, no.) I'd edge up the amount and times of medication to stay on top of his pain until we needed to move on to something stronger. He became more tired. I couldn't tell if it was the medication or the brain tumors. Whatever it was, it was okay. When no one was visiting, he'd sit in his chair and watch television or nap. He would stay up late at night and then take his medications and go to bed, then sleep until late in the mornings. (I sleep too, now, but what kind of sleep is it? It's like someone has pulled my plug. I think I'll pay for this, eventually.)

I needed to ask Andy something that had been bothering me for more than a year. "I need to know something, Honey."

"What?"

"I need to know . . . I feel like I've been unfair to you."

"How?"

"You've suffered so much and it would have been easier for you if I'd let you die when you had the heart tumor. I kept you alive because I couldn't bear to have you leave me. I think I was selfish."

"Oh, Mom."

He took my hand and said, "It was worth every second; it was worth it all."

It was getting harder and harder for Andy to move, and finally we had to use the wheelchair. His hip and back constantly hurt, so morphine tablets were begun. They made him sleepy for a day or two, but they did relieve the pain. My back had given out, so Simon, Cheryl, Paul, John and Howard all pitched in to move him wherever he needed to go.

When he became more alert again, he said the lounge chair hurt his back. We tried repositioning him without success, so Cheryl and Paul decided to go buy him a better chair. The old one wasn't going to make it.

They found a new, softer chair, but it still hurt. Cheryl and Paul loaded it up and took it back. They brought lounge chairs from their house. They didn't work either. We played musical chairs all day. Paul and Cheryl finally found one that was comfortable and we searched no more.

That night, before he went to bed, he wanted a bath. He

didn't want a bed bath and he didn't want to be washed. He just wanted to soak in the tub. That turned out to be much harder than anyone expected.

Simon and Cheryl boosted him up and turned him while I pushed the wheelchair in place. While we were doing that we were removing his sweatpants so he would be able to move quickly into the tub. Draped in a big flannel sheet, he headed for the tub.

When we got to the door, the wheelchair couldn't fit through. Simon went for his tools and we took the door off. The bathroom was too small to turn the chair around in, so we had to climb over Andy to get in.

Cheryl and Simon were going to pick him up and place him in the tub while I removed the wheelchair. Wrong. There wasn't enough room. We banged, pushed, grunted and hoisted to clear the wheelchair and swing him into the tub. Simon said he'd get him. He crossed over Andy's legs and stood with one foot on each edge of the tub.

We locked the wheelchair, and Cheryl and I lifted. Simon grabbed Andy and lowered him down into the tub. Then Simon fell in with a splash. He caught himself before hurting Andy, but ended up standing in the tub. Water had splashed all over Cheryl and me, and we howled with laughter as Simon stepped over Andy, out of the tub and on to the floor. His dignity had been lost, and Andy grinned while we tried to clean up. We added warm water and let him soak.

When he was ready to get out, we had our plan made. Simon stepped around him, reached under his arms and lifted him up, setting him on the edge of the tub. We wrapped a huge towel around him, then swung his legs out over the tub and down to the floor. Why hadn't we thought of this before? Cheryl grabbed his knees, Simon his shoulders in a fireman's carry while I wrapped the towel around him and we carried him through the doorway and on to his bed. Mission accomplished. Andy may have been more relaxed, but we were all exhausted as we sat on the floor and talked while he drifted off to sleep.

The next day his pain increased, even with boluses of liquid morphine. By the time he wanted to go to bed, Andy was unable to tolerate being lifted up. We rolled his lounge chair back as far as it would go and stuffed and pulled the flannel sheet under him. When we situated him in the center, we lifted and carried him to his room. His only comment, as we all gave orders to watch the mantle, the doorway and the refrigerator, was, "Too many chiefs."

That night was intolerable for Andy. And for Cheryl and me. We were sleeping on the floor on either side of his water bed. We couldn't control his pain at all. He couldn't tolerate the pressure of the water bed, so we let some water out. No relief.

We used the liquid morphine as often as directed and then more. No relief. His hip, back and abdomen all had tumors we could see. None of them could tolerate pressure. I took out all the egg-crate mattresses and rolled them, cut them and fitted them around him. We tried visualization and hypnosis, and for a while, all our efforts seemed to help.

With the first rays of dawn, I knew the docs would be coming in to the hospital. So I called and left a message with the staff that we needed to switch to IV morphine as soon as possible.

The phone call back said a pump had been ordered and would be set up by a home health agency later that day. Chris, the head of the oncology unit, called back explaining it would take too long for the people installing the pump to come to our house. As soon as the drugstore opened, she wanted one of us to go and pick up a vial of morphine. She'd be right out.

About an hour and a half later, Chris was at our door with the equipment to set up a line and reduce Andy's pain. She'd left her job and driven all the way to our house to make Andy comfortable.

The medication helped, but Andy's tumors still made positioning him extremely difficult. Chris suggested a bed that fills continuously with air. The air in different compartments is adjusted to ease pain in specific areas of the body. I told her I'd get one.

Cheryl called her uncle who owned a moving company, and by four that afternoon the bed was delivered and set up in the living room. Andy lay down and didn't hurt. The morphine pump and the new bed made all the difference.

It had been my sister Mello's birthday the week before, and now it was time for the onslaught of Azevedo birthdays. Cheryl started it off. Two days later Kerri's followed, and three days after that Paul had his. Brenda's followed a week after Paul's.

On the morning of Cheryl's birthday, I called a balloon company and ordered balloons to be delivered to Cheryl, from Andy. Cheryl had turned thirty-two that day, and thirty-two was Andy's number. It had to be special. Andy was groggy when I told him what I was doing but with a thick tongue, he murmured, "Thas-goood."

When the balloons arrived, I told Andy, then sent Cheryl upstairs, telling her not to peek.

The huge bouquet slapped its way through the doors. Andy grabbed it and I called Cheryl. When she came into the room, he said "Happy Birthday," and handed her the balloon bouquet. She cried and he beamed.

To this day, those balloons are still with Cheryl, deflated and sagging but one of her sweetest possessions. She says, "I'm going to be the only eighty-year-old with a bouquet of dead balloons."

32

Aloha

I don't want my son to be in pain anymore. He should be given at least that. If he isn't going to get better, let him be, let him go in peace. We'll deal with our pain (day after day after day), but he's done enough, fought hard enough, and it isn't fair that he isn't allowed to exit without the grinding, endless pain. And it's going to get worse.

It's going to get worse.

That afternoon, he asked me to call the high school and see if his wheelchair could fit in the gym for that night's graduation ceremonies. I knew it would fit. I knew if it didn't, they'd find a way. But, I also knew he wouldn't be able to tolerate sitting and had to tell him, "Oh, Honey, you can't sit up anymore."

He looked at me with an immense sadness and didn't say anything. Howard and Lisa were going because Matt was graduating, and Andy wanted so badly to go with them.

He was drifting into and out of sleep, but could wake for what was important.

That night was Cheryl's birthday and we gathered around Andy's bed. He sang "Happy Birthday" with us, thick-tongued. It couldn't have been more beautiful, and he was smiling when he finished with a crescendo and a loud "and many more."

By the time Kerri's birthday came around, Andy wasn't talking much. The tumors and the morphine were taking him deeper and deeper into some other place. All the kids had moved home by this time and the house was crowded, with little ones running around. No one argued, though, and no one fought.

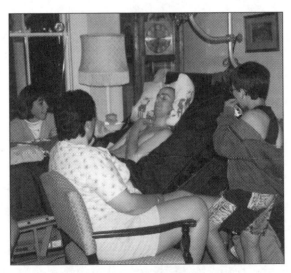

On June 14, 1991, the family gathered for Cheryl's birthday near the end of Andy's life. He is holding his comforting shark's tooth.

Kerri had looked forward to her party all year. It was Father's Day, too, but we didn't celebrate that.

The fact was, Andy was slowing down perceptibly. The whole of Andy was slowing down. Time was getting slower and lengthening simultaneously. It was flying and we knew there wasn't much left. But the moments—the sudden flashes of recognition and grief—the moments widened and dragged.

He'd complain all the time about having something stuck between his toes, and the only thing that helped was to wash his feet. So we did that in shifts as the days got fewer and stranger.

The morning after Kerri's birthday, Andy woke to talk with each of us. He told Linda he was dying. I didn't know if he felt he was dying at that moment, or was acknowledging the fact that he understood he was going to die. It hardly mattered, and we called everyone home.

We played the tape of ocean waves he loved and washed the sand he thought he felt between his toes. He couldn't tolerate covers on his body, so we used our family pareus. These Polynesian cotton cloths are used for sheets, pillows, blankets, towels, bathing suits and beach wear. When Andy had been a newborn, his blanket had been a light turquoise and white hibiscus print pareu, handmade for him by a woman from the Marquesas Islands. I had to look away briefly as I saw him again as he was, tiny and helpless in this same-type blanket (his little fingers and toes). He was helpless again in it, after all these years, after all the struggle and pain. The bright colors draped his body, kissing his skin with the lightest, softest cotton.

When he was awake, he'd ask me to talk to him. "I want to hear your voice." I'd run out of things to say (the words become hollow and your voice echoes in your own ears). I started to read to him from Jack London's stories and, when my voice would give out, someone else would take over. The hours were filled with stories about courage, strength and the will to live. When the book was finished, Andy wasn't.

I looked through the bookshelf for another and found one I'd bought him years ago on the myths and history of the Polynesian peoples. I started it and the first thing I read was about the creation of Maui. It was a beautiful story in a beautiful book filled with soft drawings.

As Andy's death came closer, I was reading to him about the birth of the culture that had always meant so much to him. His shark's tooth was on his chest, and his thumb was dreamily rubbing it. The brightly colored red and black pareu covered him, and in the background was the sound of the ocean washing onto the sand.

There was a feeling of sense to it all. The world had shrunk down to this one room, and this one life, and the important things, the things that were real in the deepest sense, were right at hand. *The way it was meant to be,* I remember thinking.

When someone is dying, a house develops a focal point. It's all arranged around the room. Going outside is a mild shock. It's like another world. It's like a huge, fancy lobby outside a small, intense theater.

That afternoon, we were standing around his bed talking. Annie had come by, and Diane, a nurse from the oncology unit. I was standing by Andy's right shoulder, near the window, when he looked past me and said, "Mom, who's that woman?" There was no one behind me. I was next to the wall. I said, "I don't know, Honey, tell me about her."

Andy shook his head, looked down the bed to his left where Annie was standing and said, "Oh, it must have been Annie."

During my hospice work, I'd seen a lot of patients who'd experienced visions. They saw strangers, or people they knew or angels. I was sure Andy had seen a guide who was waiting for him. I was sure. My own experience, added to the heightened sense of the room, lent me a certainty, a calm and an over-powering conviction that whatever Andy saw, or wherever he went, there would be nothing but good.

This whole episode was over quickly and quietly, but its importance wasn't wasted. Andy was getting closer, and someone was waiting for him.

He didn't die that day. When we went to bed that night, I leaned over to kiss him good-night. He returned my kiss and when I said, "I love you, Honey," he murmured something I couldn't understand.

The birthdays kept coming. On Paul's birthday, Andy's pain increased dramatically and I had to increase the number of boluses of morphine I gave him. In all the somber attention of the house, in all the focus of death, the only thing that couldn't be handled was the pain. It wasn't fair. And though I knew about life not being fair and that it was only for a little while longer and that everything, everything would be fine for him in death, I still couldn't stand it, I couldn't. All the years and pain and hope and struggle, his pure courage, and now it was down to this. He wasn't being allowed to slip away quietly, to just give up and drift away.

I spent a lot of time talking to him that morning telling him he needed to go, that we were all right. "Please," I said, "please, Andy, just leave, please. It's okay now, it's okay." The last, point-less round of suffering was killing me. Andy, though, had a mind of his own, and it wasn't going to let him die on Paul's birthday. He was too strong for his own good. He was still the running back, racked with cancer, breaking through the line for the final fifteen yards.

Carlos came up to spend the day and helped Cheryl, Toni and me bathe Andy. We kept washing his feet. Carlos talked for hours about his own feelings about death and his love for Andy. By the afternoon, Carlos was urging me to go take a nap. I finally seized the opportunity and fell into an exhausted sleep.

Jules had been in contact each day of his vacation. When I didn't call him, he would call me. When he called that day, I told him about Andy's pain and he said he'd order Valium to help potentiate the morphine. Someone (one of the shapes in the house, one of the watchers) drove into town to pick it up.

Late in the day, Andy grew calm with his shark's tooth held tight in his left hand. We hadn't used the Valium yet, but at least we had it. It was dark when I kissed him good-night. He didn't respond. The house was dark and silent. Even at night it seldom was silent anymore. Day and night had become odd, arbitrary distinctions. But now it was dark and quiet, and the ocean sounded softly in the background as I shut my eyes.

Around midnight Andy stirred again from the pain. Cheryl and I relieved each other through the night, sleeping that strange, open-eared sleep that mothers learn. I stayed awake as much as I could, because I couldn't stand the possibility that he'd leave without hearing again how much I loved him. I told him so many times that the words in the dark were starting to sound intrusive to me. I kept waiting for him to say, "Enough already, I know, I know," but he didn't. There was just the hiss of his air bed, his slow breathing and the sound of the waves in the dark.

When he woke from the pain, I'd give him a bolus and talk until he was comfortable. Then I'd drift back to sleep. The next time he stirred, Cheryl would wake up and repeat the process. Around 5:30 A.M., the pain was so bad the bolus didn't settle him down. He wasn't able to communicate, but his face was tense, his breathing rapid, and his feet were moving jerkily, to no purpose. The signs of his pain weren't bearable. It was time for the Valium.

I called Cheryl and told her I needed help. I was so tired. I was afraid I'd give the Valium too soon and plug the IV line. Valium can't be given in IV form with other drugs or it precipitates granules that block the tubing. Cheryl helped me clear the line, counting off a full minute while his saline ran to make sure all the morphine was out.

I slowly injected the diluted Valium and watched for its effect. I knew it was what he needed. I knew that the strength that was holding him here would relax as his muscles relaxed. It was physical. He had a body that didn't know how to give up.

I watched the liquid Valium the way you might watch a sunrise —motionless, with my head full of thoughts of painlessness and peace. Andy calmed quickly.

It was such a relief to see. It was like we all calmed with him, all breathed in his rhythm. The strain left his face and his feet stopped moving.

Paul came in to see Andy before leaving for work. He spent some time talking to him alone and just before he left, I heard him say, "Hey, Bud, it's time to get the hell out of here."

His birthday was over, and he was telling Andy it was okay to go now. Everyone had done the same thing, different words, same meaning. Maybe Paul's encouragement would be what Andy had been waiting for.

Around 8 A.M. I went out to the kitchen. Cheryl was on the phone with Michelle, another wonderful nurse from Memorial's oncology unit. Michelle wanted to know if everything was all right. She had just wakened from a dream about Andy lying on a cold wooden floor and felt sure something was wrong. Cheryl assured her Andy was fine.

Toni had been up early, baking cinnamon rolls. The smell wafting through the house brought everyone into the kitchen. Coffee was poured, the little kids snuggled in laps and we talked about Andy's night. Cheryl told us about Michelle's dream of Andy on the cold floor.

A few minutes later, Cheryl went to get dressed. She went into the living room quietly, because Lisa was still asleep on the sofa, and checked Andy. He was quiet, and she leaned closer. He wasn't breathing. She checked his face. It was barely warm. His body was perfectly still. He was calm and peaceful. He had stopped living while we were in the kitchen, with the smell of the cinnamon rolls and the rays of early light streaming through the window. Lisa hadn't stirred at all. None of us heard anything.

When Cheryl came back into the kitchen and told us, I had a sudden sensation of failure. I hadn't been with him. I felt cheated. He'd gone without anyone at his side. I hadn't been there to make sure everything was right. I thought about the woman he'd seen and hoped she'd taken his hand. I hadn't wanted him to feel afraid or lonely, and now I'd never know, though I did know, really. The Valium had done its work and he'd relaxed into death, the tension draining away. Then I thought I'd never know. That they could say what they wanted, but that nothing would make up for my not knowing. I looked at Andy and loss overwhelmed me. My head was cut loose and thoughts banged around in it pointlessly, barely perceptibly. I hadn't wanted him to feel afraid or lonely. Now, I didn't know. My hands were large and clumsy and I wasn't walking well. When the triviality left my thoughts, sorrow set in like a heavy, stifling shadow—like a heavy shadow-coat I'd wear forever.

I saw my tears falling on his body. It was something out of a dream, the way they fell—straight down, a long way off. Down there was nothing. No flicker of smile, no possible kiss, no thumb on shark's tooth, nothing, nothing.

I'd seen death many times before. This was different. Of course, of course it was. My mind knew what I was going through, but my congested heart knew nothing but pain. I didn't scream, I didn't sob hysterically. I didn't do anything.

The tears were quiet, falling all the way down there to Andy, where Andy had been. I had a huge torn, shredded hole in my chest and it was past any show of emotion. It was way past everything.

Everyone crowded around Andy's bed. Simon and John came in, Paul was called. Lisa woke and came to join us. We watched Andy's face, held his hands and talked to him. The children stood by, not knowing what they should do or how to react. Their tears fell out of huge eyes as they watched for clues. They were picked up and hugged and talked to. There was no sending them away. They were sharing a precious, beautiful and frightening time, and to send them away only would have increased their fear. They stayed, they helped and they talked.

Paul arrived. Howard received the message at the fair. The morning was spent notifying relatives, friends, leaving a message for Jules, calling the hospital, the school, and finally the mortuary.

Everyone helped wash and dress Andy. It was a chance to say good-bye in a very personal way. We dressed him in his all-star football jersey, his surfing pants and his baseball cap. We filled his pockets with mementos: a soccer patch, a shark pin, a chunk of wood from the fence in front of the house so he wouldn't forget where he had come from.

There was a guardian angel pin, too, and rattlesnake grass from Matt's grave.

When he was dressed, we wrapped him in his fuzzy, blue dairy farm blanket with the cows on it. The very last thing we did was take his shark's tooth from his neck. It was Howard's now.

The mortuary was run by friends I'd made through my hospice work. These were kind people who honored the dead in personal and meaningful ways. It wasn't just a job to them. For them it was a job to be done with care, tenderness and compassion.

When the hearse arrived, we took Andy out the front door and through the yard. It was the season for the swallowtails and the big, yellow and black butterflies were all around us in the yard, all over the roses by the fence.

33

CARRYING ON

So here I am, making an effort to remember all the moments I thought I'd never forget. The roses still bloom by the fence. The seasons come around and the responsibilities are pretty much as they always were.

That first week, my responsibilities were strange. I had to support the people who came around to offer support. I was coming down, cried out, and looking around at the world as it would be, forever, and the doorbell would ring and it would be someone who needed to hold on and cry. It was very painful, but it had to be done.

I missed Andy's aroma, being there in his room. I smelled his pillow, but it didn't work. Everything had been washed, everything was sterile. One afternoon, I drove over to Linda's. She had his letterman jacket and I wanted to smell it. But there was nothing there, either, just traces of Linda's perfume.

We had Andy cremated and then went out on Les's cousin's boat under the Golden Gate Bridge. It was a late afternoon, and the wind was blowing hard. I stayed on the deck anyway. When you don't know who you are anymore, or what there is in the world beyond failure and loss, then there's something to be said for the rush of the wind against you. I'm a failure in a strong wind, and even though I could hear my dad saying this time, "Girlie, you did just fine," I don't believe him. I waited so long, and now it's here and I don't believe him. I'm so empty, I can't think of anything I could believe.

The water was so rough at the bridge that we had to turn back into the bay. "Should we do it now?"

"I don't know. I guess."

I take the foil-wrapped box from where I'd put it, near the bow of the boat. I'm holding a box in my hand measuring eight by six inches, and that's all that remains of my child. I take off the tape, open the lid and start to pour some of his ashes into the water. The wind kicks up and blows the ashes back on us. A snicker, then a laugh. Andy would have liked it. The gray ashes trail out behind us, swirling in the air. I close the lid and save most of the ashes for other places: Hawaii, Spider Lake, Bodega Bay and the ranch. Andy was going to be every place he had ever loved.

The flowers follow. Huge bouquets, armloads and handfuls of flowers hit the water. Standing at the rail to watch the flowers is utterly anticlimactic, and we all stand there blankly as the flowers drift and sink.

There's nothing to do but head home.

The memorial service came together nicely. We wrote a Remembery for Andy, selecting poems we felt echoed his passion, spirit and kindness. Cheryl and Lisa took it to a printer, laid out the pages with Andy's graduation picture and, when it was finished, pulled out the checkbook.

"No charge," the printer said. "This is for Andy."

We decided to decorate the church Hawaiian style. The local priest would conduct the service. Ruth was asked to find the appropriate Hawaiian chants and to speak about Andy's Hawaiian spirit. Nancy was asked to speak about his spiritual beliefs. Ron, a nurse from 3-West, was asked to speak about his strength during his illness. Larry was asked to speak about the things he saw when he was his soccer coach.

I would speak first, because I was sure I wouldn't be able to hold it together if I followed anyone. Maureen would speak after me, and the rest would be however it went.

It had no form; it was perfect. We made leis to decorate the altar and the front of the church. We brought in pictures, we brought in his boogie board with his surfing stickers and all the pareus we had in the house. We brought in his huge wooden shark from Guam, and finally we brought in the extra license plates from his Jeep and truck.

The boys drove the Jeep, the truck and Andy's hot rod to church and parked right in front. When you entered the alcove, the first thing you saw was a silhouette of Andy, made from a picture Annie had taken for the newspaper.

Hawaiian chanting fell softly on our ears as we waited. It seemed like it only took a few moments for the church to fill. Father White came to ask if he could start. I looked around the church. It was full to standing. I'd had no idea so many people were there. St. Vincent de Paul Church is a huge church, and every inch was full. People who were unable to come through the doors were crowded in the back and down the steps into the street.

The priest started and spoke briefly. He explained that this was going to be a free-flowing memorial. I stood up to speak and then, for over an hour, others from the assembly added their emotions.

I talked about Andy's courage. Mainly, I wanted everyone to go away understanding that Andy had felt lucky—lucky to grow up in our family and our community, lucky to have survived so long against such overwhelming odds, lucky to have been able to speak for others locked in the same battle, lucky to have made a difference in state and national insurance-reform issues.

I wanted everyone to know, too, that Andy and all of us felt that every battle, every dose of chemotherapy, every surgery and every awful test had been worth it. And that every penny that had come in for Andy would be used to help some other child with cancer.

Then we drove out to Bodega Bay for a gathering, and I wandered pointlessly around in the trees and flowers, smiling when I had to, blurred and a little mechanical. Food was served and it started to rain lightly. Simon and I knelt down by a tree planted in Andy's memory and sprinkled a few of his ashes as people stood silently.

Kevin Sharp began to sing. Poignant songs like "The Dance" and "You Can Count on Me." His bald head nodded in time to the beat as he sat, his own cancer sapping almost every bit of his energy. We met Kevin a year or so earlier through Make-A-Wish, and he and Andy became friends. Kevin was going to be a country singer if he lived.

But he survived, we survived, I survived.

The first year is a blur. Kathy helped a lot. Simon didn't. He couldn't; he didn't have the energy to help care for my pain when he couldn't deal with his own.

Everything was an effort. It's hard to pick up a weight when you don't have any of your own, when you're just empty. Dealing with the platitudes was hard.

"He's up in heaven looking over you."

"He's in a better place."

"He's God's angel now."

The words did nothing at all.

Simon would tell me I should get dressed, but I didn't care. There weren't any more "shoulds." The only one that mattered was that Andy should be alive, and he wasn't. I didn't care.

I couldn't pay the bills correctly. Checks were sent to the wrong places or, if they arrived at all, they weren't signed. My mind was a mess. I couldn't drive because my tears obstructed the view. Every turn, every tree, every hill, everything broke my heart. I couldn't shop for groceries because I didn't care what we ate, and I was afraid I'd run into someone who expected me to be normal.

But the worst, the absolute worst was the quiet. Simon would be outside most of the day, and there'd be silence in the house. If I tried to talk to someone on the phone, I'd cry or they'd cry. The kids were trying to care for my pain as well as theirs. I was a tremendous burden.

I knew what grief was and I'd anticipated it, but it was so much more powerful, so much more intense than I'd thought possible. When I thought the worst was over, it never was.

Simon and I were at opposite poles in how we were dealing with our loss. We weren't supporting each other; we moved away from and around each other, afraid to talk or touch. Simon didn't understand my need to cry. He wanted me to get up, get dressed and do something. I couldn't understand how he could chat on the phone and laugh, how he could go outside and work. He felt that what we needed to do was move on.

I couldn't move at all.

I was terrified that I would fall apart into a pile of broken glass. I walled myself off without sunlight. Nothing warmed the cold hole in the center of my heart.

And then Andrew, Linda's baby, was born. I wasn't at the hospital, but I paced nervously through the house, wondering, hoping, that maybe this baby would come to us with some of Andy in his little heart.

Andrew was a wonderful little boy, all his own, who brought love, healing and light back into my life. He was someone to hold, someone to care about. I couldn't get enough of Drewie, and I'd spend hours looking into his tiny face and imagining who he might be.

When he was two, Andrew toddled into Andy's old room (converted by then into my office) and saw Andy's picture on the table. Andrew looked at the picture, then at me and asked, "Why Mamaw, why?"

And when he was four and Linda told him it was time to give up his baby blanket, Andrew told her he needed "to keep it for Andy." He didn't know that the baby blanket, his baby blanket, had been Andy's before him.

Andrew has turned into an adorable, freckle-faced delight, and he still has the baby blanket on his bed. Stefi is in fourth grade, involved with peer counseling and is enjoying being a big kid.

And it goes on. John and Toni gave us Ali, who's four now, a blond, dimpled bundle of energy. She follows John around feeding animals, learning how things are done and giving commands like an old farmhand.

Nick and Kerri are absorbed in high school, where Andy Azevedo is a name written in bold letters above the football field. Paul has Andy's pickup, kept up just the way Andy kept it, and sometimes he takes Brenda and the kids out for a ride. The Jeep is still running, and just last week Linda took a picture of Andrew sitting in it, in dark glasses, à la Andy.

My life is beginning to have some order, and I know I can make it now. I don't know how it will turn out, but I do know it was better for what we all went through. Andy was a very special part, one of the main threads of the tapestry of my life. The thread in my life that was Andy may have ended suddenly, but it remains in the work.

As I write, my computer has three cutout paper sharks around the screen. It's my way of asking Moho to keep him safe. The snowflake eel in the aquarium still rises to the top of the tank to take its food, and it knows me.

Twenty-seven children have had their treatments paid for by the money donated for Andy.

How did I go on? I don't know. Lord knows I didn't want to. It was just one step in front of the other. One tiny step forward, two or three steps back.

But the days pass, the weeks, even the years. And here I am.

Here I am by a blue lake in the sunlight.

Postscript

A year or two after Andy's death, I was out shopping. And just outside the door of the grocery store, a young man stood in the sun: black baseball cap; dark sunglasses; white tank top; beautifully worn-out jeans and a golden brown tan. My heart stopped, my head pounded and my breath quit inside my chest. Andy! Andy? For a second, just a second, I was filled with hope. Then the memories slammed me back. Brokenhearted, I parked the car and sobbed.

It happens sometimes—you glimpse your lost child in another and it all goes away—your heart soars, for just a moment.

And even though I came through the experience of Andy's illness and death with many raw and painful places, I can now look back and know I have been blessed and life does move on.

Returning to work in the OR didn't fill the void; somehow I wanted to give back to the broader community. To the community that supported us. Through Cheryl, I became involved with the Make-A-Wish Foundation and then with Camp Okizu. After hearing of the need, I started doing independent oncology research and consultation for people who asked for help. Years later, I returned to hospice work as a nurse case manager.

The lobbying Andy put so much effort into has paid off. In the 103rd Congress, then Congresswoman Barbara Boxer used Andy to illustrate the problems with health care when speaking in support of President Clinton's health care initiative. Congressman John D. Rockefeller IV, from West Virginia, also added his comments about Andy into the Congressional Record. (See Appendix B.) The health care initiate failed as proposed that year. But in the summer of 1996, President Clinton did sign into law a bill that makes it now illegal in the United States of America for a health insurance company to deny coverage to anyone with a pre-existing condition. It may not have been all Andy wanted, but it was a good beginning.

Annie Wells continues her extraordinary photography. In 1997, she won a Pulitzer Prize in photojournalism for a photo of a young girl being rescued by a fireman from a rain-swollen creek. Winning the Pulitzer yanked Annie into the spotlight, opening up opportunities and a new job with the *LA Times*. Though she has moved, we remain close.

Alex has stayed in touch and has moved on to earn a masters of education in Bilingual and Bicultural Education from Columbia University, New York. She plans to bring her knowledge back to the Bay Area and pursue her career. My admiration for her will never diminish. Her parents, Carlos and Rebecca, have remained a part of our lives and are dear friends.

Howard graduated college with a teaching credential, married Carey, a wonderful girl who Andy would have loved, and lives in the central valley of California, where he teaches high school.

After moving on to our ranch, and renting a mobile home for a few years, Frankie married Michelle. They have recently bought their own place in town and Frankie has started his own construction business.

Lisa has completed her master's in Latin American studies, is working in the computer industry and plans to use her skills in bringing necessary computer services to Latin America. She lives in Los Angeles with her new husband, Michael, and her two cats.

Jacob has graduated from college and plans to attend law

school in the near future. He has taken time off each year to surf the best-known waves in the world, and says he still shares his waves with Andy.

Kevin Sharp beat his cancer and continues his singing career. He is married and lives in Nashville, Tennessee. In 1997, he was nominated for New Country Entertainer of The Year. His first album, "You Can Count On Me," was dedicated to Andy and three of Kevin's other friends, who died from their cancer. He has had a television movie made about his life and has become a spokesman for the National Make-A-Wish Foundation in Phoenix, Arizona. His first "gold" album was called "Measure Of A Man."

Sonoma County still maintains an agricultural environment, although wine grapes are quickly surpassing the dairy industry. The dairy industry in Sonoma and Marin Counties, and in California as a whole, is fading. It has become more and more difficult to produce milk in this age of high costs and lowering milk prices. Simon and I still own and operate our family dairy with our son John and hope to be able to continue with dairy ranching.

Cheryl has moved on to Santa Clara. She has a new husband, Harry, who won my heart the first time he hugged me, just like Andy used to.

Paul and Brenda bought the property across the road from us and built a beautiful new home. They are involved with school activities and the running of their construction business.

Linda and Les continue to live in town, where they are both involved in their community and with Andrew and Stefanie in school and in sports.

John, Toni, Ali and Andy Michael live in their new home across the field from our house. We get to watch Ali run across the field, dogs chasing and dust flying as she makes a beeline to Mamaw and Pompa's.

Nick has graduated from Tomales High School where he played football on the Andy Azevedo Memorial Football Field and now works in his dad's construction business.

Kerri is a senior at Tomales High School where she is involved in many activities. After graduation, she plans to attend college and work in the law enforcement field.

Stefanie is in seventh grade and is also very involved in her school and most of the activities offered.

Jeff Rubnitz, M.D., Ph.D., is now the director of the Fellowship Training Program, Department of Hematology/ Oncology for St. Jude Children's Research Hospital, Memphis, Tennessee. I've known his wife Karin since she was four years old. Karin has retired from nursing for now, to raise their three children, Zac, Julia and Rebecca. Also in their "family" is one of Andy's puppies named Rex.

Jules is still in practice and he and Jennifer have discovered the aloha spirit in Hawaii, where they enjoy the culture that was so important to Andy. Jules's office now has a saltwater aquarium, a gift from our family and NorthBay Aquatics, given in Andy's memory for those patients who still have to sit and wait.

Barbara Boxer, now Senator Boxer for the State of California, serves on the Budget, Environment and Public Works and Foreign Relations committees.

John D. Rockefeller IV has also become a senator, from West Virginia, and serves on the Commerce, Science, Transportation, Finance and Veterans' Affairs committees. As a member of the Committee on Finance, he works on the subcommittees of Health Care, International Trade, Social Security and Family Policy.

U.S. Representative Henry A. Waxman (California's 29th District) serves on the House Committees on Commerce, and is the ranking member of the Committee on Government Reform and Oversight.

Congressman George Miller (California's 7th District) serves on the House Committee on Education and the Committee on Workforce and Resources.

U.S. Representative Dana Rohrabacher represents California's 45th District in Congress. He is a member of the Committee on International Relations and the Committee on Science.

Medical research has continued to move forward. Some of the programs we had hoped to get Andy into have not proven successful, while others have offered great benefits. Bone marrow transplants are considered standard care for many types of cancer, and it is now possible to receive more than one transplant. And there are alternatives to full bone marrow transplants, such as stem-cell transplant. There have also been great successes with immune therapies using vaccines and biological therapies, such as monoclonal antibodies and antiangiogenesis which inhibits the blood vessel growth to the malignancy.

New drugs have been developed that help relieve the side effects of chemotherapy and make it possible for patients to remain on schedule with their treatments.

Anyone with Internet access can search out the information they need through various available cancer support sites. Many of these sites will be listed in Appendix A of this book.

ⲟᎪppendix A: Cancer Support Groups

Community Support Organizations

American Cancer Society: Offers information, supplies and support groups. Contact them at 800-227-2345 or *http://www.Cancer.org/.*

Candlelighters Childhood Cancer Foundation: For parents of children being treated for cancer, survivors of childhood cancer and their families, and for bereaved families. 800-366-2223 or 3910 Warner St., Kensington, MD 20895 or *http://www.Candlelighters.org/.*

Corporate Angel Network: A service organization for cancer patients that provides free airplane transportation to and from recognized cancer treatment centers. 914-328-1313 or *http://www.corpangelnetwork.org/.*

National Hospice and Palliative Care Organization: Supports patients and their families with palliative care during the last months of their lives. 703-516-4928 or 1700 Diagonal Rd., Suite 300, Alexandria, VA 22314 or *http://www.nho.org.*

Parents of Kids With Cancer: This organization is no longer in operation.

Health Care Advocates

Patient Access Coalition
http://www.home.patientaccess.com/pac/.
Dedicated to putting patients first.

Patient Advocate Foundation
A national network of attorneys who help appeal when
insurance is denied. Many attorneys offer their services on
a pro bono basis.
753 Thimble Shoals Blvd., Ste. B, Newport News, VA 23606.
Phone: 800-532-5274; fax: 757-873-8999 or visit their Web
site at *www.patientadvocate.org.*
The Consumers Union—*http://www.consumer.org/.*
Provides information about health care rights.
The HMO Page—*http://www.hmopage.org/.*
Offers articles on HMO problems.

Cancer Organizations: Online Resources

National Cancer Institute (NCI)
A federally funded organization that lists comprehensive cancer
resources: databases, research information, trials informa-
tion, legislation, CancerNet and more. *http://www.nci.nih.gov/*
and the cancer information service: *http://cis.nci.nih.gov/.*
NCI's CancerNet Cancer Information
Contains a wide range of accurate, credible cancer information
by the NCI: *http://wwwicic.nci.nih.gov/.*
Medicine Online Cancer Information Libraries
http://www.meds.com/.
Oncolink
Comprehensive information resource on cancer from the
University of Pennsylvania. A superior resource for patients
with in-depth information on most types of cancer:
http://cancer.med.upenn.edu/.

Pediatric Oncology Group
Dedicated to controlling cancer in children:
www.pog.ufl.edu/.

Major U.S. Cancer Centers

Northeast
Dana-Farber Cancer Institute
Vermont Regional Cancer Center
Massachusetts General Hospital Cancer Center
The Yale Cancer Center

Mid-Atlantic
Albert Einstein Cancer Center
Cold Spring Harbor Laboratory
Columbia-Presbyterian Cancer Center
Kaplan Comprehensive Cancer Center
Memorial Sloan-Kettering Cancer Center
Roswell Park Cancer Institute
University of Rochester Cancer Center
Fox Chase Cancer Center
Jefferson Cancer Center
University of Pennsylvania Cancer Center
Pittsburgh Cancer Institute
Thomas Jefferson University Cancer Center

South
H. Lee Moffitt Cancer Center
Frederick Cancer Research and Development Center
Duke Comprehensive Cancer Center
UNC Lineberger Comprehensive Cancer Center

Midwest

University of Chicago Cancer Research Center
The Robert H. Lurie Cancer of Northwestern University
University of Michigan Comprehensive Cancer Center
Mayo Comprehensive Cancer Center
University of Nebraska Medical Center
The Ohio State Cancer Center
University of Wisconsin Comprehensive Cancer Center

Rocky Mountains

University of Colorado Cancer Center

Southwest

University of Arizona Cancer Center
The University of Texas M. D. Anderson Cancer Center
Arlington Cancer Center

Far West

Cedars-Sinai Comprehensive Cancer Center
University of Southern California Norris Comprehensive
   Cancer Center
Armand Hammer Center for Cancer Biology, Salk Institut
The Burnham Institute, formerly the La Jolla Center
   Research Foundation
Fred Hutchinson Cancer Research Center
Cancer Institute of Maui
University of California, Irvine College

ᶜᴬppendix B: Congressional Record

CONGRESSIONAL RECORD—Senate
Thursday, March 10, 1994
(Legislative day of Tuesday, February 22, 1994)
103rd Congress 2nd Session
140 Cong Rec S 2673

[Text of statement made by Barbara Boxer]

REFERENCE: Vol. 140 No. 26

TITLE: FACES OF HEALTH CARE: ANDY AZEVEDO

TEXT:

Mrs. BOXER: Mr. President, I just want to say that we are really on the verge of being able to make some progress on health care for all Americans. I think it becomes increasingly important, as the special interests pay for their very sophisticated commercials that make people believe that changes in the health care system will only harm them, that we come to the Senate floor when we can and put a face on this health care crisis. That is what I am going to do today, Mr. President, in a very personal way.

I want to talk to you about a young man whose name was George Anthony—we called him Andy Azevedo, who came to Washington and talked to many of us about health care reform when he was 17 years old.

I will never forget. He was a very strapping young man, with a potential scholarship to college. That was four years ago. He would have desperately wanted to be here with us today in

Washington, pushing us to enact real health care reform, but he cannot, because Andy Azevedo died in 1991. I think that his story is very instructive for all Americans to hear.

Andy would want us to know how hard he tried not to let down all those who cared about him. He would want us to know how his doctors never let him down, how his friends and his neighbors were there for him, how thousands of strangers from California and from all over the country gave him their love and their caring and as much money as they could.

The money was essential because the health care system did let Andy down. The insurance industry let him down. To Andy, they seemed not to care about him or people like him.

Andy died still fighting for all those who were excluded from health care like he was, or who would be excluded. It is now our fight to carry on. It is our responsibility. It is our duty to the American people to stand up and fight for real health care reform.

Let me tell you a little more about Andy.

Andy was raised in Sonoma County, California, in a very rural area of our state. He and his mom and dad, Marilyn and Simon Azevedo, and his two brothers and two sisters, spent a lot of time in Two Rock, which was their home. Andy loved sports. Football was his main love, and he played it every chance he got.

In fact, when Andy first found out that he had cancer, he thought he had a football injury. He had a sore on his finger; not much of a sore, but it would not heal. So his mom had him get it checked out. After all, here is a tough kid who bangs around all the time on the football field. What is a sore finger? As Andy said: "I just came from football practice. How can I have cancer?"

But the diagnosis was clear cell sarcoma. He had a sarcoma,

clear cell sarcoma, a rare disease that usually strikes people much older than Andy.

Illness like this can strike any of us, any American, any of our relatives, and any of our friends. A potentially fatal disease struck Andy at the age of sixteen, at the prime of his teenage years, on the way up a promising football career. A sore in his finger, and, too short a time later, Andy died.

But do you know why Andy came to see me and to sixty other offices on Capitol Hill? I was over in the House of Representatives then. Andy wanted us to know that even if he had survived his fight with cancer, he would never get health insurance again. Andy's insurance came through his parents' policy. He told us that he fully expected to survive his cancer. He said: "When I turn twenty-one, I am going to have to get my own insurance." Andy's insurance company told him that he would be uninsurable because he was too great a risk.

Andy was a fighter. He was a fighter and he fully intended to reach that twenty-first birthday and beyond. But all the time he worried about losing his insurance. So Andy came here to fight for the tens of thousands of people like him, people who have fought the fight of their lives.

Mr. President, we all have friends and relatives who have fought cancer and who have won the battle, and then after they survive the fight of their life they can never get health insurance again because of something the insurance company called a pre-existing condition.

I call it a disgrace, a shame on our country. I call it a failure of our system to keep people secure, a failure to keep faith with those who have sent us here to do the right thing.

Can you imagine what it was like for Andy, fighting every day just to be alive, and at the very time he needed all the positive thoughts he could hold on to—and anyone who has fought cancer knows that is part of the fight, a positive attitude, a positive feeling. But all the time he had to face the fact that even if he survived it he could never get his own insurance and he and his family would be in financial risk forever.

Mr. President, no one in America should ever have to face those feelings, to know that they are expendable for some company's bottom line. Every man, woman, and child deserves to know that if they will fight to survive, we will fight to make sure they are never uninsured.

Andy might be alive today if he had received better treatment from his insurance company.

He came here to tell us what life was like when he was denied a needed operation by his insurance company, and then he had to face the fact that even if he was able to raise money for this operation, and even if he survived that operation, he would lose his insurance.

Andy's family found out what it was like—extra jobs for extra money just to pay for uncovered medical costs. Andy's friends, both old and new, found out through bake sales, weekend runs, Sunday brunches, anything they could think of that earned a little money toward Andy's enormous health care bills. I know how much people cared, because I went to one of those breakfasts where we all prayed and gave what we could.

Andy went through hell. There is no other way to describe it. His finger was amputated. They found three dozen tumors in his lungs, a tumor in his heart, and then a tumor in his brain.

In his fight, Andy had surgery on both lungs, his heart, and his brain. The doctors said: "You will never walk, you will never feel; you will never play football again." They told Andy he would never survive.

But Andy survived for a period long enough to become a spokesperson for parents of kids with cancer. He was with us for less than three years, two-and-a-half years where the doctors said he would never survive. But he shared his strength with many in those two-and-a-half years.

His only hope after so many surgeries, a bone marrow operation, was denied by his insurance company. Andy went to organizations for financial help. His friends went to their savings. People from all over the country helped raise $60,000 just to get Andy admitted to the hospital for treatment. The fight took too long, and Andy died before he could get the operation.

But do you know the irony, Mr. President? The irony of our current system is that even if that transplant had been successful and Andy had survived, he would have lost his insurance coverage when he turned twenty-one because his cancer made him uninsurable.

As Andy wrote to me:

If I'm one of the lucky ones, I'll still need to be followed closely. I will need to be checked out every few months for the remainder of my life, but I can't do that unless I am able to buy the needed health insurance.

Andy did not want charity from anyone, from any company. He just wanted to be allowed to buy insurance.

He wrote, and I quote further:

The lawmakers of our country were elected with a trust of the people to do what is right for them. And to let children who have fought so hard to stay alive become victims of big business after fighting for their lives seems very wrong.

Those are the jewels, the words of a seventeen-year-old.

Andy lettered in three sports at Tomales High School. He was the student representative to the school board. He never asked much for himself. He wanted to do for himself. But he came here to Washington to ask for others. That is what the President's health care plan does. It asks for others, for all those who cannot ask for themselves, or who do not even know the trouble that may be awaiting them with the current health care system.

Andy and his mom wanted others to know how sometimes our health system caused them even more pain than Andy's cancer. They started a book together about health care. Marilyn, Andy's mom, promised to send the book for all of us when it is finished, and I am going to send it to each and every one of my colleagues. Marilyn, his mom, said:

> *If you have a rare disease like Andy's, you're blazing a trail because the treatment that you will get will help others. Helping Andy would have helped others.*

And she said further:

> *Insurance has to be there for all of us when we need it. Isn't that what it's for?*

We are going to debate this issue. There are those who are fighting for the status quo.

And I am going to again quote Marilyn Azevedo, a mother who lost a son, who put it all in two sentences:

> *Insurance has to be there for all of us when we need it. Isn't that what it's for?*

I hope that I can tell her, and I will fight to tell her, that we are going to make certain that insurance will be there for everyone, regardless of pre-existing conditions.

And here is another terrible irony. Marilyn, Andy's mom, told us that the company she works for changed insurance carriers and that her new carrier rejected her—high blood pressure, they told her.

During one of his remissions, Andy was talking about his career. He said, "I'm interested in forestry because I like the outdoors. But, who knows, after all this, I could get into politics."

Andy never made it. He never made it here. But we have, and let us listen to his plea.

An illness may have beaten Andy, but nothing except our lack of courage on health care reform can beat the spirit that he shared with so many of us.

Andy's courage in the fight against cancer is legendary. Now let us find the courage to stand up to the special interests and to those who fight for the status quo, and to Harry and Louise on television, a couple of actors who want to turn Americans against health care reform. Andy has given me the courage, and I hope Andy will give each and every one of my colleagues the courage.

Mr. President, I yield the floor.

The ACTING PRESIDENT pro tempore. The Senator from California yields the floor.

Mr. ROCKEFELLER addressed the Chair.

The ACTING PRESIDENT pro tempore. The Senator from West Virginia Mr. Rockefeller is recognized.

Mr. ROCKEFELLER. I thank the Chair.

Before the good Senator from California, Mrs. Boxer, leaves, I think we are all very conscious of Andy and I hope we get around finally to doing something about Andy.

What strikes me about this place is our ability to put politics above people, to put party above people, and to put all of those above Andy. Andy would not have been happy about that.

I think that is one of the reasons that you were elected and that is one of the reasons that the Senator from California is such a strong advocate. And if we can just focus the American people's attention on Andy, on health care, we will get this done, because we know they want us to do it, just as Andy's family wants us to do it.

So I really thank the Senator.

Mrs. BOXER. Mr. President, if I might ask the Senator to yield to me for just a moment to comment on his leadership on this.

This has been a very long and difficult struggle. The Senator from West Virginia has stayed focused on this issue to the point where I think sometimes it pays a price.

I want to say to him that the more we can bring these real stories to the floor of this U.S. Senate and talk about real people and talk about our responsibilities, I think the quicker we will succeed.

With the Senator's leadership—I will be by his side—we will pass real health care reform, and we will all be proud, and we will do it in Andy's memory and for all those children and adults who had to go through really the kind of hell that he went through; again, at one point saying that this fear of losing insurance was more painful at times than the cancer. It is an extraordinary comment, is it not?

I yield the floor.

Mr. ROCKEFELLER. I thank the Senator from California.

What People Are Saying About
Defending Andy . . .

"I read *Defending Andy* in one long sitting, feeling as if I had loved and lost Andy myself. Azevedo paints every emotional moment with remarkable clarity. The result is unmistakably important, honest and human. The real blessing of this story is that it left me feeling not despondent that Andy died, but gratified that he lived."

—**Catherine Ryan Hyde**
author, *Pay It Forward* and *Electric God*

"I can't imagine a more beautiful tribute for a mother to give her son. As a cancer survivor myself, I found the emotions and the reactions so honest and true. Andy's life continues to make a difference in the world we live in. This book needs to be required reading for all those in the medical and insurance fields."

—**Kevin Sharp**
country music singer

"Andy's courage in the fight against cancer is legendary."

—**Barbara Boxer**
U.S. Senator (D-CA)

"Andy Azevedo and his family changed my life. The handsome, funny and sweet Andy won my heart the first day I went to the Azevedo Dairy to photograph him for a newspaper article about his fight with insurance companies. I was not prepared for the next year and a half when he would lose his war with the cancer that killed him. It wasn't his death I was unprepared for, but the strength of his mother Marilyn. The constant vigil, one filled with life, love and more determination than I had ever seen, allowed me, through some messy miracle, to become more connected and more determined in my own life."

—**Annie Wells**
Pulitzer Prize–winning photographer

About the Author

Marilyn Azevedo, R.N., and her husband, Simon, own a 230-acre dairy with four hundred head of dairy cattle and young stock. Marilyn has milked cows, baled hay, fed field hands, raised newborn calves, rounded up cattle and harvested crops before and during her return to school, where she graduated as an R.N. in 1980.

Marilyn has volunteered at the local level, helping in school and in service organizations. She was named Marin County Volunteer of the Year 1974, for establishing a medical center for local townspeople.

She was employed as an operating-room nurse for six years, a hospice staff nurse for one year and as a hospice nurse—a case manager for eight years.

Andy's illness brought other issues into her life. Marilyn, Andy and a small group of parents lobbied in Sacramento and Washington, D.C., for health insurance reform for children and patients diagnosed with catastrophic illnesses. President Clinton signed a bill into law August 1996, making it illegal for any health insurance company to deny coverage to anyone with a pre-existing medical condition. This was as a direct result of the efforts taken by Andy, Marilyn and the Parents of Kids With Cancer Foundation.

For people who call requesting her help, she volunteers on-cology research and referral services for treatment options through the Internet and the National Cancer Institute. She also aids parents whose children have a newly diagnosed cancer or a terminal prognosis.

As an inspirational speaker, she has lectured in many capacities, including professional nursing symposiums, nursing classes, "I Can Cope" cancer classes and for various charity and community organizations. She was one of eight national speakers for the Make-A-Wish Foundation of America, Phoenix Arizona, and also spoke for the Make-A-Wish Foundation of the Greater Bay Area.

With the Greater Bay Area Make-A-Wish Foundation, Marilyn volunteered as wish coordinator for eight years and served as a member of the board of directors.

Marilyn volunteers at Camp Okizu, a camp for children with cancer, where she helps cook for 250 campers and participants. The high points of camp are the hugs from the participants, who understand, without explanation, the emotions involved when cancer invades your family.

Marilyn is an active member of a committee on end-of-life issues at Santa Rosa Memorial Hospital.

Marilyn is an avid outdoors person who enjoys daily hikes, backpacking in the mountains, swimming in the ocean and traveling. She also loves art, music and reading. She is a seamstress, tailor and has a broad background in antiques, collecting both antique, as well as contemporary, art glass and paperweights.